DATE DUE

Why Red Doesn't
Sound Like a Bell

Why Red Doesn't Sound Like a Bell

Understanding the Feel of Consciousness

J. KEVIN O'REGAN

OXFORD
UNIVERSITY PRESS

*Oxford University Press, Inc., publishes works that further Oxford University's objective of excellence
in research, scholarship, and education.*

Oxford   New York
Auckland   Cape Town   Dar es Salaam   Hong Kong   Karachi   Kuala Lumpur   Madrid   Melbourne
Mexico City   Nairobi   New Delhi   Shanghai   Taipei   Toronto

With offices in
Argentina   Austria   Brazil   Chile   Czech Republic   France   Greece   Guatemala   Hungary   Italy
Japan   Poland   Portugal   Singapore   South Korea   Switzerland   Thailand   Turkey   Ukraine
Vietnam

Copyright © 2011 by Oxford University Press, Inc.

Published by Oxford University Press, Inc.
198 Madison Avenue, New York, New York 10016

Oxford is a registered trademark of Oxford University Press
Oxford University Press is a registered trademark of Oxford University Press, Inc.

Library of Congress Cataloging-in-Publication Data

O'Regan, J. K.
Why red doesn't sound like a bell : understanding the feel of consciousness / J. Kevin O'Regan.
p. ; cm.
Includes bibliographical references and index.
ISBN 978-0-19-977522-4
1. Consciousness—Physiological aspects. 2. Visual perception. I. Title.
[DNLM: 1. Consciousness—physiology. 2. Psychomotor Performance. 3. Vision, Ocular.
4. Visual Perception. WL 705]
QP411.O74 2011
612.8'2--dc22   2010042381

. . . to my parents,
(and to Lazula) . . .

It was spring, and I was a PhD student, sitting with my supervisor in a café in Paris, idly watching the tourists walking by. As I watched the tourists, I realized that the scene in front of me looked quite stable despite the fact that the image inside my eyes was shifting as I moved them back and forth. Why did the scene seem steady even when I moved my eyes?

My supervisor was an extremely good supervisor.[1] Inclining his head to see some particularly attractive tourists, he mumbled distractedly: "Yes, why don't you try and figure it out."

It took me 30 years, but I think I've now figured it out. And doing so has led me by an indirect route to a better understanding of consciousness.

The journey began with vision. The problem I discussed with my supervisor is just one of many puzzles posed by vision. Engineers know well that the eye seems to be a catastrophic piece of apparatus,[2] and its shortcomings lead them to raise questions like: Why do we see things right side up? Why don't we see that we have a blind spot in each eye? Why do we see things in focus, in color, undistorted, and generally veridical, despite the multiple defects of our eyes?

While investigating these puzzles, I came to realize that I had been thinking the wrong way about vision. I had fallen into a trap that has snared scientists since ancient times: mistakenly believing that vision is generated in the brain. Given the eye's defects, it is often difficult to avoid this trap, and in the first chapter of the book, I'll illustrate exactly how easy it is to fall into it. In the next four chapters, I'll show how to get out of the trap by adopting a "sensorimotor" approach to vision. This approach solves the puzzles about the eye's defects and predicts some interesting new phenomena, including "looked but failed to see" and "change blindness." Both of these phenomena have received considerable attention recently, partly because of their importance in traffic safety and surveillance.

In the second half of the book, I show how the sensorimotor approach to vision can be extended to a new way of thinking about consciousness. I begin by reviewing the generally accepted notion of consciousness, and I show that there is an aspect of consciousness that, though very difficult, can be understood through scientific investigation. This aspect involves different levels of knowledge that a person has about what he or she is doing or thinking. It includes awareness and self-awareness, and it is related to attention. It is this first aspect of consciousness that engineers are already starting to build into robots.

There is, however, a second aspect of consciousness, namely its "raw feel": what it's like to experience the smell of a rose, the redness of red, the feeling of pain. Such inherently private experiences seem to elude scientific investigation. These raw feels are part of what philosophers call the "hard" problem of consciousness.

I explain how we can begin to understand raw feel by taking the same sensorimotor approach I take toward vision in the first part of this book. As I go on to illustrate, the sensorimotor approach to raw feel allows us not only to develop a general classification and understanding of the peculiarities of sensory feel but also to make surprising predictions about color perception, the localization of touch, and what is known as sensory substitution, in which, for example, it becomes possible to see via the skin or the ears.

Given how much progress the sensorimotor approach allows us to make in understanding raw feel, perhaps we are on our way to solving the "hard" problem of consciousness.

Note: *For interesting supplements to the book, see the Web site http://whyred. kevin-oregan.net.*

Notes

1. My supervisor was John Morton, a well-known experimental psychologist then at the Medical Research Council Applied Psychology Unit in Cambridge, UK. He was my official supervisor at Cambridge while I finished my PhD in Paris in Jacques Mehler's laboratory. I will remain eternally grateful to John Morton for helping me understand how to understand.
2. The idea that from the engineer's point of view the eye would seem to be an atrocious piece of apparatus had been mentioned by Hermann von Helmholtz in his "Physiological Optics," which though written at the end of the 19th century is full of inspirations for us today (Helmholtz, 1867).

ACKNOWLEDGMENTS

Writing this book has been an arduous process taking more than 15 years, with many people who have kindly contributed time and encouragement to me. Benedicte de Boysson Bardies was the person who suggested I embark on the venture, and I thank her warmly, as I thank Abel Gerschenfeld and Marco Vigevani, who provided further encouragement. My parents, brother, son Elias, and daughter Lori, as well as Hasna Ben Salah have given me extraordinary support, as have, in different ways and at different times, Alva Noë, Ed Cooke, David Philipona, Erik Myin, and Jacqueline Fagard. The following people read parts or all of the manuscript and provided valuable suggestions: Malika Auvray, Aline Bompas, Jim Clark, Jan Degenaar, Thi Bich Doan, Jérôme Dokic, Shaun Gallagher, Abel Gerschenfeld, Andrei Gorea, Sylvain Hanneton, Tomas Knapen, Ken Knoblauch, Sid Kouider, Charles Lenay, Tatjana Nazir, Peter Meijer, Pasha Parpia, Frédéric Pascal, Daniel Pressnitzer, Joëlle Proust, Paul Reeve, Ronan Reilly, Martin Rolfs, Eliana Sampaio, and Aaron Sloman. I warmly thank them. I also warmly thank Marion Osmun and Catharine Carlin for their expert editorial work at OUP.

CONTENTS

PART ONE

The Feel of Seeing

Chapter 1

The Catastrophe of the Eye

Vision comes so naturally to us that it is easy to forget what a problem it poses. How can two small spheres filled with transparent jelly (our eyes!) encapsulate the whole world before us and allow the shape and position of far-off objects to be effortlessly apprehended?

The ancient Greek philosophers devoted much work to this question,[1] and in the Middle Ages the study of "Perspectiva," which included all aspects of optics and the study of light, was one of the main scientific pursuits alongside the study of Aristotle and Euclid.[2] But little progress was made. A kind of curse lay over the study of optics and vision: Although all the pieces necessary to understand the puzzle were available well before Christian times, no one had been able to put those pieces into a coherent theory.

The situation changed suddenly in the first years of the 17th century. The astronomer Johannes Kepler is generally better known for his discovery of the elliptic orbits of the planets around the sun, and for thereby contributing, with Galileo, to starting the scientific revolution.[3] But Kepler also started a second revolution.[4] He and other astronomers had noted that observations of the sizes of the sun, the moon, and the planets sometimes yielded inconsistent values depending on how the measurements were made. Kepler intuited that part of the problem might lie in errors introduced by the human eye.

Kepler set aside his astronomical calculations for a while and devoted himself to studying the eye. In 1604 he published a remarkable book[5] showing that the eye worked like what we today call a camera, by using a lens to form an image (Kepler called it a *pictura* or "painting") on the inside surface of the eyeball (Fig. 1.1).[6]

Kepler's discovery of the image at the back of the eye was a revolution in the understanding of vision. The fact that the eye could be the origin of perceptual errors forced people to realize that it was an *optical instrument*, not the *seat of vision*. The function of the eye was not *to see*, but *to make an image*. Now the eye could be studied with scientific methods: It could be analyzed, measured, and understood.

Upside-Down Vision

Immediately after the publication of Kepler's book, the philosopher René Descartes proceeded to verify Kepler's prediction that there should be an image at the back of

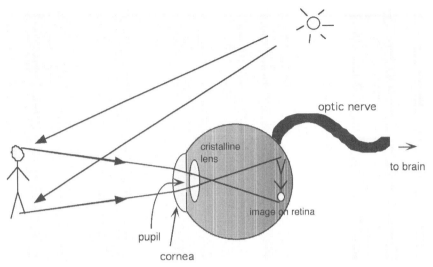

Figure 1.1 Kepler's discovery as depicted in terms used today. Rays of light from a source like the sun reflect off an object like a man and penetrate through the pupil at the front of the eyeball into the eye. They are first deviated by the corneal surface and then by the crystalline lens, and then fall on the retina at the back of the eye, where they form an upside-down image. The retina is composed of about 130 million microscopic photoreceptor cells that are more numerous but whose function is similar to the 8–12 million pixels that sample the image in today's digital cameras. Each photoreceptor is connected to a nerve fiber. All the nerve fibers come together and leave the eyeball at one point at the back of the eye to form the optic nerve, leading to the brain.

the eye. By cutting away the outermost coats of the back surface of the eye of an ox, leaving only a thin, translucent layer, he was able to see the image of a bright scene, just as it would be received in the living animal's eye.[7] In fact, Descartes mentions how, by lightly squeezing the eye, he could modify the focus of the image, exactly as Kepler predicted.

The trouble was—and Kepler had predicted this, too—the image at the back of the eye *was upside down*.[8] "I tortured myself for a very long time" about this problem, Kepler writes:

> Here then is how I wish those who are concerned with the inversion of the image and who fear that this inversion might produce an inversion of vision, should appreciate the problem. The fact that illumination is an action does not make vision an action, but rather a passion, namely the passion contrary to this action: and similarly, so that the loci should correspond, it must be that patients and agents should be opposed in space . . . . One need not fear that vision should err in position: Since to look at an object placed in a high position, one simply directs one's eyes upwards, if one has realized they are too low, and, as concerns their position, facing the object. On the contrary, it is rather the case that vision would be in error if the image were right-side up. (. . .) There would no longer be opposition (between the object and the image) . . . .[9]

Did you manage to get to the end of that paragraph? Kepler's book is wonderfully clear except at this one point where his writing becomes confused. This is evident in the last statement, in which Kepler proposes that if the image were *not* inverted we *would* see the world inverted. It seems that he thinks the absolute orientation of the image on the retina is important after all.

Kepler was not the only person to be confused. Al Hazen, the great 10th–11th century Arab thinker on whose work much of medieval optics was based, tried to avoid what he called a "monstrous" theory of vision in which rays of light crossed over each other when they came into the eye through the pupil and thereby ended up in the wrong order.[10] Four centuries later, Leonardo da Vinci also worried about the problem. Not yet knowing the true function of the lens, he actually suggested that its purpose was precisely to uncross the rays.[11]

And now consider what Descartes had to say, working in the same period as Kepler. As evident in Figure 1.2, which is taken from his *Traité de L'homme*, Descartes made use of what Kepler had shown only a few years earlier. The paths of the light rays coming into the eye are just what Kepler had suggested, and what modern optics confirms: Light from the arrow ABC is projected on the inside of the eyeballs, and the image is indeed *upside down*.

What does Descartes do about this? From the eyeballs he depicts nerve fibers leading to the inside surfaces of the ventricles of the brain. He suggests this inside surface serves as a kind of theatre where the image from the eye is displayed. Here the image can be analyzed by the pineal gland, which Descartes considered to be the seat of the soul.[12] The contemporary philosopher Daniel Dennett has coined the now widely used term "Cartesian theatre" to refer to the little theatre or cinema screen in the brain that the "mind," materialized in the pineal gland, is supposed to look at in order to see.[13] But note something interesting in the figure, consistent with the theatre analogy: The lines connecting the nerve endings in the ventricle to the pineal gland are *crossed*, presumably so that the image seen by the pineal gland should be *right side up*.

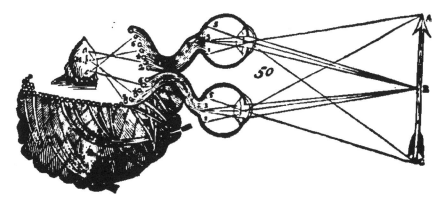

Figure 1.2 The illustration shows how Descartes' engraver has the nerve fibers cross as they go from the inside surface of the ventricle (empty cavity inside the brain) to the pineal gland (the drop-shaped organ inside the cavity). Reprinted from Descartes, R. (1965/1637) with permission of Hackett Publishing. Original work published in 1637.

At least based on his figure, it looks like Descartes thought that to solve the problem of the inverted retinal image, it was necessary to postulate some kind of compensating mechanism, in particular, the crossing of the connections going from the ventricles to the pineal gland. But Descartes seems to have changed his mind between when he had the figure engraved and when he wrote his text. In his text he says something quite close to what we think today, namely that the inverted image is not a problem at all.[14]

After all, what is meant by "up" and "down"? By "up" is meant, for example, the direction we have to move our hands if we want to move them from the center of our bodies to near our heads, or near the ceiling. The notion of "up" (or "down") has nothing to do with the way the retina codes information; it is determined by the way the information on the retina relates to actions.

More generally, the code used to register information in the brain is of little importance in determining what we perceive, so long as the code is used appropriately by the brain to determine our actions. For example, no one today thinks that in order to perceive redness some kind of red fluid must ooze out of neurons in the brain. Similarly, to perceive the world as right side up, the retinal image need not be right side up.

Whereas vision scientists no longer consider the inverted retinal image to be a problem, there are other defects of the visual system for which it seems necessary to find compensatory mechanisms analogous to the crossed connections of Descartes' figure. Perhaps in these cases researchers unwittingly have fallen into a way of thinking in which they implicitly presuppose the existence of something like Descartes' pineal gland, that is, the existence, inside the head, of what philosophers call a "homunculus" (a "little man") who perceives the information brought in by the visual system. The following discussion examines some cases in which the ghost of the homunculus still haunts scientific thought and insidiously influences research on vision.

Filling in the Blind Spot and Vascular Scotoma

Humans have about 130 million densely packed light-sensitive nerve cells, called photoreceptors, lining the inside surface of the eyeball. Images from outside the eye fall on this network or "retina" of photoreceptors. Each photoreceptor gathers up the light falling in its tiny spot of the image and sends off nerve impulses to tell the brain how much light there was at that point.

To get to the brain, the nerve fibers from each retinal photoreceptor come together in a bundle and go out of the eyeball in a thick cable called the optic nerve. At the spot where the cable comes out of the eyeball there is no room for photoreceptors, and there is thus a *blind spot*. The blind spot is large enough to make an orange held at arm's length disappear (see Fig. 1.3).

In addition, the retina must be supplied with blood. To do this, Nature seems to have just blithely strung blood vessels over the retina, right in the way of the incoming light. The blood vessels emerge from inside the optic nerve cable and spread out all over the retina. This is not a problem where the blood vessels are very fine and

Figure 1.3 Instructions to make an orange disappear: Close your *left* eye. Look with your *right* eye directly at a reference point ahead of you. Hold an orange at arm's length and bring it in line with the reference point. Keep looking at the reference point with your right eye and move the orange slowly to the *right*, *away* from and slightly below your line of sight. When the orange is about 15 cm away from your line of sight, you will notice in peripheral vision that parts of the orange start disappearing. You can then maneuver it so that the whole orange is no longer visible.

nearly transparent, but the thicker vessels where the cable emerges at the blind spot obscure vision seriously (see Fig. 1.4).[15]

Thus, not only is there a large blind spot in each eye, but emerging from this spot is a network of blood vessels like legs stretching out from the body of a giant spider. This is the vascular scotoma. Why do we not see it?

Scientists have an obvious answer: "filling in." They say we don't see the blind spot and the vascular scotoma because the brain fills in the missing information. The idea is that the brain takes the information available around the edges of the blind spot and vascular scotoma and uses that as filler pattern, so to speak, to plug up the adjacent blind regions.

How "intelligent" is this filling-in process? Presumably filling in holes in a uniformly colored surface is not too much to ask. But what about filling in the missing bits in an object that falls in the blind spot? The "IQ" of the filling-in mechanism can be tested by holding a pencil at arm's length. If it is held so that it crosses the blind spot, it will not appear to be interrupted, but if only the tip goes into the blind spot, the tip will appear to be missing.[16]

This seems to make sense. Any filling-in mechanism would have to have been hard-wired into the visual system by eons of evolution. It is conceivable that such a mechanism could connect contours, lines, or regions that cross the blind spot.[17] But it would be extraordinary if such an age-old, genetically predetermined brain process somehow "knew" about pencil tips.

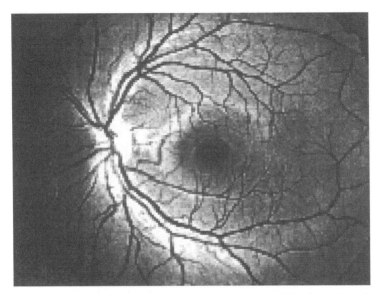

Figure 1.4 Photograph of the surface of the retina on the inside back surface of my eye, taken from the side facing the light. Visible is the black network of blood vessels spreading out from a point on the left of the picture. This is the blind spot. Also spreading out from this point are white streaks. These are the nerve fibers carrying nerve impulses out of the eye. At the blind spot these nerve fibers form a thick cable that goes out of the eyeball. The blood vessels are lodged in the middle of the cable. In the center of the picture is the fovea, the area of the retina most densely packed with light-sensitive photoreceptors, corresponding to central vision. The blood vessels are finer there, and so do not excessively obscure central vision. (Thanks to J.-F. LeGargasson for taking the picture with his laser scanning ophthalmoscope.)

A particularly interesting example to test the IQ of the blind spot is the "hole in the donut" experiment invented by vision researcher V. Ramachandran. Consider a texture made up of "donuts" as shown in Figure 1.5, presented in such a way that the hole of one of the donuts falls in the blind spot. Since the other donuts have holes, the filling-in mechanism should, if it is clever enough, be able to deduce that it should paint in a hole.

But the filling-in mechanism is not clever enough. It fills in the black hole with white, so that the donut in the blind spot seems to be uniformly white and stands out as a holeless intruder among the other, normal, donuts. It is as though the filling-in mechanism fills in the blind spot with material taken from the immediately surrounding area, in this case, the white ring of the donut.

But something quite different happens if the figure is held far enough away so that the donuts form an overall texture (case B in the figure). Now the blind spot engulfs not just the hole in the donut, but a whole donut. And curiously, the impression one gets is that nothing is missing in the texture, as though now the filling-in mechanism is clever enough to fill in all the details of a complicated texture of donuts.

There is a wealth of experiments on filling in the blind spot, showing that sometimes the filling-in mechanism is clever, sometimes not.[18] To explain these effects, some scientists invoke a mechanism that involves more a kind of "knowing

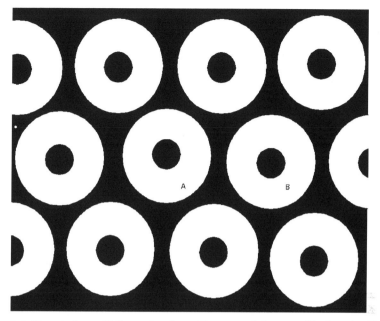

Figure 1.5 Donuts due to V. Ramachandran. Close your left eye and look with only your *right* eye on the very small white dot on the left edge of the figure. Move your head very close to the page (about 5–10 cm) so that the donut marked A falls in the blind spot. You will have the impression that it has lost its black hole, and so this holeless donut pops out as an empty white disk among the other donuts. Now bring the page about twice as far away from you so that whole donut marked B falls in the blind spot. The fact that a whole donut is missing is hardly noticeable, and you see something like a continuous texture of donuts.

something is there" rather than an actual "painting in" of material in the blind area. They compare what happens in the blind spot to the phenomenon of amodal completion, shown in Figure 1.6, where, even though one does not actually see the black square on the left, one is sure it is lurking behind the white squares that cover it.[19]

Other scientists believe that filling in is a real painting in of material. They compare the phenomenon with the Ehrenstein and Kanizsa illusions, shown in Figure 1.7, where the sensation of really seeing contours bounding a light disc or triangle is almost palpable.[20] But whether the filling in is of the "knowing-something-is-there" or the real "painting-in" type, vision researchers generally agree that filling in exists.[21]

Is there not something suspiciously "homuncular" about filling in, particularly the "painting-in" variety? The notion seems to require that after the filling in has occurred, some kind of perfected picture of the world is created. Who or what would then be looking at this picture? Might scientists be falling into the same trap that many people fell into as concerns the inverted retinal image: the trap of thinking that there is a little man in the brain, a homunculus, looking at the internal screen where the outside world is projected?

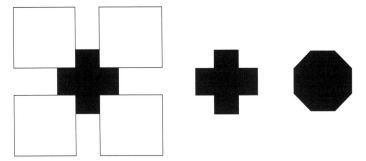

Figure 1.6 Amodal completion. On the left it palpably seems like there is a black square underneath the white ones, even though the shape could just as well be a cross or octagon as on the right. But the presence of the square seems less "real" than the contours in the Ehrenstein and Kanisza figures (see Fig. 1.7).

Other Design Flaws of the Eye

There are other examples of where apparent design flaws of the eye raise the spectre of the homunculus.

Optical Defects

Even the cheapest camera lenses are carefully shaped so that the images they create are in focus everywhere. There is very little so-called spherical aberration. Furthermore, there is little color aberration because the lenses are made out of composite materials so that light rays of different wavelengths all come properly into focus together.

But the optical system in the human eye is a catastrophe. Photos made using the human cornea and lens would be totally out of focus everywhere except in the middle of the picture. Furthermore, even in the middle, the picture would be in focus only for one color, and not for the others. If the optics are adjusted so that, say,

Figure 1.7 On the left, the Ehrenstein illusion: The abutting lines create the effect of a whiter-than-white disk floating above the background. On the right, the Kanizsa triangle: The white triangle formed by the pacmen and the interrupted black lines seems whiter than the white of the page, and it seems to have a real boundary, whereas in fact there is none.

red objects are in focus, then blue objects are out of focus. The error in focus between red and blue in the eye is about 1.7 diopters. This is a large error: Opticians daily prescribe spectacles correcting smaller errors than this.

Yet we think we see the world as perfectly in focus. We don't see things in peripheral vision as out of focus, nor do we see multicolored objects with bits that are in focus and others that are out of focus. The natural explanation would be that some kind of compensation mechanism corrects for these errors. For example, the focus problem outside the center of the image could perhaps be dealt with by a deblurring mechanism similar to the deblurring filters that are used in photo processing software packages. Perhaps there could also be a way of compensating for the color focus problem.[22]

Would proposing this be succumbing to the homunculus?

Nonuniform Sampling

The image at the back of the eye falls on the retinal network of photoreceptors lining the inside surface of the eyeball. Each photoreceptor samples a minute region of the image and sends a signal to the brain to say how much light fell on that region. An engineer would probably arrange the photoreceptors so that they sampled the image in a uniform way like the pixels on a television screen.

Nature didn't follow such a banal approach. It chose to arrange the photoreceptors more artistically, in a nonuniform mosaic resembling the heart of a sunflower. At the center of the retina, the photoreceptors are very small and densely packed. But further away from the center they get larger and larger. There is no central part of the retina where the cells are uniformly packed.[23]

A consequence of this arrangement is that when we look at an object, the part we look at directly is sampled very densely, but immediately next to that precise point, sampling density diminishes drastically. As a test, one can look fixedly at the middle of a long string of letters: Without moving one's eyes, one can only accurately recognize two or three letters on either side of the fixation point. One can see that there are lots of other letters, but one can't quite make them out or see exactly which is next to which.[24]

|
XHUDHEKLGHDJSUIRGABDPFHDRITYZNDKGHZSXPUMLKLNJUR
|

And yet this tremendous drop-off in visual quality is not readily apparent. Only in careful tests like this do we realize how little we actually see. Generally when we look around, we don't have the impression that the world looks somehow grainier in the regions we are not looking at directly. Why not? Will it be necessary to appeal to another compensation mechanism to clean up the part of the image seen in peripheral vision? Would this be invoking the homunculus again?

Bad Color Vision in Periphery

Another odd thing about vision concerns the way the retina samples color. The receptors that allow us to distinguish colors are concentrated only in the center of the eye.[25] As a consequence, and as can be demonstrated by the method shown in Figure 1.8, color vision, even just slightly away from the fixation point, is severely limited.[26]

This is very surprising to many people. After all, if we look at a red object and then look away from it, we don't have the impression that the redness fades away. The world doesn't seem to lose its color in the areas we are not looking at directly. Why not? Is there some kind of color filling-in process that compensates for the lack of color in peripheral vision?

Geometric Distortions

Suppose you look at a horizontal straight line: Its image will fall on the inside of your eyeball, say on the eye's equator. Now if you look upward, the same straight line no longer falls on the equator but projects onto a different arc on the inside of your eye. If you were to cut out a little patch at the back of the eye and lay it flat on the table, the shape of the projected lines would be quite different. The line on the equator would be straight, but the line off the equator would be curved. In general, the same straight line seen ahead of you changes its curvature on the retina depending on whether the eye is looking directly at it. But then how can we see straight lines as straight when they wriggle around like spaghetti as we move our eyes over them?

The situation is actually much worse. We have seen that straight lines in the world project as arcs with different curvature at the back of the eye. But we have also seen

Figure 1.8 To show that color vision is very poor in peripheral vision, ask someone to take five or six colored pencils in random order, and to hold them out at arm's length to the side without your seeing them. You now look at the person's nose, and try and guess the colors of the pencils he is holding out to the side. The person brings the pencils gradually closer and closer to the side of his face, until they are touching his ear; all this time you continue looking at his nose. You will find that if you don't move your eyes, you will perhaps be able to pick out a red pencil or a green one, but you will not be able to identify all the colors, and you will not be able to accurately judge the order in which they are arranged.

that the retina samples the image at the back of the eye in a totally nonuniform way, with photoreceptors densely packed at the center of the retina, and fewer and fewer photoreceptors as we move out from the center into the periphery. There is even a further nonuniformity introduced by "cortical magnification": Nerve fibers originating from the center of the retina have direct connections to the visual cortex, but nerve fibers originating from peripheral areas of the retina converge together on their way to the cortex so that many retinal neurons come together at a single cortical neuron. This has the consequence of essentially magnifying the cortical representation of central vision as compared to peripheral vision. With the already very strong nonuniformity due to the arrangement of photoreceptors, the final representation of the straight lines that ends up in the brain is extremely distorted.

As shown in Figure 1.9, how is it possible that two straight lines, of equal length, equal thickness, and equal spacing all along their length should be seen that way

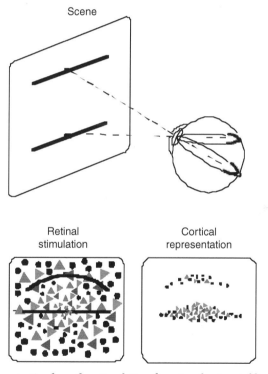

Figure 1.9 Demonstrating how the stimulation from two horizontal lines projects in the cortex. At the top is shown how the two lines project as great arcs at the back of the eyeball. When laid out flat, the arc lying on the eyeball's equator gets mapped out as straight, but the other arc is curved. These lines on the retina are sampled by photoreceptor cones (symbolized as triangles) and rods (symbolized as dots). The cones are small in the center of the eye, but get larger toward the periphery. The rods are concentrated only in periphery. Cones and rods connect, via the optic nerve and visual pathways, to the cortex. Because there are more cones sampling the middle of the central line, and much fewer sampling the other parts of the lines, and because of convergence of neural pathways along the way to the cortex, the cortical representation is highly distorted.

when in the brain they look like two totally dissimilar blobs? Should we search for a compensation mechanism for this distortion? Suppose there were such a mechanism. Its purpose would be to correct the distortion and create a perfected picture of the world. But who or what in the brain would look at this perfected picture? Again, proposing a compensation mechanism may be to succumb to the homunculus error of thinking there's a little man in the brain looking at an internal screen.

Blur Caused by Saccades
When we look at the world around us, our eyes flit from thing to thing like a butterfly stopping on flowers here and there. One might say it is a supersonic butterfly, because the jumps or "saccades" are extraordinarily fast. A large saccade might have a speed of about 600 degrees per second, fast enough to track bullets or follow a supersonic aircraft passing 20 meters in front of us.

As a consequence, the information provided on the retina by the image of the world is totally smeared out during saccades.[27] Why do we not see this smear? The natural answer to give is: a compensation mechanism.

The idea of "saccadic suppression" is a serious proposal for a compensation mechanism that has received considerable attention over the last decades.[28] The idea is that since the brain commands the saccades that it makes, it can ensure that at the same time as it gives each command, it turns off something like a switch or "faucet" that prevents the perturbations caused by the saccades from getting into the brain areas that do visual recognition (Fig. 1.10). But again, who or what would be looking at what comes out from the other side of the faucet? Is it a homunculus?

Shifts in the Retinal Image
Saccades have another unfortunate consequence. Say you are looking at one particular thing in the scene in front of you. If you now make an eye saccade to another

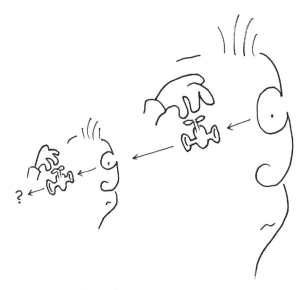

Figure 1.10 The principle of saccadic suppression.

thing, after the blur subsides, you have a clear image again on the retina. But the image is now shifted. Why does the world not appear to shift?

You can get an idea of the kind of shift that occurs in the image by closing one eye and placing your finger on the eyelid near the corner of the other, open, eye. Now if you quickly press hard on the eyelid, your eye will move in its socket. You will see that the world appears to shift.

Normal saccades are much faster and can be much larger than the shift caused by pressing with your finger. So why do you see the world shift when you push your eyes with your finger, but not when the eyes do it by themselves?

The tempting answer is to suggest a compensation mechanism. Since the brain knows when it's going to make a saccade, and since it knows what the size and direction of the saccade are going to be (after all, it commanded it), it can shift the image of the world back into place so that the final picture remains stable despite eye movements.

Since the 1980s there has been a large amount of experimental work on this issue. Researchers have assumed that a compensation mechanism exists, and they have gone ahead to find ways to measure it. One simple method you can use on yourself is this. Look for a few seconds at a small bright light, like a lightbulb. Now close your eyes, and you will see an afterimage of the bulb floating in front of you. The afterimage is caused by the fact that the retinal photoreceptors remain slightly "irritated" after having been exposed to the bright light, and they keep sending impulses to the brain, which ends up thinking the light is still there. Now, with your eyes closed, move them left and right. You will see the afterimage move as well.

Why does the afterimage move? Scientists will tend to answer that it is because of the compensatory shift. That is, to keep the world apparently stable, the brain usually must add in a compensatory shift every time you move your eyes. It keeps doing this now when your eyes are closed, causing the perceived motion of the afterimage. So this experiment appears to provide a way of materializing the compensatory shift (assuming it exists).

Now do the following. Move your eyes very quickly back and forth as fast as you can. A curious thing happens. Suddenly the afterimage *no longer appears to move*. It now seems to be stuck straight ahead of you, in a single location.[29] It seems that when the eyes move too quickly, the compensatory signal can't keep up, and you see the afterimage as straight ahead.

In the laboratory, various more precise methods of measuring the supposed compensatory shift have been used.[30] The main finding is that the compensatory shift made by the brain is not accurate. The brain seems to get wrong the moment when it commands the compensatory shift, so that the actual eye saccade and the compensatory shift are out of sync. It also gets wrong the size of the shift. Furthermore, the shift that it makes is not the same everywhere: The place that the eye is aiming for seems to shift into place faster than other parts of the visual field, which lag behind.[31]

Such laboratory measurements seem to contradict our subjective impression that the world remains steady when we move our eyes. If it were true that the compensatory shift is inaccurate, then as we move our eyes around, errors in the perceived location of objects should accumulate, so that in the end we should see the world where it isn't. Also, if it were true that different parts of the visual field shift into place faster than others as we move your eyes around, we should see the visual scene squish and unsquish at every eye movement. Neither of these things is observed under normal conditions: We see the world where it is, and it does not appear squishy.

One suggested explanation for these discrepancies is that information about what is out in the real world can itself be used to help patch together the successive snapshots that the brain receives at each eye fixation. As if aligning sheets of patterned wallpaper, the brain adjusts the positions of overlapping snapshots that it receives of the world so that they fit together nicely into a composite image.[32]

But this is not what happens either. Several experiments in past years have tested the idea of a composite image. The overwhelming evidence is that information gathered at one eye fixation cannot be combined accurately with information gathered at the next. There is no composite picture that is formed from overlapping snapshots of the world.[33]

The most striking experiment that really brought home the idea that something was seriously wrong with the notion of a composite picture was done by George McConkie at the University of Illinois at Champaign in the late 1970s. McConkie and his student John Grimes displayed pictures on a high-quality color video monitor. Using the technical wizardry that only McConkie and a few others in the world possessed in those days,[34] McConkie managed to set things up so that as people freely viewed the pictures, every now and then, coincident with an eye movement made by the viewer, some element in the picture would change. For example, in a picture of two people wearing top hats, the hats would be interchanged (see Fig. 1.11).

McConkie and Grimes consistently observed that even very large or obvious changes would *simply not be seen* if they occurred during an eye movement. Table 1.1 is a list given by Grimes of the percentage of viewers that failed to see such changes.

Figure 1.11 Example of picture change in Grimes' and McConkie's experiments done in the late 1970s, published later in Grimes (1996).

Table 1-1. PERCENTAGE OF FAILURE TO DETECT CHANGES IN
GRIMES & MCCONKIE'S EXPERIMENT

Image Manipulation Description	Detection Failure (%)
A prominent building in a city skyline becomes 25% larger.	100
Two men exchange hats. The hats are of different colors and styles.	100
In a crowd of 30 puffins, 33% of them are removed.	92
In a playground scene, a child is enlarged by 30% and brought forward in the depth of the picture by approximately 5 m.	83
In a marketplace, brightly colored fruits switch places among their four respective baskets.	75
A celebrity, leaning upon an air conditioner, is rotated approximately 40 degrees to lean the other direction.	67
Two cowboys sitting on a bench exchange heads.	50
A parrot, comprising roughly 25% of the picture space, changes from a brilliant green to an equally brilliant red.	18
The castle at Disneyland rotates around its vertical axis so that what was visible on the left is now present on the right, and vice versa.	25
The swimsuit of one of four people posing for a swimsuit advertisement changes from bright pink to bright green. The subjects begin viewing the picture while fixated on that person.	58

Source: From "On the Failure to Detect Changes in Scenes Across Saccades," by J. Grimes, 1996, in *Perception: Vancouver Studies in Cognitive Science*, Vol. 2 (edited by K. Akins), pp. 89–110, New York: Oxford University Press. Reprinted with permission.

Following is an extract from Grimes' article in which he describes these phenomena, showing the degree of bafflement that he and other researchers expressed about them, particularly in cases when the observer was looking directly at the location that was changing in the picture:

Perhaps the oddest cases of all were those in which the subject was directly fixated upon the change region before and immediately after the change and still failed to detect the image manipulation. Among these instances, one of the most puzzling and striking involved an image of a boy holding up to the camera a parrot with brilliant green plumage. The parrot occupied approximately 25% of the scene and yet when its plumage changed to an equally brilliant red, 18% of the subjects missed it. Examination of the data revealed that of the 18% who missed it, two of the subjects were directly fixated upon the bird immediately before and after the change, and still failed to respond. Their eyes left a large, brilliant green parrot and landed, 20 msec later, upon a brilliant red parrot and yet nothing in their experience told them that anything unusual had happened. The data from this and related experiments are full of such events. These are the data that I consider truly interesting. Somehow the subject was either completely insensitive to, or was able to completely absorb, the sudden presence of the new visual information without any awareness or disturbance. How can these changes occur right in front of awake adults without their awareness? What is the nature of the internal visual representation and why does it accept the appearance of radically different information without a hiccup, just because the visual world happens to change during an eye movement? What mechanisms in the visual system can ignore, absorb, or accommodate changes in the visual world of this magnitude? Is it not important to inform the viewer of such a change, just because it happened to have occurred during an eye movement? And finally, is this phenomenon just a scientific curiosity that has no place in, and teaches us nothing about, real everyday life? Or is it a real characteristic of the visual system that has implications for human vision and theories of visual processing?[35]

McConkie's picture change experiments dealt the final blow to the idea that there is some kind of composite picture that accumulates information across successive eye movements. If there were a composite picture, then surely it would get messed up if changes occurred during eye saccades, and people would immediately notice something wrong.

We thus have a serious problem for visual stability. How can we see the world as stable unless we have some way of compensating for the perturbations caused by eye movements? These perturbations are another set of design flaws like those of the blind spot, optical defects, sampling, color problems, and distortions I mentioned previously. How can we see the world as perfect if the eye is such a catastrophe? The tempting answer is, once again, to invoke compensation mechanisms, but this would imply that a homunculus lurks within to contemplate the picture that is perfected by the compensation mechanisms.

The solution that I finally came upon was a turning point in how I understood vision. It is also the key to the question of feel. We need to look at it.

Notes

1. As supplementary information for this book, I have posted on the Web site http://whyred.kevin-oregan.net an essay in which I attempt to explain why the ancient visions of optics and the eye propounded by Plato, Aristotle and Euclid, and Galen prevented medieval thinkers from understanding the operation of the eye.

2. "Perpectiva" was a broader domain than what we call "perspective" is today, and it included all aspects of optics, vision, and the eye. It was considered an important field of study. Thirteenth-century Franciscan philosopher Roger Bacon says in his *Opus tertium*: "It is necessary for all things to be known through this science." Sixteenth-century mathematician, astronomer, and occultist John Dee, supposedly one of the most learned men of his time, says in his *Mathematicall Praeface*: "This art of *Perspectiue*, is of that excellency, and may be led, to the certifying, and executing of such thinges, as no man would easily beleve: without Actuall profe perceived. I speake nothing of *Naturall Philosophie*, which, without *Perspectiue*, can not be

fully vnderstanded, nor perfectly atteinded vnto. Nor, of *Astronomie*: which, without *Perspectiue*, can not well be grounded: Nor *Astrologie*, naturally Verified, and auouched." Given the fairly minor role played by optics in universities today, it is surprising to learn that historians of science have catalogued long lists of medieval universities that acquired costly copies of manuscripts on optics and organized lectures on optics. At Oxford, for example, throughout the 15th and 16th centuries, the study of optics was listed as an alternative to Euclid in the BA syllabus (Lindberg, 1981, p. 120). Another example showing the importance of optics as a field of study in the Middle Ages and the Renaissance is the fact that Descartes' first concern, after conceiving his famous "Discourse on Method," was to bring his new method to bear on the problem of optics and vision; in fact, the full title of the Discourse on Method mentions "Dioptrics" as its first application ("Discours de la methode pour bien conduire sa raison et chercher la verité dans les sciences. Plus La dioptrique. Les météores. et La géométrie. Qui sont des essais de cette méthode").

3. The story is well told by Arthur Koestler in his admirable book *The Sleepwalkers* (Koestler, 1968).

4. On the supplementary information Web site: http://whyred.kevin-oregan.net, I have a more detailed account of how Kepler came upon his discovery, and why it was so revolutionary.

5. "Ad Vittelionem paralipomena, quibus astronomiae pars optica traditur" ("Extensions to the work of Witelo, representing the optical part of astronomy"), or "Paralipomena" as it is often called. I obtained it in a French translation by C. Chevalley (Kepler, 1604/1980). Paralipomena is really the beginning of the modern study of vision. Whenever I show the title page of Paralipomena in a class, I get a surge of emotion in respect for the sad, hypocondriac genius that Kepler was.

6. Until Kepler came along, almost nobody had actually realized that lenses can create images. It's true that lenses were already being used in spectacles at that time to correct presbyopia and myopia, but curiously, it was not known how they worked. Galileo had recently fixed two lenses in a tube and made a telescope, but he didn't know why that worked, and anyway there was no visible image involved. It may be that lenses were considered unworthy of scientific inquiry—indeed it has been suggested that this might explain why they bear the name of a vulgar vegetable, the lentil, which they resemble in shape, rather than a ponderous Latin name that any self-respecting scientist would have given them (Ronchi, 1991). Still, if lenses were known, you might wonder why no one had noticed that they form images. Perhaps the explanation lies in the fact that if you fiddle around with a lens, it's actually quite hard to obtain an image. The image doesn't just float visibly in midair behind the lens. The room has to be quite dark and you have to put a piece of paper at exactly the right place behind the lens before you see the image.

7. The Jesuit astronomer Christoph Scheiner performed a similar experiment, also at the beginning of the 17th century.

8. And inverted left to right.

9. Kepler, 1604/1980, ch. V, prop XXVIII, section 4, pp. 369–370, in French translation.

10. Al Hazen had proposed that the first stages of sensation occurred at the front surface of the crystalline humor *before* any crossing of the visual rays had occurred. He thereby obviated what he says would be a "monstrous" distortion of sensation that would be provoked by inversion of the image. But he nevertheless also claims that the incoming light does propagate deeper into the ocular media, where further consolidation of sensation occurs. Because it is known that the visual rays must

ultimately cross, this evidently drove an anonymous student of vision to write "dubitatio bona" in the margin of a 14th- or 15th-century Latin manuscript of Al Hazen's *De Aspectibus* to be found in the library of Corpus Christi College at Oxford. And to this it seems a second glossator of the manuscript added a diagram suggesting a solution in which rays crossed over yet again within the eye "ut forma veniat secundum suum esse ad ultimum sentiens" (in order that a form arrive at the *ultimum sentiens* in accord with its true being (i.e., right side up). Eastwood discusses these glosses in detail in an article in which he considers the question of retinal inversion, as seen by Al Hazen and Leonardo (Eastwood, 1986).

11. According to Lindberg (1981, p. 164). Thus, in his treatise *On the eye*, Leonardo suggests six schemes by which the path of light rays within the eye might cross to arrive correctly oriented at the back of the eye. He even contrives a demonstration of this which involves putting your face into something like a fishbowl partially filled with water, as shown in the picture in the section on the inverted retinal image in the supplement Web site, http://whyred.kevin-oregan.net.

12. "Further, not only do the images of objects form thus on the back of the eye, but they also pass beyond to the brain, [. . .]. [. . .] And that, light being nothing but a movement or an action which tends to cause some movement, those of its rays which come from [the object] have the power of moving the entire fiber [leading to the brain]. . . so that the picture [of the object] is formed once more on the interior surface of the brain, facing toward its concavities. And from there I could again transport it right to a certain small gland [the pineal gland] which is found about the center of these concavities, and which is strictly speaking the seat of the common sense. I could even go still further, to show you how sometimes the picture can pass from there through the arteries of a pregnant woman, right to some specific member of the infant which she carries in her womb, and there forms these birthmarks, which cause learned men to marvel so" (Descartes, 1637/1965, Optics, Fifth Discourse, p. 100).

13. Dennett, 1991.

14. For a more detailed treatment of what Descartes actually says, see the section on the inverted retinal image in the supplementary Web site for this book: http://whyred. kevin-oregan.net. Many people today take for granted the idea that Descartes himself fell afoul of the idea of the homunculus, and that he himself believed in what is called the "Cartesian theatre." But in his text at least, this is clearly not true. I speculate that the crossing of the lines in Descartes' diagram may have been an error on the part of the engraver. Preparing a figure for a text was probably a much more tedious process than it is today, and errors made by artists or engravers may have been harder to correct. An example of such an occurrence appears in Kepler (1604/1980, Paralipomenes, ch. V, section 2), who reproduces a table containing a set of figures from Plater illustrating the parts of the eye and complains: "There are 19 figures, the last two (showing the organs of hearing) were added by the engraver although I had not requested it."

15. It is interesting that blood pressure and emotional state may modify the size of the blood vessels and thus the size of the blind spot by as much as a degree or so. See various references in Legrand (1956, ch. 9 of Vol 3).

16. To do this experiment, close your left eye and look at your left thumb held at arm's length with your right eye (admittedly this is a bit confusing!). Take a pencil in your right hand and hold it against the right side of your left thumb, still at arm's length. Gradually separate thumb and pencil, still looking at the left thumb with your right

eye. When your hands are about 15–20 cm apart, the pencil disappears. (It helps to hold the pencil about 2 cm lower than the left thumb. Remember you are looking at your *left* thumb: The pencil disappears in periphery, in indirect vision.) Depending on whether the pencil crosses the blind spot or just sticks into it, you will either see no gap or see the tip missing, respectively.

17. For recent information on neural correlates of illusory contours in humans and animals, see Murray et al. (2002). For a review, see Komatsu (2006).

18. A similar phenomenon occurs in audition where it has been called "phonemic restoration" or the tunnel effect of the continuity illusion. See Warren, Wrightson, and Puretz (1988) and Petkov, O'Connor, and Sutter (2007). There is also an analog with touch; see Kitagawa, Igarashi, and Kashino (2009).

19. See Durgin, Tripathy, and Levi (1995).

20. There is also the Craik-O'Brien-Cornsweet illusion, which is a brightness illusion; for example, see Todorovic (1987).

21. See the reviews by Pessoa, Thompson, and Noë (1998) and Komatsu (2006).

22. An interesting experiment has been performed to test this. It is possible to equip people with special lenses that improve the quality of the eye's optics, so that there are no colored fringes. People who put on these special lenses now see colored fringes where in fact there are none. If they wear these lenses for a few days, they gradually adapt, and no longer see the fringes. Their vision is back to normal. But then, when they take off the lenses, they see the fringes again, except the colors are in the reverse order. Then gradually people adapt back to normal again, and the fringes go away. It really seems like there is some process in the visual system that detects the fringes and the very complicated laws that determine how they are formed and gets rid of them. When the fringes start obeying new laws, the brain adapts, so that after a while the colors are again no longer seen (Kohler, 1974). See also Held (1980). The McCollough effect is another well-known example of a low-level neural adaptation mechanism in which perceived colors are modified by the presence of nearby oriented edges (e.g., Vladusich and Broerse, 2002).

23. This fact is surprising even to many experts on vision. There is a widespread belief in the vision science community that there is a thing called the fovea, which is an area in the central part of the retina with high acuity, and outside that area, acuity falls off. The fovea, it is usually thought, corresponds to a region in the visual field that is about the size of half a thumbnail, when seen at arm's length. But this is very misleading. It leads one to believe that the fovea is a uniform area of high acuity, and that there is a sudden drop in acuity as one goes out of the fovea. In fact what happens is that acuity drops off in a uniform way, even within the fovea, and going out to about 10–14 degrees. In Figure 4 of O'Regan (1990), I have compiled data from a number of acuity and retinal density studies showing this.

24. Suppose you are looking at a word in the newspaper, say the word "example," and suppose your eye is at this moment centered on the first letter, the letter "e." It turns out that the patch of retina that would be sampling this "e" would contain about 20 x 20 photoreceptors. But two letters outwards from the center of the retina where the "a" in the word "example" falls, the photoreceptors are less densely packed. Here the patch that would be sampling the "a" would contain only about 15 x 15 photoreceptors. And still further out, in the region of the "p" of "example," there would only be 10 x 10. Figure 4 in O'Regan (1990) gives an illustration of this. Thus, when we look at a word, the quality of the information the brain receives about the letters degrades extraordinarily rapidly, even within the very word we are looking at.

A letter situated only four letter spaces away from the fixation point is being sampled by a 10 x 10 pixel grid: about the same number of pixels as used to define letters on a television screen—and we all know that this is quite tiring to read.

25. The cones are less sensitive to the light than the rods. Having the highly sensitive rods located only in periphery has the odd consequence that, in the dark, you can't actually see where you're looking. For example, if you look directly at a very dim star at night, it disappears. You have to look slightly away from it to actually see it.

26. For a review, see Hansen, Pracejus, and Gegenfurtner (2009).

27. It is, of course, not the image on the retina itself that is smeared, but the information provided by the photoreceptors. These have an integration time of 50–100 ms, and so cannot track fast-moving contours. You can check the existence of saccades by closing one eye and placing your fingers gently on your eyelid. If you then look around the room with the other eye, you will feel the closed eye moving under your fingertips. You can get an idea of the speed of eye saccades as you travel in a train. You look out onto the track next to you and observe the wooden sleepers under the rails. Because the train is moving fast, you cannot see them clearly. But every now and then, when you make an eye saccade toward the back, suddenly you will have a perfectly clear, stationary flash of them. This is because when your eye is moving at nearly the same speed as the sleepers, they remain still on your retina, and you see them clearly.

28. A very large literature on saccadic suppression has developed since Volkmann and collaborators coined the term (see review by Volkmann, 1986). People have tried to distinguish a central suppression mechanism (which may be either a copy of the motor command or information deriving from proprioception) in which the brain actively inhibits sensory influx, from masking of the retinal signal by the strong retinal perturbations created by the saccade. There is also an ambiguity between suppression of visual sensitivity and suppression of detection of motion. A recent, balanced review overviews this very contentious topic (Castet, 2009). See also Ibbotson and Cloherty (2009).

29. This experiment is due to Grüsser (1987). See also the very clever "eye press" experiments by Stark and Bridgeman (1983).

30. These often involve displaying a small, brief flash of light at some moment during or just before or after a saccade, and asking people to judge where they see it. Errors in localization observed in such experiments give information about the mismatch between what the eye is really doing and the compensatory shift. For a review, see Matin (1986) and more recently, Bridgeman, Van der Heijden, and Velichkovsky (1994).

31. This very important finding, published in German (Bischof and Kramer, 1968), seems to have been largely ignored in an imposing literature on saccadic mislocalization. For a recent model, see Pola (2007).

32. See http://photosynth.net for an application that combines photos in this way.

33. For reviews, see Irwin (1991) and Wurtz (2008).

34. In those days color monitors were costly, computers slow, and eye-movement measuring devices extremely cumbersome. Changing a whole high-definition color picture during an eye movement was much more difficult than just changing letters in a text. McConkie's systems programmer, Gary Wolverton, managed to set up this delicate system so that picture changes would occur within 4 milliseconds of an eye movement being detected. For a historical description of some of the work in McConkie's lab, see Grimes (1996).

35. Grimes, 1996, p. 105.

Chapter 2

A New View of Seeing

When I was about 14 years old, we had periodic "science lectures" at school where local scientific celebrities would come and give talks. I don't know why Donald MacKay, who years later I discovered was the author of some very profound papers about perception,[1] conceded to give a lecture to a bunch of unruly school children. But he conveyed to us a point of view about perception that was extremely innovative. In fact, he said something that must have prepared my mind for understanding the problem of how we can see so well despite the catastrophe of the eye. MacKay said that the eye was like *a giant hand that samples the outside world.*

I later learned[2] that this point had also been made by the psychologist James J. Gibson, and by the philosopher Merleau-Ponty, who had said that seeing was a form of *palpation.*

To understand the idea, consider a game.

The Hand-in-the-Bag Game

Suppose someone secretly puts a household object, like a cork, a pocket knife, a potato, or a harmonica, in an opaque bag, and then you try, by putting your hand into the bag, to guess what the object is (Fig. 2.1). At first you feel disconnected sensations of roughness, smoothness, cavities, or cool surfaces on your fingertips. Then suddenly the "veil falls," and you no longer feel these disconnected sensations, but a *whole harmonica,* say. Yet despite this change in what you feel, your fingers are still in contact with the same bits of the harmonica as before. There has been a qualitative shift in the feel, even though there has been no change in the sensory input you are getting from your fingers. Suddenly instead of the jumbled parts of an unidentified puzzle, you have the whole object.

What is happening here?

First, and this is a well-established point in the scientific literature, recognizing an object involves knowing how its parts fit together. Until you put the parts in the right relation to one another, you merely have a jumble. Suddenly when you have discovered the relational structure between the parts, you have a kind of "aha" experience, and the object materializes out of the mess.

Another fact that is well accepted by cognitive scientists is the *active, exploratory* aspect of the recognition process. You will have a much harder time recognizing the harmonica if you are not allowed to move your fingers over it. An eminent cognitive

Figure 2.1 You feel the whole harmonica in the opaque bag, even though your fingers are only touching a few parts of it.

scientist, Whitman Richards, illustrated this to me in an amusing way once. We were talking in a café near MIT, and he asked me to hold out my hand with my palm upward. He placed an object on my hand and asked me to guess what it was without moving my hand around it. I was totally unable to guess.

But the situation was quite different when I moved my hand. You can imagine my surprise, and the sidelong glances of the other people in the café, when I realized, instantly upon moving my hand and wielding the object, that it was one of Whitman's nicely polished shoes that he had quietly removed under the table and placed on my hand.

So recognition is much easier if you are able to explore. But there are some additional, more subtle points worth noting about the recognition process.

The Feeling of Wholeness

At any moment during your exploration of the harmonica, you are only in contact with those few bits of it that happen to be touching your fingertips, your palm, and so on. And yet you have the feeling it is a whole harmonica. The parts that you are not in contact with at any moment do not appear to be missing. The harmonica does not appear to have gaps in it where there are gaps between your fingers.

The reason for this is that the feeling of the whole harmonica derives not from your being in complete contact with all its parts, but from knowledge of the fact that all the parts are potentially accessible to your exploration. You feel a whole harmonica because you have implicit knowledge that if you move your fingers this way, you will encounter this particular smoothness or roughness, and if you move your fingers that way, you will encounter that particular depression or bump.

The feeling of having the whole harmonica is like the feeling of being at home. You cannot be everywhere at once in your house, but you nevertheless feel quite at home sitting on your couch, because you know that if you *want* you could go into the kitchen or the basement and encounter the things you know to be in those rooms. Similarly it could be said that the feel of the whole harmonica derives not from being in simultaneous contact with all of its parts, but from being at ease, comfortable, at home with all the things you can do with your fingers and hand with respect to the harmonica.

Thus, you can get a feeling that the object you are exploring is a spatially continuous and coherent whole, despite the fact that the exploration is done with a tool (the hand) that touches only parts of the object and has significant spatial discontinuities. The reason for this is that the feeling of wholeness derives from your knowing that all the different aspects of the object are immediately available to you via your exploratory actions.

The Feeling of Temporal Continuity

There is a similar point to be made about temporal discontinuities, or gaps in time. Once you have realized that you are holding a harmonica, the feeling of holding it is there, and it continues to be there, even though, in the process of exploring it, your fingers may actually briefly lose contact with it. During that gap you have no sensory input from the harmonica at all, and yet you are still in the process of manipulating it. The harmonica is still *present* to you. If you pay careful attention to what you are doing with your hand, you may discern certain moments where you are in contact and certain other moments where you are not in contact, but even during the gaps in time you consider yourself to be in the presence of the harmonica.

This is a very important point, and it shows that the feeling of continuousness, ongoingness, or "presence" of the harmonica does not require continuous contact with the harmonica. What it requires is for you to be *engaged* in the action of exploration or obtaining contact. You are *poised* to do the actions of exploration; you need not actually be doing them now. The feeling of continuousness arises not because you are at this moment actually in contact with the harmonica, but because you have in the past explored it, and you can, if you will, explore it again right now. Like an explorer in unknown territory, you're still an explorer even while you rest.

Extending the Analogy to Vision

In summary, the classical way of thinking about perception emphasizes its active, exploratory aspect, and the need for a construction process that puts the parts of an object together to give a coherent representation. But two additional, more subtle points are generally not stressed: First, the feeling you get of the *wholeness or completeness* of the object resides in the immediate accessibility of sensory information, not in the current presence of sensory input. Second, the ongoingness, continuousness, or "presence" of the feel resides in being engaged in the process of acquiring sensory input, not in the presence of sensory input itself.

We shall soon see the tremendous counterintuitive implications of these two subtle points when applied to vision. But first consider the more obvious points about the constructive and exploratory aspects of perception, as applied to vision.

People studying vision agree that it involves a construction process. Under normal conditions this is perhaps not quite so obvious, but in conditions where vision is impeded for one reason or another, it becomes clear that recognizing objects in the world requires putting together the perceived bits into a coherent whole. An example is provided by certain "difficult" pictures. At first you see only meaningless patches or contours. Then suddenly they take form, fit together, and the whole image emerges (see Fig. 2.2).

The situation is analogous to what happens sometimes when you are lost in a town, and you come upon some familiar landmarks. Suddenly things now fit together and you get the feeling of knowing where you are, as though the whole environment, previously strange, somehow clicked into place. Nothing has changed in your sensory input, yet now you have the feeling of knowing the lay of the land. You feel you're on familiar ground. What previously looked just like another mailbox on the corner now becomes your old familiar mailbox. There is a qualitative change in your perception not just of the mailbox, but of the whole scene. Thus, despite vision being a constructive process, you generally have the impression of seeing everything all at once.

And, of course, vision is also an *exploratory* process. Because the eyes have high acuity only in the central fovea, it is usually necessary to move them around to get all the information needed to recognize an object.

So far so good. The trouble is, this is where most theories of visual perception stop. They say that visual recognition of an object occurs in the following way: After active *exploration* of its constituent parts through eye movements, and after fitting

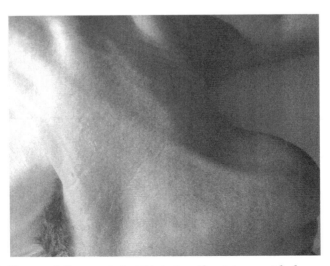

Figure 2.2 If you can't figure out what this is, turn the picture upside down.

these together into a coherent mental *construction*, a global mental representation of the object is created, and the object is thereby perceived.

But what exactly does it mean to say that "a global mental representation is created"? Does it mean that somewhere in the brain a little picture of the object is created that brings together the pieces into a coherent whole? People who work in visual perception are not so naïve as to imagine something like that. So instead of saying a little picture is formed in the brain, they say a "representation" is formed. But I think the word *representation* is misleading. It makes people think they have an explanation, when in fact they have nothing.

For how could the creation of a "representation" make us *see* the object? Presumably a representation is some kind of neural inscription that represents the object, somewhat like the pits engraved on a CD that represent the music you hear when you play the CD. But just having the pits in the CD doesn't make music: You have to *play* the CD. You need a device, a CD player, that reads the special code that corresponds to the pits in the plastic and transforms that into music. Similarly, just having a representation of an object in the mind isn't going to make you see the object. Something more is needed that reads out the representation. It seems we are back to having to postulate a little man in the brain that somehow *decodes* what's in the representation: a homunculus that looks at the internal picture.

I suggest that thinking in terms of representations leads to the need to postulate compensation mechanisms to get rid of the various apparent defects of vision identified in the preceding chapter. If we assume that what the homunculus sees is the representation, then to see things as perfect, the representation has to be perfect.

And this is where the two more subtle points about tactile perception help to avoid the "internal picture" idea, and to make a theory of vision that doesn't depend on the idea of looking at an internal representation.

Seeing the Whole Scene

The first subtle point about tactile perception was the fact that we can get the impression of holding a whole harmonica, even though we are only in contact with parts of it. If we extend this idea to vision, we can see that it will be equally possible to have the impression of being in the presence of the whole visual scene despite the fact that our eyes provide extraordinarily poor information about it. This will happen when we are in a mental state in which we are "at home" with the various things we can do with our eyes to visually explore the scene.

Imagine I am looking at an indoor scene with a table and chair near a window and door. Suppose my eyes are centered on a vase on the table. Because my central retina has good acuity, I have high-quality information available about the vase. But other things in the scene, like the window, the chair, and the door, fall in peripheral vision, where I only have low acuity. Only poor-quality information will be available to me about them. Nevertheless, there will be some cues available. For example, the bright square shape of the window will be there off to the side. The top of the chair stands out and contrasts with its surroundings. If I want to get more information about the chair, for example, I can use such coarse cues to orient an eye movement to it. Like signposts on a road that tell me which towns are coming up on my route, the cues available in peripheral vision serve as signposts for the information that is immediately accessible through the slightest flick of an eye saccade. After I've made a few eye movements around the scene, even parts of the scene for which no visible cues are available from my current vantage point can be attained, because I have now become familiar with the lay of the land in the scene, and I now know how to move to parts of the scene I want to get more information about. Having the knowledge I have accumulated, plus those peripheral signposts, becomes equivalent to actually having the real visual information. Because the information is available on demand, I have the impression of seeing everything.

Seeing Continuously

The second subtle point about tactile perception was that we feel the presence of the harmonica continuously, despite the fact that we may not be in continuous contact with it. Applied to vision, this means that despite the fact that I frequently blink, that my eyes are continually hopping around, making saccades from one place to another, and that this causes perturbations and momentary blanks in the visual input, I nevertheless have the impression of seeing the scene continuously. If I attend to my blinks or my eye movements and ask myself at that moment what I see, I can become aware of perturbations in my vision. But most of the time, if I am attending to the scene, I am unaware of the blinks and eye movements and have the impression of a continuously present visual world.

The important point is that the reason I see things continuously is not because I have built up an internal picture that is continuously present in my mind. The impression of continuity derives from the immediate availability of information about the objects I see. Having this impression does not require continuous neural input.

It's like the light in the refrigerator (Fig. 2.3).[3] I open the door of the refrigerator, and the light is on. I close the door. I quickly sneak the door open again, and the light is still on. It seems like the light is on all the time. But, in fact, the light only turns on when I open the door. Similarly, we think we are seeing continuously because if we so much as vaguely wonder, or open our minds to the question of, whether we are seeing, we are indeed seeing. That is because seeing is precisely this: probing the outside world with our eyes.

Is There a Representation?

Admittedly there is some information being built up in the brain, namely the information about all the things I can do with my eyes and the changes that will occur as I move them around. You could argue that this information constitutes a kind of representation. But the *seeing* is not caused by the existence or "activation" of this information or representation. It is caused by—I had better say *constituted by*—being engaged in making use of this information to explore or *visually manipulate* the visual scene.

Note that even when my eyes have moved to the region where I want to extract information, and when they are fixating precisely the information I am interested in obtaining, even here there is no "image" that is being seen all at once. Rather, I am actively making use of the information available on my retina to answer my interrogations: "Is it an 'A'?"; "Is it in Times Roman?"; "Is it black on white?"; "Is that a

Figure 2.3 The refrigerator light illusion: The light seems always to be on.

speck on the crossbar?". . . At any moment, even without moving my eyes, a multitude of questions can be asked about what is out there, and among all the possible things to see, I am only "seeing" what pertains to those particular questions that I am currently asking. There is no little image of an "A" with all the possible properties simultaneously "activated," with all the possible questions answered, in my brain.

Why does this idea get rid of the homunculus problem of requiring a little man to contemplate the representation? Because the seeing is no longer considered to occur by virtue of the mere existence or activation of the representation. There is no final image. Instead, seeing is considered as something that the person *does*. Seeing is the process of being engaged in asking and answering questions about what is before us, if need be by exploring the changes in visual input that occur as we move our eyes around. There is no end product to be contemplated by a homunculus.

What then is in the brain when I am seeing something? The questions I am currently asking, and their answers, plus a framework of exploration-instructions applied to the particular scene I am contemplating. These instructions allow me to access any of the details in the scene, relying partially on cues from peripheral vision as signposts to the details that interest me, partially on information already gathered about which way to cast my attention.

Seeing Versus Remembering and Imagining:
The World as an Outside Memory

Now compare the experience of seeing with the experience of remembering. In my memory I've stored lots of knowledge. For example, I have knowledge about Latin verbs, about history, about how to dance the tango. . . But at any moment, even though all this knowledge is stored, I am not currently aware of it. Only if I think about some aspect of my stored knowledge am I actually remembering it. Remembering is not conjuring up a picture or representation whose activation brings the memory to life. Remembering consists in actively engaging in a form of mental manipulation. It is being in a state where you know you can answer questions about the things you are remembering.

This asking-and-mentally-checking process even occurs for the case of imagining. Suppose I want to imagine my grandmother's face. The mental image does not light up instantaneously as when you switch on your television. In fact, just as for remembering nonvisual things about my grandmother (her friendliness, the story of her life), making a so-called mental image of her face consists, more or less implicitly, in going through this or that question about her face and answering it to myself. The details of her face are not all "painted in" simultaneously to some kind of inner picture that contains these details. The details remain implicit until I ask myself about each particular item: Is she wearing her gold or her silver earrings? Is she wearing her glasses? The more I consider her face, the more parts of it I can detail, and after a while I have detailed most of the ones I'm interested in. Finally when I'm in a state of mind in which I know that all these details are immediately mentally available to myself, I can say I am having a mental image of my grandmother. I am at that point "at home" with all the possible things about her face that I have just attended to and might at any moment want to call to mind again. But those details have not all come together into some kind of composite internal image to be presented to myself or to some internal homunculus for seeing all at once to occur. On the contrary, having a mental image of my grandmother's face consists in being in a mental state of particular confidence that all those details are immediately available to me when I turn my mental powers to recalling them.

This view of remembering and imagining is therefore very similar to the view I have been putting forward about actual seeing, because I have been claiming that seeing a real scene is also a process of checking that you have information about the scene. In the case of seeing, however, the information you are checking on can be confirmed in the outside world. In seeing, the world serves as a kind of outside memory store.[4]

The "Presence" of Seeing Determined by Four Important Concepts

If seeing is really the same as remembering or imagining, except confirmed with information from the world, then the feel of seeing should be very much like the feel of remembering or imagining. Why then does seeing provide an impression of "reality" that we don't get when we are just remembering things? Even imagining things does not give the same impression of "presence" as seeing. Where does the feel of presence or reality of seeing come from? The answer lies in four important concepts that I will also be making use of extensively when discussing the "what it's like" of consciousness.

Richness

First, the real world is *richer* than memories and imaginings. When I imagine my grandmother's face, I cannot really be surprised by what I imagine, since it is myself who is reconstructing it. Furthermore, there are large uncharted territories where I'm unable to answer questions about her face: "Are her eyebrows equally thick?"; "Is her hairline asymmetrical?"

On the other hand, when I'm actually seeing her face in front of me in the real world, I can ask myself any question about what is visible and obtain the answer through the mere flick of my eyes or my attention.

Bodiliness

Second, vision has *bodiliness*: Whenever I move my body (and in particular my eyes), there is an immediate change in the incoming visual input: The retinal image shifts. Seeing therefore involves an intimate link between my body motions and resulting sensory input. On the other hand, when I'm *remembering* or *imagining*, moving my eyes or my body doesn't in any way change the information available in my sensory input. Later in this book we shall also see the importance of bodiliness when applied to other sense modalities.

(Partial) Insubordinateness

Third, the sensory input is not totally controlled by my body. It is insubordinate, and *partially escapes my control*, in the sense that there are times when sensory input can change by itself, without my bodily motions causing this change. This happens when the thing I'm looking at moves or changes in some way. Except in certain mental pathologies, such a situation cannot occur when I remember something, for in that case there is no independent outside agency that can cause a change.

Grabbiness

Fourth, vision has *grabbiness*. The human visual system is wired up with an alerting mechanism that can imperatively grab our cognitive processing on the occurrence of sudden outside events. The alerting mechanism works by monitoring neural input in the visual pathways and detecting sudden changes (so-called transients) in local luminance, color, or contrast of the retinal image.

The word *transient* is borrowed from electronics, where it denotes a transitory current surge in a circuit. In electronics, transients are nasty things that should be filtered out, because they tend to destroy sensitive components. In vision (and indeed in the other sense modalities), sudden changes often signal dangerous and unexpected events, like lions shifting behind bushes and mice flitting across rooms. It is natural that biological systems should possess detectors for tran- sients. Furthermore, these detectors are wired up so as to interrupt other forms of cognitive processing and provoke automatic orienting responses: When a sudden,

Figure 2.4 Vision (on the left) has grabbiness—the slightest flicker or flash attracts our attention. Memory (on the right) has no grabbiness—we forget things without being aware that we have forgotten them.

unexpected loud noise occurs, we cannot help but to orient our heads and eyes to the source of the sound. The visual system has detectors that continuously monitor the incoming information, and whenever there is a sudden change, our eyes are automatically drawn to the location of the change.

Thus, if I am visually manipulating one part of the scene and a transient occurs somewhere else, then I am forcibly stopped from manipulating the original part and caused to start manipulating the new part. As a consequence, I go from seeing the original part to seeing the new part.

The grabbiness of vision means that transients in the visual world exercise a form of *authority* on our mental activity. They incontrovertibly cause us to orient our cognitive processing toward sudden disturbances. Imagine that suddenly my grandmother's hair changed to purple while I was looking at her face. This would immediately grab my attention and I would see it.

On the other hand, memory has no grabbiness. Those neurons that code the third person of the Latin verb *amo* might die in my brain, and no bell will ring or whistle will blow to warn me . . . the memory just will quietly disappear without my noticing it. I will only discover I've forgotten the conjugation of *amo* if I try to recall it (Fig. 2.4).

In summary, the reason seeing seems more real to us than remembering or imagining is because the activity of seeing involves four properties that provide it with its particular perceptual "presence": richness, bodiliness, partial insubordinateness, and grabbiness.

As mentioned, these four concepts will also be very important in explaining the "what it's like" of other sensory feels.

Notes

1. For example, see MacKay (1967, 1972).
2. Whenever I give a talk about the idea now, a few philosophers always come up to me and say, "You know, so-and-so said something like that a long time ago" (you can replace "so-and-so" by Plato, Al Hazen, Bergson, Husserl, Ryle, Minsky, Dennett ... to name but a few). This illustrates the principle that once you latch on to a good idea, people always like to spoil the thrill by telling you that everyone knew about it already.
3. I mentioned this idea in several lectures I gave in the United States in 2000, notably in a plenary lecture at the conference "Toward a Science of Consciousness," in Tucson, Arizona, April 8–15, 2000. Block (2001, 2007) has also discussed it. The idea is due to Nigel Thomas (Thomas, 1999), but he has not been given as much credit as he should for it.
4. I proposed this in my article "Solving the mysteries of visual perception: The world as an outside memory" (O'Regan, 1992). A similar idea had been proposed by Minsky (1988) and Dennett (1991), and it has also been taken up by Rensink (2000).

Chapter 3

Applying the New View of Seeing

The new view of seeing described in Chapter 2 considers seeing to be an exploratory activity, somewhat like touch. The experience of seeing is not something that is generated in the brain, but it consists in the very fact of engaging in this visual-exploratory interaction with the environment. The experience of seeing the whole scene, and of seeing it continuously, derives not from the spatial extent or temporal continuity of some internal representation, but from the fact that anything in the scene that might be of interest can be immediately accessed by making the appropriate movements of the eyes or attention.

Now consider how this new view can be applied to understand why we don't experience the multiple defects of the visual system enumerated in Chapter 1.

Inverted Vision

The first defect of vision that I discussed was the fact that the image on the retina is upside down. I surveyed the views of several authors on this question, reaching the conclusion that this "defect" really is no problem because what counts is the relation of sensory input to actions that can be effected. Provided the observer has learned the effect of his actions on his sensory input, it will appear correctly oriented to him.

But this suggests that the perceived right-side-upness or upside-downness of vision should not be something that applies across the board to all parts of a scene: rather, whether we see some particular thing as correctly oriented should depend on the proficiency with which we engage in actions with respect to that thing. When we are adept at interacting with one particular thing, then the aspects of vision which are necessary for that interaction should seem "correct" to us. But at the same time other aspects of the scene, for which the associated exploratory skills are not fully mastered, may appear uncomfortable or abnormal to us.

These predictions are confirmed by research done on "inverted vision." At the 1896 International Congress for Psychology in Munich, George M. Stratton, a psychologist from the University of California, read a paper that sparked the interest of generations of researchers. Stratton had constructed a special tube which, when worn over one eye, made the visual world look upside down and left-right reversed. Because this meant that inside the eyes the images of the world were now right side up instead of being inverted as they usually are, his paper was entitled "Some preliminary experiments on vision without inversion of the retinal image,"[1]

He wore the apparatus continuously for 3 days and noticed that while everyday actions were at first very awkward, he gradually adapted to the apparatus, and at certain times actually felt that things looked right side up again: ". . . all things which under the conditions could be seen at all repeatedly appeared to be in normal relation; that is, they seemed to be right side up."[2]

In a paper published the following year Stratton described a second, 8-day experiment, in which he confirmed that there were times when the world seemed normal. For example, on the seventh day of the experiment, he wrote: "The general outlines of the room, and the more important points of reference, arose in harmony with the new sight-perceptions."[3]"During the walk in the evening, I enjoyed the beauty of the evening scene, for the first time since the experiment began."[4]

Since Stratton's day, numerous researchers have done similar adaptation experiments where an observer (very often the investigator himself) will, for a number of days or even weeks, wear some peculiar instrument that radically alters or distorts his perception of the world (see Fig. 3.1). People have, for example, worn goggles fitted with prisms, lenses, or mirrors that reverse left and right, that shift the whole visual scene to the right or left, that cause the top half and bottom half of the scene to be shifted in opposite directions, or that shrink horizontal dimensions so that everything looks squashed. Goggles with prisms will, in addition to shifting the scene, often introduce additional effects like making straight lines look curved, making flat objects look concave or convex, changing the apparent distance of objects, and making colored fringes appear on the edges of objects. In the 1950s at the University of Innsbruck in Austria, Ivo Kohler was a champion of such

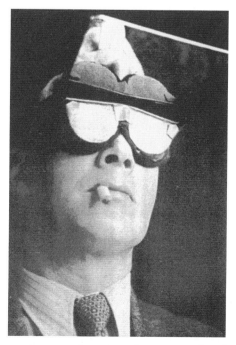

Figure 3.1 A person wearing a top-down inverting mirror, taken from the book by Ivo Kohler's colleague Heinrich Kottenhoff (Kottenhoff, 1961). Reprinted with permission.

experiments. He equipped people with inverting mirrors or prisms and observed how they adapted over periods lasting as long as several months.[5]

Wearing a device that inverts your vision does much more than just make things look upside down. It interferes profoundly with everything you do. Most dramatically, you first have a very hard time standing up. Under normal circumstances, your brain uses information from peripheral vision to detect any slight swaying of your body, and to adjust your balance so that you don't fall over. But if you are wearing goggles that invert your vision, the information being provided to your peripheral vision is incorrect. For example, it says that you are swaying backward when you are actually swaying forward. As a result, the subtle correction that the brain sends to your leg muscles to get you back to vertical actually causes you to sway even more in the wrong direction, which in turn causes even more incorrect corrections to be made. Consequently, you rapidly fall flat on your face, or, rather, you energetically throw yourself flat on your face in a useless attempt to avoid doing so. A similar thing happens when you try to ride a bicycle with crossed hands: All your normal reflexes act to accentuate errors in balance and you throw yourself to the ground.

But gradually, as you continue to wear the goggles, you adapt to the situation and you are able to stand up and walk around. If you look down at your feet (which is confusing because it requires looking in a direction that seems upward to you), you see them not as sticking out from under you, but as facing toward you. Furthermore, when you move one foot, you have the impression that you see the other foot move, or that the foot that is moving is someone else's, not yours, since the moving foot is moving toward you instead of away from you.

There is a film made by the Innsbruck researchers where a person wearing inverting goggles tries to walk through a gateway to shake hands with a friend. He boldly walks toward the open gate, and then instead of simply walking through it, makes an enormously high leg movement, as though he were stepping over a very large obstacle. Evidently he sees the top of the gate as being below him, and he thinks he has to step over it. Having dealt with this obstacle he strides confidently forward and reaches out to shake his friend's hand. But unfortunately he again misjudges the directions of up and down and energetically stretches his arm out at about the level of the friend's head, who recedes in alarm to avoid being knocked in the nose.

Figure 3.2 is a photograph of another researcher, Hubert Dolezal, trying to shake hands with someone. Dolezal is one of the people who submitted themselves to an extended investigation of the effect of wearing reversing prisms. Dolezal evidently wanted to combine work with pleasure, and he decided to spend his holidays on a Greek island while continuously wearing a helmet equipped with the prisms. Notwithstanding the reactions of the local population as he swam at the beaches and walked around the villages, he was able to conduct a careful investigation that formed the material for his PhD thesis, later published as a book.[6] Some of Dolezal's descriptions of his difficulties adapting to the apparatus are worth quoting in full.

After first putting on the inverting prisms, Dolezal describes his encounter with a hook as follows:

> Pulling down is visually confused with lifting up, and vice versa: The problems with hanging or removing some clothing article from a hook are unbelievable.

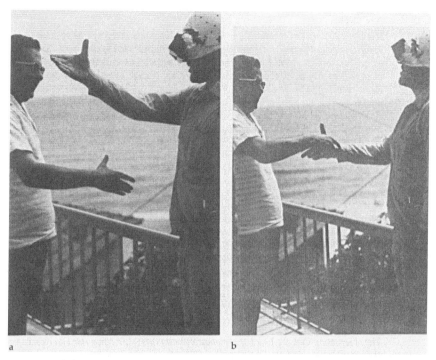

Figure 3.2 (*a*) Hubert Dolezal attempting to shake hands wearing up-down reversing prisms; (*b*) success is finally achieved by assuming a novel head position, which keeps the reaching arm-hand in the field of view. (From Figure 8.2 in Dolezal, 2004.) Reprinted with permission of The Blackburn Press.

Visually, a hook's open (receiving) part appears to be pointing toward the ground so that anything that one might hang on it would immediately drop to the ground. Also, the visual meaning of the correct hand movement which needs to be executed to hang something on a hook—the one I have been using for years—is that it is incorrect or awkward. Thus, under visual guidance, this hand movement is "corrected." Hence, in order to take something off the hook, I have been pulling wildly, almost taking the hook with me. This action was invariably accompanied by surprise, then disbelief (that the shirt wasn't doing what a shirt in that situation should be doing visually), and finally, frustration. It took me minutes of pulling to convince myself that I needed to lift the shirt in order to get it down in one piece. This "convincing" required engaging in an arm movement, the visual meaning of which is contrary to its actual effect. Lifting, of course, looks like (visually affords) pulling, and pulling looks like lifting. Ten hours after this initial encounter, I'm not so sure anymore. If nothing else, my "hook" behavior is more appropriate on Day 4 to what hooks require as well as afford. It must be noted that the gains made in this task are virtually wiped out unless I stand directly in front of the hook; when I'm off to the side—when the hook is no longer in the sagittal plane (i.e., directly in front of my body)—the old problems spring up.[7]

This last remark is particularly interesting: It shows that the adaptation that has occurred after 10 hours is not a global righting of the visual field. For if it were, then it should make no difference whether the hook is in front of Dolezal or to the side. In fact, what we see is that adaptation is restricted to particular situations and behaviors.

Another example is given by the experience of subject Kottenhoff in one of Ivo Kohler's studies. Kottenhoff had after several days of wearing left-right inverting goggles adapted sufficiently to be able to drive a car. When asked to judge on which side of the road he perceived the car ahead of him, he answered correctly. When asked on which side of the car he perceived the driver to be sitting, he also answered correctly. But at the same time as all these aspects of the scene seemed normally oriented to him, when asked to read the license plate, he answered that he saw it in mirror writing.

Similar phenomena have been observed with inverting goggles. After adaptation, the observer's impression of uprightness depends on context. A cup is seen as upside down until coffee is poured into it, when suddenly, because logically coffee can only flow downward, the scene is now perceived as being correctly oriented. A cigarette is seen as upside down until the smoke that rises from it is noticed, when it is perceived as right side up.

It is as though the observer has an ambiguous perceptual experience: She is not sure whether the image is right side up or upside down, and she sees it in some sense as both. But when contextual information is provided, this helps precipitate her perception into one or other state. A good example of how perception can be ambiguous in this way is provided in a study done in the 1950s with a man wearing left-right inverting spectacles.

> Another of the training procedures he adopted was to walk round and round a chair or table, constantly touching it with his body, and frequently changing direction so as to bring both sides into action. It was during an exercise of this kind, on the eighth day of the experiment, that he had his first experience of perceiving an object in its true position. But it was a very strange experience, in that he perceived the chair as being both on the side where it was in contact with his body and on the opposite side. And by this he meant not just that he knew that the chair he saw on his left was actually on his right. He had that knowledge from the beginning of the experiment. The experience was more like the simultaneous perception of an object and its mirror image, although in this case the chair on the right was rather ghost-like.[8]

Instead of considering the adaptation that takes place as consisting in a righting of the visual field, it would seem that in many cases the observer will conceive of what is going on in terms of a modification of her body schema. This is illustrated by the following example from Dolezal:

> Eating with my forehead: My luncheon companion just spoon fed me. The spoon with food was seen to be coming directly toward my forehead, and I experienced great surprise when the spoon touched my closed lips.

While the spoon was on its way, I recall thinking angrily, "What's the idea of trying to stick food onto my forehead?" On Day 12, the same thing happened. This time her hand never entered the FV and haptically, the "feel" of the food on my lips was wrong— haptically, my mouth should have been somewhere else. . . up there somewhere. . . at the top of my head. [9]

Dolezal provides an illustration in which he tries to sum up his experience: It was as though his head were attached upside down to his shoulders, or floating between his legs (see Fig. 3.3).

It would seem therefore that rather than perceiving the world as correctly oriented, Dolezal adapted to the apparatus by conceiving of his head as being inverted. Other investigators have also described similar impressions, and the results are compatible with recent careful replications.[10]

What is interesting about all these studies is that adaptation takes place in a piecemeal fashion, with perception of objects and even the observer's own self being fragmented. Each different activity the observer engages in has its own, different adaptation process with its own particular time course. Thus, balancing and standing up constitute an activity that adapts relatively quickly, but doing fine manual manipulation takes much longer. As concerns the *perceptual* impression people have, it is less that they think the world is either upside down or right side up, but more that they are familiar or unfamiliar with how things look, that things are easy or difficult to deal with. To the observer the location of objects in space is not a

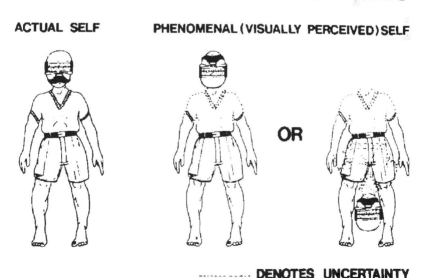

PERCEIVED ORIENTATION AND LOCATION OF THE HEAD AND OTHER BODY PARTS

ACTUAL SELF   PHENOMENAL (VISUALLY PERCEIVED) SELF

OR

---------- DENOTES UNCERTAINTY

Figure 3.3 Dolezal's feeling of the location of his head and other body parts seen while using the up-down reversing prisms. (From Figure 9.2 in Dolezal, 2004.) Reprinted with permission of The Blackburn Press.

simple matter of knowing their x,y,z coordinates. Objects seem to possess a variety
of coordinate systems that need not be logically coherent with one another and that
evolve at different rates during adaptation. So, for example, an object like a man's
face can be correctly localized as being in the top portion of the visual field, yet his
eyes may nonetheless be perceived as being upside down inside his face.

The situation can be compared to an upside-down picture of Margaret Thatcher
(Fig. 3.4). You may notice that the image has been somehow doctored, but you nevertheless clearly recognize the iron lady. However, if you now turn the picture right
side up, the horror of her expression suddenly becomes evident. What this shows is
that recognition of a picture does not involve recognition of all its parts in a uniform
way. The facial expression and the face as a whole are not recognized and rotated
simultaneously to their correct orientations, and they clearly involve independent recognition mechanisms. This is similar to Kottenhoff's finding that the whole
car looked normally oriented but that the license plate was nevertheless in mirror
writing.

Another example is looking in the mirror. I distinctly remember the trouble I had
learning to shave. I would continually move the razor in the wrong direction, confusing left and right, near and far. Now after many years I am very adept at shaving
and thought I had a perfect perception of the topography of my face. But recently
I was going to a party and thought my hair needed trimming. I tried with a razor
to adjust my sideburns so that they were nicely horizontal. I realized that although
I could see them perfectly well in the mirror, and though I could see that they
were slanted and not horizontal, I was unable to say *which way* they were slanting.

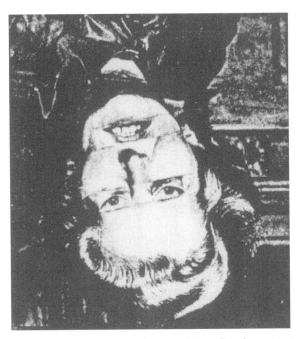

**Figure 3.4 Peter Thompson's "Margaret Thatcher illusion" with permission from Pion
Limited, London (Thompson, 1980).**

Furthermore, I was unable to adjust the razor to correct for the slant. It was extremely frustrating. I think I must have ended up going to the party with one side burn slanting one way and the other slanting the other way.

What is the conclusion from all these considerations? It would seem that it is incorrect to conceive of the visual field like a picture that may or may not be "the right way up." Thinking about the visual field in terms of this "picture postcard" analogy is merely a convenience that makes sense when we have mastered all the different ways of interacting with our visual environment, and when these different skills blend into a coherent web. But even when they do, as we have seen with the Margaret Thatcher phenomenon, the "visual field" actually is not perfectly coherent.

All this is understandable in the light of the new view of seeing that I have put forward. Under this view, seeing does not consist in passively registering a picture-postcard-like representation of the outside world. Instead, seeing involves actively interacting with the world. Saying that we have the impression of a coherent visual field is simply an abbreviated way of saying that we are comfortable with all the ways that we visually interact with the world.

The Blind Spot and Retinal Scotoma

I shall now look at how the new view of seeing deals with the problem of the blind spot and the retinal scotoma: Why do we not have the impression of seeing the world with vast empty spots, as though it is under the body and legs of a giant spider?

Instead of answering this question directly, first consider another question. Suppose you are a blind person exploring a table with your hands. You touch it with your fingers, your palm. Now ask yourself: *Do you feel that there are holes in the table in the places where there are gaps between your fingers?* Answer: Obviously, no. Do you think this is because the brain fills in the bits of the table that are missing between your fingers? Answer: Probably not. Feeling the table consists in using your hand as a tool to explore an outside object, namely the table. There is no question of confusing the defects in the tool you use (i.e., the gaps between the fingers) with defects in what you feel (i.e., holes in the table).

But then why is it so natural to think the brain should have to fill in the gap in the blind spot, when we don't think this is necessary for the gaps between our fingers? Presumably it's because we usually consider vision to involve something like taking a photograph, whereas we consider touch to be an *exploratory* sense.

But let us take the view that vision is an exploratory sense like touch. Seeing is then like exploring the outside world with a giant hand, the retina. The fact that there are parts of the retina like the blind spot and the retinal scotoma where there are no photoreceptors is then of no consequence. Just as the holes between the fingers don't make us think there are holes in the table, the gaps in the retina will not make us think there are gaps in the world.

This is not to say that we cannot become aware of the retinal scotoma. Just as we become aware of the gaps between our fingers by noting that we can put something in the gaps, we can become aware of the blind spot by noting that we can make things disappear into it. But, again, just as we cannot feel the gaps *themselves* between our fingers, we cannot see the blind spot *itself*.

Indeed, under the new view of seeing, there is no reason why we should see the blind spot. Seeing involves exploring the outside world with a tool, namely the retina. You cannot use the tool to inspect the tool itself: You cannot measure whether a ruler has changed length by using the ruler itself. You cannot grip your own pliers with your own pliers. You cannot see your own retina, let alone the holes in it.

Filling in

If filling in is not necessary for the blind spot, what should we make of phenomena like the Kanizsa and Ehrenstein illusions described in Chapter 1, where the filling in seems somehow more "active" or real, and where there is neurophysiological evidence for filling-in mechanisms? I claim that in these cases, what look like active neurophysiological filling-in mechanisms are actually instances of the way the brain extracts information about the outside world. This can be understood in the following way.

What the brain does when we see is to probe the environment, checking whether this or that thing is present. To do this, the brain uses a battery of neural "detectors" or "filters" that it applies to the sensory input. Such filters have evolved through the course of evolution and are additionally tuned by our everyday interaction with the world so as to detect things like lines and borders and local motion cues, which constitute a useful vocabulary of features with which to describe the outside world.

Now, when the visual system applies its filters to the world, it may happen, because of the way the filters are wired up, that they will respond even if the cues are only partially present. Special situations may even arise when the filters can be made to respond when in fact there are no lines or borders or surfaces or motion at all. This may be what happens in the case of virtual contours of the Ehrenstein or Kanizsa illusions, where abutting lines excite line detectors that are oriented perpendicularly to them. Analogous explanations may apply for brightness filling-in phenomena as in the Craik-O'Brian-Cornsweet illusion, or in the phi phenomenon or cinema,[11] where rapid sequences of static images cause motion detectors to respond in a way that is indistinguishable from when real motion is present.

Thus, the apparent neurophysiological evidence for active filling in can be accounted for in terms of basic feature detection mechanisms whose purpose is to extract regularities in the environment. These processes can, under certain circumstances, be tricked into signaling the presence of information that is in fact not present in the environment. When that happens we may see virtual contours where there are no lines, brightness changes where there are no brightness changes, extended surfaces where there are no surfaces.[12]

Optical Defects and Aberrations

Why do we not notice the strong optical defects of the visual apparatus, which cause those parts of the retinal image which are off the line of sight to be out of focus, and which, at high-contrast edges, create rainbow-like color fringes oriented tangentially to a circle centered on the optic axis? There are two aspects to this question. One aspect concerns the existence of adaptation mechanisms in the visual system. Another aspect concerns what we see.

Adaptation Mechanisms

As I said for filling-in mechanisms, there may indeed be mechanisms in the visual system that are sensitive to blur and to color fringes and that transform the incoming sensory data in such a way as to take account of these defects. However, such mechanisms are not "compensation" mechanisms that re-create a perfected image of the world which can subsequently be projected onto an internal screen and contemplated by a homunculus. They are instead part of the process of extracting information about the outside world from the sensory input.

What the visual system must do in order to provide information about the outside world is to differentiate sources of information in the world from sources in the visual system itself. If a point of light on the retina is systematically associated with a circle of blur around it, or if edges are systematically associated with colored fringes, it is most likely that these phenomena are not part of the world, but artifacts of the way the visual system operates. The statistical mechanisms in the visual system which are continually searching for the most efficient ways of coding neural input would ensure that such phenomena would tend to be ignored in further, higher order processing.[13]

Such neural mechanisms might exist in relation to the blur[14] and color aberrations caused in the eye by the poor optical quality of the lens.[15] In experiments where people are fitted with spectacles having prisms that create colored fringes, they adapt to these fringes and come to no longer see them. But when they remove the spectacles, inverse fringes are seen which correspond to no real fringes on the retina.[16]

In short, mechanisms may well exist in the visual system that adapt to the statistical structure of the incoming sensory data and decrease sensitivity to artifacts that are likely to be produced by optical defects of the visual apparatus.[17]

What We See[18]

When I look through a dirty window, I don't see the outside world very clearly. But I don't have the impression that the outside world is itself somehow dirty. When I wear my glasses, I'm not usually aware of their rims. But if I put on someone else's glasses, their rims, which are in a new place, are suddenly much more obvious.

As with tactile manipulation, seeing is actively manipulating, probing, and testing the way my visual inputs react to motions of my eyes, body, and external objects, with a view to extracting information from the environment. When I'm in this way palpating certain features of the environment, I see those features. This is part of the explanation of why I don't see the outside objects as dirty or as blurry, and why I don't usually notice the rims of my glasses.

Take again the tactile example of holding the harmonica. Question: Without moving your hand, can you feel the gaps between your fingers? Answer: No, you can only come to know there are gaps between your fingers if you first detect a part of the harmonica, and then note that that you are no longer in contact with that part. You can only become aware of the gaps between your fingers indirectly, by virtue of how these gaps modify your perception of outside objects.

The same is true of the blind spot. The only way to become aware of it is to note that for certain special positions of your eyes you cannot get information about things in the outside world which you normally would be able to get.

Take another example. You hold your hand out in front of you without moving your fingers. Can you feel how soft the skin on your fingertips is? Obviously not. Try touching an object now. Can you tell how soft your fingertip skin is? Again, no. You can feel how soft the *object* is, but not how soft your *fingertip* skin is. To feel how soft your fingertip skin is, you have to feel it with the other hand.[19] Or you have to know previously how hard an object is and, by comparison, judge how hard your finger is by touching that object.

Perception is oriented toward objects in the environment. To perceive the deficiencies of the organ you use to perceive with, you have to make use of known facts about the environment to reveal them.

Nonuniformities in Retinal Sampling, and Perception of Color

Touch involves actively exploring with your hand. You can stroke and tap a table with your fingertips, your palm, your fingernails, and each part of your hand provides further confirming evidence about the hardness of the table. Despite the different sensitivities of the different parts of your hand, objects do not appear to change their hardness when you explore them with these different parts. On the contrary, part of the feeling of hardness actually resides precisely in the different ways that different parts of the hand interact with the table.

The same argument holds for spatial resolution. The fact that my vision is highly detailed only in the center of the visual field doesn't make the things I look at seem highly detailed at the center of my visual field and more granular in peripheral vision. To expect this to be the case would be like expecting things to feel differently smooth depending on whether you touch them with your fingertip or with your palm or fingernail.

In a similar way, the fact that I have good color resolution only at the very center of my visual field doesn't mean I see objects as losing their coloredness when I move my eyes away from them. On the contrary, part of the sensation of the color of an object lies precisely in the way the quality of the sensory information concerning color gets modified as I move my eye near and close to the object.

Another example in relation to the sensation of color concerns the changes that occur as you move a colored object around in front of you. A piece of paper is perceived as red if it behaves like red things behave when you move it around under different light sources. For example, depending on whether you hold the red piece of paper in the sun, under the lamp, or next to another colored surface, the changes in the shade of light reflected back to you obey a different pattern than if it had been a green surface. What characterizes red is the set of all these typical red behaviors.

In Chapter 11, I show the surprising fact that these ideas allow us to predict what colors people tend to give names to and see as "basic."

Deformations and Cortical Magnification

In Chapter 1, I described the geometrical distortions that affect straight lines because of the shape of the eyeball and cortical sampling of that shape, and I asked why we nevertheless see straight lines as straight. Under the new view of seeing, however, it is clear that the shape of the cortical representation has little to do with the perceived shape of the lines. The reason is that what defines a straight line is something special about the laws that govern how you can interact with a straight line: What defines a straight line is the fact that if you sample information about a straight line, and then move along the line, the new sample you get will be the same as the old one.[20] It doesn't matter if the optics of the eye produce horrendous distortions, with the image totally bent or exploded. And it doesn't matter that the cortical representation is distorted. The retina doesn't have to be flat; in fact it can be any shape, even corrugated. It is simply a property of straight lines that if the eye moves along them, there will be no change in the excitation pattern, and this is true no matter how the eye or brain represents the information.

There are subtleties about these ideas that would require discussion beyond the scope of this book. Suffice it here to say that it is possible to deduce things about the structure of outside physical objects by studying the laws relating movements that an organism makes to the resulting changes in sensory input.[21] These "sensorimotor laws" are not affected by any distortions caused by defects of the sensory apparatus.

But then you might ask, If we can get perfectly good information from a totally defective sensory apparatus, why then is our sensory apparatus not even more catastrophic? Why are our retinas constructed with some resemblance of order instead of simply being made up of gobs of mixed up neural tissue with random structure? The answer is that differences in the quality of the sensory apparatus make information harder or easier to obtain. The efficiency of neural processing may depend on the organization of the sensors and the codes used to represent information. But whatever the efficiency and whatever the code, we perceive the world, not the code.

Perturbations Due to Eye Movements

Why do we not see the blur caused by eye saccades, and why does the world not appear to shift every time we move our eyes? The analogy with tactile exploration once again provides the answer. When you manually explore an object, at different times your hand can lose contact with the surface. Despite this, you do not have the feeling that the object disappears from existence. The reason is that the feeling of the presence of the object resides not in the continuous presence of tactile stimulation through your skin, but through your being continually "tuned" to the changes that might occur when you move your fingers this way and that. Stopping the finger motion or even removing your hand from the object and checking that tactile sensation ceases are actually ways of further confirming that you are indeed exploring an external object. Were you to remove your hand from the object and find that tactile sensation nevertheless continued, you would have to conclude that the object was somehow sticking to your fingers. Were you to stop moving your hand and find that the sensation of movement continued, you would conclude that the object was moving of its own accord.

Similarly with vision, the feeling of the presence of an outside object derives precisely from the fact that by moving your eyes, you can produce predictable changes on the incoming signal. Were you to blink, for example, or move your eyes, and find that there was no change in the retinal signal, you would have to conclude that you were hallucinating. Just as with touch, the feeling of the continual presence of an outside visual object resides in the very fact that eye movements and blinking allow you to control, in a predictable way, the signal that the object provides.

Thus, far from creating a perturbation in vision, eye movements are the means by which we can ascertain that neural stimulation truly corresponds to a real, outside object and is not simply some artifact of the sensory apparatus like an afterimage or a hallucination.

Of course, for this to work, the brain must know when it makes eye movements. Indeed, evidence for the fact that the brain is taking account of eye movements comes from the discovery of neurons in the cortex whose sensitivity to visual stimulation shifts when the eye is about to move. For example, such a neuron might be sensitive to information 10 degrees to the right, but then just when the eye is about to move, say, 3 degrees to the right, the neuron shifts to being sensitive to information 7 degrees to the right. This means that the same area of outside physical space (that first was located at 10 degrees and now is located at 7 degrees) is being sampled by the neuron, despite the shift caused by eye movement.

The trouble is that the eye doesn't always move exactly to where the brain tells it to move. There may be inaccuracies in the execution of the muscle command, caused by fatigue or obstructions. For that reason there are sensors in the muscles themselves that tell whether the command has been properly executed by measuring the actual degree of extension or contraction that has occurred. Such so-called proprioceptive information is also available to help keep tabs on where the eye has moved.

Taken together, both the eye movement command signal itself and the proprioceptive feedback signal from the muscles contribute to allow the brain to estimate where things are located in space. That does not mean there is an internal picture of the outside world that is being shifted around. The representation that the brain maintains of the outside visual environment need not have accurate position information. This is because seeing does not involve reconstructing an internal picture of the outside world with accurate metrical properties. Seeing involves *being able to access* information in the outside world. If we need to know the position of some object accurately, we can just move our eyes and our attention to the parts that we are interested in and estimate the position that way. We don't need to expend costly brain resources to re-create an internal picture of what is already available outside in the world. All we need is to know how to get our eyes focalized on regions that we are interested in seeing[22].

Notes

1. Stratton (1896). A second paper was Stratton (1897).
2. Stratton, 1896, p. 616.
3. Stratton, 1897, p. 464.
4. Stratton, 1897, p. 466.
5. Kohler also investigated adaptation to much more bizarre devices. For example, he got people to adapt to spectacles mounted with prisms that were continuously rotated by an electric motor attached to the forehead. The result was that people perceived regular "optical earthquakes" at a rate that diminished gradually as the battery that drove the motor discharged. Predictably he had to discontinue this experiment because people rapidly became nauseous. Another experiment involved wearing a hat equipped with elastic bands connected to the shoulders, forcing the head to remain continually turned to the side. Both these devices are mentioned in Kohler (1974). All these experiments had the purpose of creating distortions of the perceptual world, whereas more recently, electronics and computers are being used to modify perception in order to provide conditions of what has variously been called augmented reality, virtual reality, or mediated reality. One of the earliest proponents of the idea that human perception might be aided by the use of modern computer technology was Steve Mann with his wearable "mediated reality" devices. In the 1990s Mann could be seen gingerly making his way around MIT wearing a helmet equipped with goggles and an antenna. Instead of seeing the world directly, Mann was seeing the world via the goggles he was wearing. The images captured by miniature TV cameras mounted on the helmet were transmitted back to the MIT media lab. There the images were processed and modified by a computer and transmitted back to the goggles. The images could be modified in various ways; for example, text could be added providing identity information if the user had difficulty remembering faces, or colors could be added or modified to highlight interesting or important aspects of the scene. At the time, CNN broadcast an article about Mann, which can be seen on http://www.cnn.com/TECH/9604/08/computer_head. The Web site http://www.wearcam.org is an amusing collection of information about mediated reality that was run by Mann. Today the use of wearable aids to perception is commonplace in the military, for example, providing night vision or information about potential targets.
6. Dolezal, 1982. Originally published by Academic Press in 1982, the book was republished in 2004 by the Blackburn Press.
7. Dolezal, 1982, pp. 170–172.
8. Taylor, 1962, pp. 201–202. The observer here was Seymour Papert (early director of the MIT Artificial Intelligence lab, well-known proponent of the logo programming language, and, with Marvin Minsky, destroyer of the perceptron) wearing left-right inverting spectacles, during an experiment he subjected himself to while visiting Taylor in Cape Town in 1953.
9. Dolezal, 1982.
10. In particular, a recent study using functional brain imaging shows that while certain everyday tasks are rapidly adapted to, others that involve fine haptic manipulation do not easily adapt. Also perceptual biases in shape-from-shading tasks did not adapt, nor was there any evidence for "righting" of the cortical representation of the visual field (Linden, Kallenbach, Heinecke, Singer, & Goebel, 1999).

11. We all know that the pictures in motion pictures are not in actual motion. Movies consist of sequences of still shots, clicking away in succession at a rate of around 24 frames per second. We see this as smooth motion because the neural hardware that detects smooth motion in the retina actually happens to react in the same way whether an object moves smoothly from A to B or simply jumps from A to B—provided the jump takes place sufficiently quickly, and provided A and B are sufficiently close. A particularly interesting case is when the object changes its color as it jumps. Say a red square at A is followed in rapid succession by a green square at B. The subjective impression you have is of a red square moving to B, and changing its color to green somewhere in the middle along the way between A and B. The philosopher Daniel Dennett has devoted considerable discussion to this example in his book *Consciousness Explained* (Dennett, 1991). What interested Dennett was the philosophical difficulty this finding seems to present: The nervous system doesn't know in advance that the square is going to change to green when it arrives at B. Thus, how can it generate the perception of changing to green *in the middle* of the path of motion, *during* the motion, before the information about what color will occur in the future has been received? From the philosopher's point of view, there seems to be a problem here. But from the neuroscientist's point of view, there is no problem at all: The neural hardware responds in the same way to the jump from A to B, with the color change, as it would if there were smooth motion from A to B with a color change in the middle. The neural hardware has been tricked. Or rather, the neural hardware provides the same information to the observer as when smooth motion occurs with a change in the middle. The observer thus interprets the scene in that way.

12. More detail on how the new view deals with filling in can be found in the supplementary information Web site for this book: http://whyred.kevin-oregan.net.

13. This idea has been extensively developed by Barlow (1990).

14. The fact that the visual system is sensitive to the statistics of blur has been very nicely shown in chicks (and monkeys). For example, when chicks are fitted with lenses that make them strongly shortsighted, their eyeballs will, in the course of a few days, change their shape so as to bring images into better focus. The phenomenon appears to be a local, retinal phenomenon, capable of adapting independently to different degrees of blur at each retinal location. (Smith, 1998; Wallman, Gottlieb, Rajaram, & Fugate Wentzek, 1987; Wildsoet & Schmid, 2001). This example shows that the visual system of chicks is sensitive to blur and tries to eliminate it by differential growth of the eye. The example makes it seem quite plausible that adaptation mechanisms might operate also at a purely neural level to eliminate blur in humans.

15. For example, see Vladusich and Broerse (2002); Grossberg, Hwang, and Mingolla (2002).

16. Held, 1980; Kohler, 1974.

17. For an overview of different mechanisms, neural and optical, of compensating for optical defects, see Hofer and Williams (2002).

18. Philosophers: please be tolerant with a mere scientist who does not want to get embroiled in issues of "seeing as" and "seeing that"! I hope what I mean by "what we see" will be clear enough from the use of the phrase in this section.

19. And actually it's not so easy to distinguish *what hand* you are feeling when you do this. Husserl (1989) and Merleau-Ponty (1962) have made interesting distinctions between using the fingers to actively feel something else and passively feeling

something on the finger. Feeling one's own hand with one's other hand is a more difficult, ambiguous case.

20. This idea was suggested by Platt (1960) and further developed by Koenderink (1984). More detail can be found in the filling-in and geometrical distortions section in the supplementary information Web site for this book: http://whyred. kevin-oregan.net.

21. David Philipona worked on this for his PhD with me, and it is partially described in two articles (Philipona, O'Regan, & Nadal, 2003; Philipona, O'Regan, Nadal, & Coenen, 2004). See also http://www.kevin-oregan.net/~philipona

22. Cavanagh et al. (2010) have a very promising account of how this can be done without appealing to shifting pictures in the head.

Chapter 4

The Illusion of Seeing Everything

The new view of seeing suggests that there is no "internal replica" of the outside world where all aspects of the scene are simultaneously "projected" for us to "see all at once." On the contrary, seeing is constituted by the fact of using the tools provided by our visual system to extract and cognitively "manipulate" parts of the scene.

This makes an important prediction: We will only effectively see those parts of a scene that we are actively engaged in "manipulating." Furthermore, the parts that are seen will be seen in the light of the particular type of manipulation we are exercising, with the knowledge and mental background which that involves. Everything else in the scene will not actually be seen. This surprising claim has received impressive confirmation from recent research.

Looked But Failed to See: Inattentional Blindness

On a slightly foggy night at Chicago O'Hare airport, Captain F was bringing his 747 in for a landing. Captain F was an exceptionally good pilot, with thousands of hours of flying to his credit. He had a lot of experience using the "heads-up display" that projected instrument readings on the windshield, allowing him to check the altimeter while at the same time keeping his eyes on the runway. At an altitude of 140 feet, he indicated over the radio his decision to land and then tried to do so. At 72 feet and 131 knots, the runway was clearly visible and Captain F eased back the throttle. Suddenly everything blacked out.

An aircraft was standing in the middle of the runway, totally obstructing it. Evidently not seeing it, Captain F had simply landed through the aircraft (see Fig. 4.1).

Luckily no one was hurt in the accident. The event had taken place in a flight simulator, not in real life.[1] After the blackout Captain F sat there in the simulator wondering what had happened. The First Officer said: "I was just looking up as it disappeared [the simulator image], and I saw something on the runway. Did you see anything?" Captain: "No, I did not." On later being shown a video of what had actually happened, the captain was astounded. Other experienced pilots in this experiment, which was done at the NASA Research Laboratories at Ames, California, had similar experiences. Pilot F said: "If I didn't see it [the video], I wouldn't believe it. I honestly didn't see anything on that runway."

Figure 4.1 The view from Captain F's cockpit. (Photo courtesy of NASA.) Reprinted from Haines, R. (1991) with kind permission of Springer.

Such events are not isolated occurrences: They occur in real life. You're driving down the road, for example, and come up to an intersection. You're just moving into it when you suddenly slam on the brakes: A bicycle is right there in front of you. You realize that you had actually been looking straight at it but somehow didn't see it.[2]

"Looked but failed to see," or LBFTS as it's called by researchers studying traffic accidents,[3] is a curious effect that has been receiving progressively more attention in recent years. An overview[4] commissioned in 2002 by the Department of Transport in Great Britain, discusses three extensive studies (in 1975, 1996, and 1999). One study showed that LBFTS was third in rank among a survey of 3,704 driver errors, after "lack of care" and "going too fast," and that it occurred more frequently than "distraction," "inexperience," or "failed to look," among others. Another study examining 51,261 perceptual errors made by drivers concluded that LBFTS came after "inattention" and "misjudged others' path/speed" and before "failed to look" and "misjudged own path/speed." The effect seems to occur among experienced drivers rather than beginners, and it seems to involve the driver looking directly at something and somehow simply not seeing it.[5]

Another typical example is cited by a British study of police cars parked by the road side.[6] The statistics show that despite very conspicuous markings and flashing lights, stationary police cars quietly sitting on the side of the highway in broad daylight were, until recently, being systematically rammed into by drivers who simply "didn't see them." The rate of such accidents reached more than 200 a year in Britain, and again, seemed mainly to involve experienced drivers who didn't even brake before they hit the back of the police car. Making the police cars even more conspicuous had no effect: It would appear people were somehow just "looking through" the cars. The problem was solved by having police cars park at a slight angle, so that they looked different from a normal car driving along the road and could more clearly be perceived as being stationary, presumably thereby alerting the driver's attention.

A similar finding concerns accidents at railway crossings. One would think that people would not be so stupid as to drive into a train that is rolling by right in front of them. Yet a large number of accidents at railway crossings (36% in a survey in Australia between 1984 and 1988)[7] seem to concern people who drive directly into the side of a train passing in full view.

The "thimble game" is a safer version of "looked but failed to see," described by Daniel Dennett in his book *Consciousness Explained*.[8] You take a thimble and place it in full view somewhere in a room, ideally in a place where the thimble blends in with its background so that, though perfectly visible, it plays the role of something other than a thimble (e.g., masquerading as the hat of a statuette, or as a lamp switch button), or at least is not in its normal thimble context. You then ask a friend to find the thimble. As often as not you will find that the person looks directly at the thimble but does not see it. A commonplace example of this occurs when you look in a drawer for, say, the corkscrew and don't see it even though it is right in front of you.

Dan Simons and Chris Chabris, at the time working together at the University of Harvard, did particularly impressive work on LBFTS, or, as psychologists call it, "inattentional blindness." They produced an astonishing demonstration based on an experimental technique invented in the 1970s by well-known cognitive scientist Ulrich Neisser.[9] A video shows six people, three dressed in black, three in white, playing a ball game in a confined area. The white and black teams each have a ball that they are passing from person to person within their team. Everyone is continuously moving around, making it difficult to follow the ball. Simons and Chabris ask an observer to count the number of times the white team exchanges their ball. The task is hard and the observer concentrates. In the middle of the sequence a person dressed in a black gorilla disguise walks into the middle of the group, stops, pounds his chest in a typical gorilla fashion and then walks out of the room (see Fig. 4.2).

As many as 30%–60% of observers will not notice the gorilla despite the fact that it was totally visible and occupied the very center of the display for a considerable period of time.[10]

Simons and his collaborators have established[11] that the phenomenon depends on the visual conspicuity of the object that is not seen and its relation to the task being performed: If instead of counting the white team's ball passes, the observer counts the black team's, he is almost certain to see the gorilla, who is dark colored. It seems that people define a "mental set" that helps select the aspects of the scene which are important for the task at hand. Things that do not correspond to this mental set will tend to be missed. More prosaically, when you don't see the corkscrew in the drawer, it may be that you have a mental set of the normal, old-fashioned type of corkscrew, and the one in the drawer is a newfangled one. Seeing requires cognitively "manipulating"; how and what you manipulate depends on your expectations.

Another example of the influence of mental set is seen in Figure 4.3. Do you think you see "The illusion of seeing"? Check again! That is not what it says.[12] What we see is strongly determined by our expectations and prior knowledge.

Figure 4.2 Frame from video of Gorilla pounding its chest in Simons and Chabris's 1999 experiment. (Figure provided by Daniel Simons.)

Yet another example of the influence of mental state is seen in Figure 4.4. If I position my eye near the center of the Figure, then both black and white profiles will be projected on my retina and be potentially equally visible. Yet I can cognitively manipulate only one or other of the two profiles, so I only see one at a time.

Processing by the Brain

In these demonstrations, perfectly visible things are not seen. Does that mean that those things are not processed *at all* by the brain? The answer is no. It has been shown that in inattentional blindness tasks, even if observers do not "see" the intruding element, detectable changes in their later behavior may indicate that the element was nevertheless processed to some extent.[13]

This should not surprise us. In experimental psychology there is ample evidence that subliminally presented information can nonetheless influence later decisions and behavior. Even quite sophisticated processing can go on unconsciously.

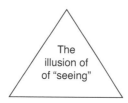

Figure 4.3 This does not say: "The illusion of seeing."

Figure 4.4 It's virtually impossible to see the black and white profiles at the same time.

After all, it happens to all of us that, for example, immersed in a conversation with a friend, we drive for minutes on end without being conscious of the complex maneuvering we do to get through the traffic.

Eye Movement Trajectories

Under the new view of seeing, you only effectively "see" what you are cognitively manipulating at a given moment. Eye movement trajectories in scene perception support this idea.

The left of Figure 4.5 shows a typical trajectory, corresponding to where a person's eyes first went when inspecting a picture for 5 seconds. On the right are the eye movements that occurred in the following minute of observation. We see that the eyes are simply going round in circles.

Under the new view of seeing, this makes sense. If a person looks at a picture and sees it as a picture of a man and a woman having dinner, then in order to see the picture as such, the eyes must continually test and "manipulate" that fact. The impression that

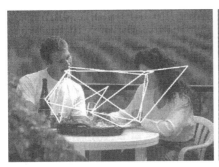

Figure 4.5 Eye movements in the first 5 seconds (*left*) and following (*right*) minute while scanning a scene.

a viewer will have of "seeing everything" in the scene derives from the *potential* accessibility of everything else in the scene. But until the observer actually does wonder more precisely about these other aspects, the eye just goes around concentrating on the parts that the person is currently "manipulating." It is nevertheless important to realize that while eye movement traces identify where a person has *looked*, they do not guarantee that that is what the person has *seen*, as indicated by Captain F in his cockpit, the "looked but failed to see" results, and the gorilla experiment.

Change Blindness

A phenomenon called change blindness that we discovered in the 1990s with colleagues Ron Rensink and Jim Clark has been particularly important in relation to the new view of seeing, because it so dramatically suggests that something might be wrong with the conception that seeing involves activating an internal representation.

In change-blindness experiments, an observer looks at a first picture on a computer monitor. The picture is then replaced by a changed version. The change can be an object that has been moved, or modified (for example, a tree disappears or shifts in position), or it can be a whole region of the picture that has been changed in some way (for example, the sky is changed from blue to red, or the reflection in the water of a lake is removed).

Under normal circumstances such a change is perfectly visible; in fact, it pops out just as a sudden motion in the corner of your eye will catch your attention. But in change-blindness experiments, a brief blank is displayed in between the two pictures. This blank has a devastating effect: Large differences in the two pictures now sometimes become very hard to detect, even if the sequence is shown repeatedly and the observer is told in what region of the picture to look. Demonstrations may be seen on my Web site.[14]

Consciousness researcher and writer Susan Blackmore is really the person who should be credited with doing the first experiment on change blindness.[15] She had already shown, before the flurry of work on this phenomenon, that you can get change blindness by displaying first one picture, then a second, changed picture, but slightly shifted, as though the eye had moved. In fact the effect is not much different from just putting two slightly different pictures side by side and trying to spot the change by moving your eye back and forth between the two pictures. This is the "spot the differences" puzzle found in newspapers, with the difference that here there is just one, much bigger difference (see Fig. 4.6). We shall see below that all these methods produce change blindness because there is always a brief interruption that creates visual "transients" that disrupt your ability to see the difference between the two pictures to compare.

Most people are amazed by change blindness, but on closer consideration, it should not be so surprising. Certainly when you look at a scene, you have the impression of *seeing* it all, but you also know that you cannot *remember* every single detail even for a very short time. It's amusing to check this by asking a friend to go out of the room and change an article of clothing or jewelry. When he or she comes back, you may find it extremely difficult to know what has changed, even though

Figure 4.6 Two different pictures that are displayed successively, with a blank in between them, in change-blindness experiments. The same effect can be achieved as here by simply making an eye saccade between them. Find the difference in the two pictures.

you carefully checked how the person was dressed beforehand. As another example, I have a colleague whose wife and children had pressed him for years to shave his beard. One day on an impulse he excused himself during dinner and came back without his beard. No one noticed. It was only on the following day that his wife remarked that something had changed in the way he looked.

The limitation in memory capacity shown by these kinds of example is confirmed by a whole literature in experimental psychology that has investigated our ability to remember visual details over a short time period. The conclusion from these studies is that even over a time interval as short as a tenth of a second, our so-called visual short-term memory capacity is only about four items.[16] Thus, it should not come as a surprise that we cannot accurately compare two pictures, since to do so we would have to remember many more than four items across the interval between the two pictures.

The reason people find change blindness so surprising[17] is that the phenomenon seems to contradict the fact that we so easily notice even small and unexpected changes in real life. For example, if a mouse suddenly flits across the floor, even if you weren't looking that way or thinking about mice, you will immediately see it. So the real question is not actually about change blindness, but about normal conditions: Why can we so easily detect changes under normal conditions when it's well known that memory capacity is limited to four items? And then why is this capacity disrupted when there is a blank screen between original and changed pictures?

The answer is: visual transients. As mentioned in Chapter 2, one of the things that gives us the impression of really seeing rather than just remembering or imagining is the fact that when there is a sudden event in the visual scene, it creates a visual "transient." When these transient detectors register a sudden event, they interrupt and grab ongoing cognitive processing, and our attention and processing resources are automatically oriented to the event. This is what I mean by saying that vision is "grabby."

But what happens in change blindness, when there is a blank screen between the original and the modified pictures? At the instant the first picture is replaced by a blank, all the elements in the picture disappear, thereby creating numerous transients at each location in the visual field where an element is replaced by a blank. A fraction of a second later, when the modified picture appears, further transients occur all over the visual field, corresponding to the transition from blank to each of the picture elements. In both cases a large number of visual transients are generated in the visual field. As a result, your attention is more likely to be attracted to one of the multiple other transients than to the one corresponding to the change you are looking for.[18]

Slow-Change Experiments

Change blindness makes normal visual transients hard to detect by flooding the visual field with other, extraneous transients. But there is another way of disrupting the normal action of visual transients: Make the changes so slow that there no longer are any transients. This is the technique used in experiments on slow or "progressive" changes.[19] If a change in a picture occurs so slowly that nothing attracts your attention to the changing location, unless you know what is changing, or unless you ask yourself explicitly what there is at that location, you can stare at the picture endlessly and not discover the change. It's particularly noteworthy that you may even be looking directly at the thing that is changing and still not discover it.

The point is that when your eyes are centered on something, what you see is not everything that falls on the retina. You see only what you are currently (implicitly) asking yourself about.

The Impression of "Photographic Vision"

In these last sections I have shown that there are situations in which much of what our eyes fall upon is actually, in some sense of the word, not "seen"—or at least not available for report. This is precisely what is expected from the new view of seeing that I am promoting, since under this approach, seeing does not involve passively receiving all the information available in the visual field. Rather, seeing involves using the tools provided by our visual system to interrogate the visual field in search of information we are currently interested in seeing. It is only what we are interested in seeing at any moment that we actually "see."

Yet the subjective impression we have when we see is absolutely not of only seeing a minute fraction of what is before us. If the theory is right, how can it account for the fact that we have the distinct impression of seeing everything within our field of view, as if in a photograph? Is this impression some kind of illusion?[20]

The impression of "photographic vision" is related to the question already discussed in Chapter 2 of why vision seems "real" or "present" to us, and for which I had invoked the concepts of richness, bodiliness, insubordinateness, and grabbiness. Here I want to extend my treatment to look more closely at four particular aspects of visual experience that underlie its "photographic" quality.

One aspect concerns the *extent* of our vision: We think we perceive things as highly detailed and perfect *all over* the visual field. How are we so sure that we really do perceive those details all over the scene? The answer must be because we know we can answer any questions about all these details if we ask ourselves about them. But to do this we needn't actually have any information stored in the brain about these details. All we require is to be able to immediately access the information in the world by using the instruments that our visual apparatus provides. If our eye movements and attention movements are immediately mobilized as soon as we ask ourselves a question about what detail is over there, then that information will be immediately available on demand.[21] We can then also have the impression of perceiving the detail all over.

Another aspect of our "photographic" impression of seeing everything is that the details seem *simultaneously* present. This means that if we ask ourselves about one detail here and then very quickly ask ourselves about another detail over there, we can do it easily, confirming that all the details are simultaneously present. But again, we don't require any information to be stored in the brain, be it simultaneously or not, for this to be the case. If information about any detail can be obtained instantaneously on demand through a flick of the eye or of attention whenever we ask ourselves about it, we will also have the impression of everything being simultaneously visible.

Thinking we see everything "photographically" seems to also entail the notion of *ongoingness*, that is, that the details in the scene appear all to be *continuously present*. How do we know? Because whenever we ask ourselves whether the details are present, we find them to be present. But again, to have this impression, we merely need the information to be available at every demand. The information doesn't actually have to be continually present in order to seem continually present to us, provided that whenever we do inquire about it, it is available. It might be thought that to have the impression that vision is "ongoing," it would be necessary to have a neural mechanism that is somehow "buzzing" like a running motor, continually active, somehow continuously "refreshing" the internal representation. But in fact, no. We would still have the impression of ongoingness if the visual areas of the brain went to sleep after each eye movement, provided that whenever we ask, "Is the information there?" they wake up and move the attention or the eye over to get the information we want.

The impression of seeing everything "photographically" also seems to entail the idea that things out there *impose themselves* on us, in the sense that when something happens we automatically see it. The fact that the visual scene imposes itself on us is part of visual "presence," already discussed in Chapter 2. Along with richness, bodiliness, and insubordinateness, this presence is mainly brought about by transient detectors built into the visual system that capture our cognitive resources whenever there is a sudden change in the visual input. The grabbiness provided by this setup gives us the impression that vision of everything is somehow forced upon us.

This then is the view that I propose to take about what seeing is. It is using the tools provided to us by the visual system to probe those parts of a scene that interest us. Our impression of seeing everything in the scene as though it is in front of us like a technicolor picture postcard or movie is a sort of illusion. The detail all over, the simultaneous presence of everything, and the impression of temporal continuity provided by the visual scene are in fact consequences of the immediate accessibility of anything we are interested in seeing through a flick of the eye or of attention. The feeling that vision imposes itself on us as being perceptually "present" derives partially from the grabbiness of the visual system in capturing our cognitive resources when transients occur.

Taking this view solves problems that have preoccupied scientists since Kepler and Descartes discovered the upside-down image of the world at the back of the eye. It relieves us of having to postulate "compensation mechanisms" that correct for the upside-down image, for the fact that the retina has a giant hole in it, as well as a spidery network of blood vessels that obscure vision, for the fact that the image is blurry and color smeared everywhere except in the middle and that the retina samples the image in a totally nonuniform manner, and for the fact that eye movements continually smear and displace the image. It relieves us of having to find mechanisms that compensate for these defects because now, instead of having to suppose the existence of a perfected internal brain representation, we can simply assume that the task of the brain is to *make use and make sense* of the information that our different visual tools and filters provide us with.

In particular, if I should ask myself: Does what I see appear to me "like a photograph?"[22] then I will check to see if the outside world has properties that make it seem like a photograph: That is, does it have detail all over? Is the detail all there simultaneously? Is it there continuously? Does it impose its presence on my visual senses? And indeed, because it really is out there available on demand through the slightest movement of attention or of the eye, I will perceive the outside world as looking like a photograph. The photographic appearance of the outside world thus derives from the way our visual instruments can exploit the information the world provides, and not through the "activation" of some inside replica that has photograph-like properties.

Notes

1. Haines, 1991.
2. This type of accident with a bicycle or motorcycle has been discussed by Herslund and Jørgensen (2003). There is also the Web site: http://www.safespeed.org.uk/smidsy.html

3. Cairney & Catchpole, 1996; Sabey & Staughton, 1975. Citations from Cairney, 2003.

4. A review of the "looked but failed to see" accident causation factor, by I. D. Brown, Ivan Brown Associates, 21 Swaynes Lane, Comberton, Cambridge CB3 7EF. Available on the Web site of the British Department for Transport: http://www.dft.gov.uk/ stellent/groups/dft_rdsafety/documents/page/dft_rdsafety_504574-13.hcsp

5. In the case of not seeing bicycles certainly, see Herslund and Jørgensen (2003).

6. The study was conducted with the University of Sussex Human Factors Group. This result is reported by the company Conspicuity, which is associated with researchers from the University of Sussex, including J. Heller-Dixon and M. Langham (see http://www.conspicuity.co.uk/resources/index.html).

7. Cited by Cairney (2003). I have heard informally that the U.S. Department of Transportation has statistics showing that actually the *majority* of accidents at railway crossings in the United States involve cars hitting trains rather than trains hitting cars, but I have been unable to confirm this. I did a search on the Web for occurrences of the combination "car hits train" and found hundreds of them, mostly news stories from small English-language newspapers the world over. Admittedly, many of them corresponded to cases where the accident occurred in the night, in fog, or on slippery roads. But a significant proportion were in full daylight and remained unaccounted for by any visibility problem.

8. Dennett, 1991.

9. Simons & Chabris, 1999. Simons and Chabris' work is also described in their successful book *The invisible gorilla* (Chabris and Simons, 2010). The gorilla demonstration is based on Neisser & Becklen, 1975. See also Mack & Rock, 1998. Neisser used two film sequences that were transparently superimposed; see an example from Becklen and Cervone (1983) on youtube: http://www.youtube.com/watch?v= nkn3wRyb9Bk. Here the interloper is a woman carrying an umbrella instead of a gorilla.

10. The video can be seen on Dan Simons' Web site (http://viscog.beckman.uiuc.edu/ djs_lab/demos.html) or on his youtube channel http://www.youtube.com/user/ profsimons. There is also a youtube version made by Transport for London to warn drivers that they don't see as much as they think (http://www.youtube.com/ watch?v=1_UuZQhlZ5k). For the demonstration to work, the observer must not suspect that anything bizarre is going to happen, and he or she must be trying hard to follow the white team's ball. When I show the video in a lecture, I start by saying that this is a test to see whether you can concentrate on one thing while another thing is going on. I tell people that it is quite hard to follow the white team's ball because of the interference from the black team, and that people will have to concentrate. Generally about a third to half of the audience does not see the gorilla. I have another demonstration using a different task on my Web site: http://www.kevin-oregan.net/demos/BONETO.MOV. The movie was created by Malika Auvray. If you ask people to follow the coin, many will fail to see the green pepper.

11. Using carefully controlled experimental procedures; see the examples on his Web site.

12. The word *of* is repeated.

13. Evidence for this is somewhat controversial and has been gathered mainly in the context of change-blindness experiments; see, for example, Fernandez-Duque and Thornton (2003).

14. http://www.kevin-oregan.net. Early papers made the change coincident with an eye saccade (Blackmore, Brelstaff, Nelson, & Troscianko, 1995; McConkie & Currie, 1996), but the phenomenon became widely known as "change blindness" when it was demonstrated to occur with a flicker between the two images (Rensink, O'Regan, & Clark, 1997, 2000). Following that it was shown that the phenomenon occurred also during blinks (O'Regan, Deubel, Clark, & Rensink, 2000), with "mudsplashes" superimposed on the images (O'Regan, Rensink, & Clark, 1999) during cuts in video sequences (Levin & Simons, 1997) or even in real-life situations (Simons & Levin, 1998). For reviews of the extensive literature, see Rensink (2002); Simons and Ambinder (2005); Simons and Rensink (2005).

15. Blackmore et al., 1995. Philosopher Daniel Dennett had also proposed that one might not easily be able to see isoluminant changes in background colors in peripheral vision if the changes are made during eye movements (Dennett, 1991, p. 467–8).

16. What is meant by "item" in this claim is a delicate issue: Can an item be composed of a large number of elements, all of which are remembered? See Luck and Vogel (1997).

17. See also the following well-named article ("Change blindness blindness") for further discussion of why change blindness is so surprising: (Levin, Momen, Drivdahl, & Simons, 2000).

18. On the Web site for supplementary information for this book, there is a description of how to make your own change blindness demonstration using office presentation software. See http://whyred.kevin-oregan.net.

19. Dan Simons should be credited with this brilliant realization (Simons, Franconeri, & Reimer, 2000; also Auvray & O'Regan, 2003). For demonstrations made by artist Renaud Chabrier and by Malika Auvray see http://www.kevin-oregan.net and http://www.malika-auvray.com

20. The use of the word *illusion* here is loose. In a strict, philosophical sense, it can be argued that seeing can, by definition, not be an illusion (Noë & O'Regan, 2000).

21. Ron Rensink makes the analogy with "just-in-time" industrial procedures of manufacturing, for example, in Rensink (2005).

22. It would be more accurate to ask: "Why do photographs and the visual world seem to look so similar?" since the only way we can know what a photograph looks like is by looking at it as an entity in the outside world.

Chapter 5

Some Contentious Points

The new view of seeing provides a solution to the question of why various defects of the visual apparatus pose no problem to us. It also explains results that are otherwise surprising, namely cases in which we fail to see what would normally be very obvious elements in the visual field, as in the phenomena of looked but failed to see (or inattentional blindness) and change blindness. It's worth addressing here in more detail some points already mentioned in earlier sections that my colleagues tend to get wrong about the approach.

Representations

Many people who have heard about my approach to vision and the idea of the "world as an outside memory," and who have seen the change-blindness demonstrations, think that I am claiming that the brain has no representations of the world. Certainly I claim that in order to see the world, we don't need to fabricate any kind of "internal picture" in our brains. But this doesn't mean that the notion of representation is altogether useless. Indeed, the notion is ubiquitous in cognitive science. Scientists who try to understand how the brain works, and how people think, perceive, and talk, use the notion frequently.[1]

But when used carelessly, the notion of representation leads to confusion. The upside-down representation of the world on the retina led scientists to fall into the trap of thinking that this implies we should also see the world upside down. The blurs, distortions, or other defects in the information provided by the visual system have led people to think that our perception should suffer similar defects and to postulate compensation mechanisms to remedy these defects. But this is to make what Daniel Dennett called the "content-vehicle" confusion. It is to make the mistake of thinking that the way information is represented (the vehicle) determines how it is perceived (the content). It is an error that Descartes already had taken pains to avoid in his *Traité de l'homme* when discussing the upside-down image. Thinking that we somehow "see" the representation rather than making use of its content is equivalent to supposing that seeing involves a homunculus looking at something like Dennett's "Cartesian theater."

On the other hand, this doesn't mean there are no representations. Colleagues who misunderstand me often stop me in my lectures and say that I must be wrong about representations, since, for example, it is known that there really is a "cortical map" in area V1 which represents the outside world in a picture-like fashion (see Fig. 5.1). There are also other brain areas where the representation is not so picture-like.

Furthermore, people remind me that there is a whole literature in cognitive psychology, starting in the 1970s with Roger Shepard and Jacqueline Metzler's famous "mental rotation" experiments, developed and extended by Harvard cognitive

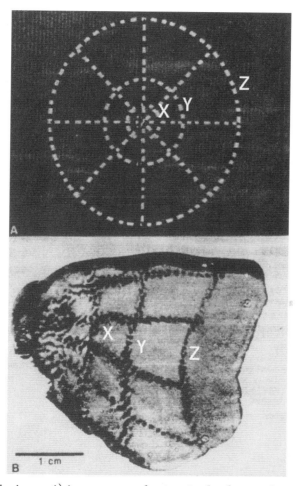

Figure 5.1 (Top image, A) A macaque monkey is trained to fixate at the center of this pattern of circles. The monkey is injected with a radioactive sugar that is taken up by brain cells in proportion to their recent activity. (Bottom image, B) After sacrificing the monkey, its occipital cortex shows recent neural activity as dark stripes. The radial pattern in A appears projected in distorted form on the cortex (here only a single brain hemisphere is shown), showing the existence of a "map" in the cortex that represents, in topographic form, the information that stimulated the retina. Half circles X, Y and Z in the visual field (A) are represented as vertical lines X, Y and Z in the cortex (B). (From Tootell, Silverman, Switkes, and De Valois. 1982. *Science, 218* [4575], 902–904.) Reprinted with permission of AAAS.

scientist Stephen Kosslyn,[2] that show that our mental images really do behave like pictures. For example, if we want to rotate an object in our mind's eye, the time it takes is proportional to the amount of rotation we want to achieve.[3]

In response, I wish to stress again that I have nothing against representations *per se*. Information from the outside world must be processed in the brain, and thus it must somehow be represented. The way information is represented will play a role—obviously we cannot see something if there is insufficient information available in the representation. What is important is not the representation itself, but how it is used.

Why then is it that in area V1 of the cortex, the information is represented in a topographic way? This seems so close to looking like an "internal picture" that it is hard not to think that V1 is indeed the locus of our picture-like vision of the world.[4] The reason information is represented topographically in V1 presumably has to do with the particular calculations that the brain does to make use of the information. A topographic representation like this cortical map may be useful so as to facilitate the extraction of meaningful local cues like contours, edges, local motion, depth, and color.

All this does not mean, however, that activation of the cortical map generates the impression of vision. For if activation of the cortical map were indeed to generate the experience of seeing, then we would be faced with the problem of explaining what exactly it is about the map that generates the experience. Neuroscientists will reply by saying that it's "obviously" not the mere activation of the map that generates the experience. They will say that other structures of the brain also participate. That raises the question of what is it about the other structures that generates the experience? People may say that the sensation is actually generated by the interaction with the other structures.[5] But then that raises yet another question: What is it about the interaction with the other structures that provides the sensation? We seem to be in an infinite regression.

Another difficulty is the notion of "activation." In a computer, a transistor that is turned off in the computer memory might represent a binary "zero," which is just as important as a binary "one" represented by a transistor that is turned on. In the brain, neural activation presumably codes information in a similar way. Thus, a neuron that is *not* "active" or firing at a given moment may be just as important as a neuron that is firing. So what people mean by a representation being "activated" may have nothing to do with actual neural firing. What people mean by "activated" must have to do with the fact that a representation is being accessed by other parts of the brain. But then we are back to having to explain how this accessing by other parts of the brain generates experience.

For all these reasons I think it is better to avoid words like *representation, activation*, and *generate*, and to think more carefully about what we really mean when we say we are having the experience of seeing. And I think what we really mean is just that we are currently involved in extracting information from the environment in a way which is peculiar to the visual sense modality. Obviously the brain is involved in this, and we would like to know exactly how. The empirical work being done using sophisticated imaging techniques will certainly contribute to the answer.[6]

The Brain

Neuroscientists are generally upset with my account of vision because they have the impression that I'm minimizing the brain, as though in some mystical way it were possible to see without a brain. To them it's obvious that the brain is the seat of consciousness, thought, and sensation, and to say that the experience of seeing is not generated in the brain seems to them nonsensical.

An argument people will bring up in favor of the brain generating vision is the fact that we can dream, hallucinate, or imagine things with our eyes closed and have the impression of seeing things almost like pictures. There are also the well-known experiments of the Canadian neurosurgeon Wilder Penfield, who, working with epileptic patients, showed in the 1950s that electrical stimulation of certain brain areas can generate visual experiences[7] and memories. And there is a growing body of literature showing that when we imagine things, visual cortex gets activated in different, predictable ways depending on the different things we imagine.[8] Doesn't all this show that visual experience is generated in the brain?

The problem is a misunderstanding. In my statement: "Visual experience is not generated in the brain," the important point is not the word *brain*, but the word *generated*. Visual experience is simply not generated *at all*. Experience is not the end product of some kind of neural processing.

I think the comparison with "life" is useful. Where is life generated in a human? Is it generated in the heart? In the brain? In the DNA? The question is meaningless, because life is *not generated at all*. It is not a substance that can be generated; it is nothing more than a *word* used to describe a particular way that an organism interacts with its environment.

In the same way, "visual experience" is not an end product, a substance, an entity that is secreted or generated by the brain.[9] It is a *phrase* used to describe the way humans potentially interact with their visual environment. The brain enables the form of interaction with the environment that we call vision, and we can and should investigate how this works. We should look for the brain mechanisms that underlie those particular characteristics of visual interaction that provide vision with its peculiar visual qualities: The fact that access to information in the environment is so immediate as to give us the impression that the information is continually present and displayed before us in infinite detail; the fact that when we move, there are systematic and predictable changes in the sensory input; the fact that there can also be changes in the input that are not due to our own voluntary acts; and finally, the fact that we are exquisitely sensitive to changes that occur in the information before us, because any change causes an incontrovertible orienting reflex and automatically engages our cognitive processing.

Each of these facts about the mode of interaction we call "seeing" is a consequence of the way we are built and the way our brains are wired up. To explain what it's like to see, we need to look in the brain for the mechanisms that enable each of these properties of visual interaction. We should not try to find particular neural structures in the brain that *generate* the experience of seeing.

Dreaming and Hallucinations

But then how does one explain hallucinations, dreams, and the Penfield brain-stimulation experiences, which seem so much like normal vision, clearly are entirely generated in the brain, and don't require any interaction with the environment? Don't these experiences suggest that there must be an internal picture that is activated?

The answer is no. In *normal* vision the world appears to us as having the detail and continual presence all over of a picture *not* because there is an internal picture that is activated, but because, as is also the case for pictures, *whenever we ask ourselves about some aspect of the world, it is available* to us visually (and the change blindness and other demonstrations in Chapter 4 show that the detail we think we see is in a certain sense illusory). I suggest that exactly the same is true about dreams and hallucinations. The reason they look so detailed is that, through the special action of sleep or drugs or trance, a dreamer's or hallucinator's brain is in a state in which it makes the sleeper think it can provide any detail that is required. This is sufficient for the dreamer or hallucinator to have exactly the same feel of highly detailed presence that she has in normal vision.

Dreaming and hallucinating therefore pose no problem for the new view of seeing that I am proposing. Indeed, the approach actually makes it easier to envisage brain mechanisms that engender convincing sensory experiences without any sensory input, since the sensation of richness and presence and ongoingness can be produced in the absence of sensory input merely by the brain being in a state such that the dreamer implicitly "supposes" (in point of fact incorrectly) that if the eyes were to move, say, they would encounter more detail. This state of "supposing you can get more detail" would be much easier to generate than having to really recreate all the detail.[10]

Seeing Versus Imagining

Usually people consider imagining as a reduced, poorer form of seeing. Seeing is considered to be the "real thing," and imagining is an inferior species. But the new view of seeing, rather than stressing the differences, emphasizes the similarities: Seeing is actually almost as poor as imagining—we (in a certain sense) see much less than we think. Under the new view, imagining and seeing are essentially the same, sharing the same basic process of actively exploring and accessing information.[11] The only difference is that whereas imagining finds its information in memory, seeing finds it in the environment. One could say that vision is a form of imagining, augmented by the real world. The experienced "presence" of seeing as compared to imagining derives from the fact that the environment is much richer than imagination, and from the fact that in addition to this richness, vision has bodiliness, insubordinateness, and grabbiness.

Action

My philosopher colleague Alva Noë, with whom I wrote the main paper expounding this theory of vision in 2001, has since published two books in which he has adopted the name "enactive" or "actionist" for his brand of the theory, and where he strongly emphasizes the role of action in visual consciousness.[12] Nigel Thomas has a "perceptual activity" theory of visual perception and imagination[13] that resembles mine, and which says that visual perception necessarily involves real or at least covert exploratory eye movements, and he attempts to muster evidence from recent experiments in support of this theory.[14]

On the other hand, though in my own approach I also take action to be very important, I am not claiming that action is *necessary* for vision. I am claiming that seeing involves obtaining information from the outside world by using the visual apparatus. Usually indeed this involves action in the form of eye movements, but there are cases, as when you recognize something in a briefly flashed display, where eye movements are not used. There need not be any covert eye movements either: All that is necessary is that you should be interrogating the information available in the visual world. You have the impression of seeing because the way you are obtaining that information is the way you usually obtain information from vision. You may not actually be moving your eyes, but you are poised to move your eyes if you want more detailed information. Furthermore, if something should change abruptly in the visual field, it will probably cause your eyes and even your cognitive processing to move toward it: You are poised to allow this to happen. If you were to move your body or your eyes, the information you are obtaining would change drastically (because it shifts on the retina). You need not move, but you are poised for the occurrence of this particular interaction between body motions and the resulting changes on the retina.

The idea is similar to the idea of feeling at home. When I am sitting on my sofa, I feel at home because there are a variety of actions I can undertake (go into the kitchen and get a coffee, go to the bedroom and lie down, etc.). But I need not undertake them. It is because I'm poised to do these things that I have the feeling of being at home. Feeling at home does not require actual action. In the same way, seeing does not require actual action. It requires having *previously* acted, and it requires having the future *potential* for action.[15]

But there is an even more important point about action that has not been sufficiently stressed: Action gives vision its "presence."[16] I have discussed other aspects of seeing that contribute to making the experience of feel "real," like the richness, the insubordinateness, and the grabbiness of the visual world. But action plays an essential role since it determines what I have called "bodiliness." If I move (but I needn't actually do so), I (implicitly) know there will be a large change in my visual input. This is one of the major distinguishing properties of the mode of interaction with the environment that we call seeing. When I have a hallucination or a dream, I may temporarily and incorrectly also be in the state of mind where I think I am seeing, but as soon as I do the appropriate "reality check," in which I move in order to verify that this motion produces the expected changes on my sensory input, I become aware that I am having a hallucination or dream.

Thus action, with the sensory consequences it produces, is one of the aspects of visual interaction that provide vision with its experienced "phenomenality" or presence. The experienced quality of visual experience is determined by the particular laws that visual input obeys as we move. But action *right now* is not necessary for vision.[17]

Implications for Consciousness

There are two very interesting points that arise from my treatment of seeing that I will use later in the book. The first is that by treating vision as an experience constituted by the ongoing process of interacting with the environment, I have escaped the logically insoluble problem of trying to understand how neural machinery might generate the feel of seeing. The second is that by noting four criteria that distinguish the feel of seeing from the feel of imagining and memory (richness, bodiliness, partial insubordinateness, and grabbiness), I have provided steps toward understanding why vision has its particular feeling of "reality" or "presence."

In the next part of the book, I shall be looking at feel in general. We shall see that the mystery of how feel might be generated in the brain can be solved by taking the same strategy that I have taken toward the feel of seeing: Abandon the idea that feel is generated! Feel is something we do. And we will also be able to explain why feel has "presence" or "something it's like" by noting that its qualities share the same four criteria of interaction with the environment that are involved in vision.

Notes

1. Even if the notion of representations poses logical problems, and even if some philosophers consider it to be problematic or vacuous (Press, 2008), there are certainly ways of using the notion that are helpful in understanding cognition and perception (Markman & Dietrich, 2000). On the other hand, there is a philosophical movement called "enactivism" that strongly rejects the use of representations in cognitive science, and which perhaps takes its origin in works like *The Embodied Mind* (Varela, Thompson, & Rosch, 1992). For a review of enactivism, see a special issue of the journal *Phenomenology and the Cognitive Sciences* and the introduction to it by Torrance (2005). My colleague Alva Noë once considered himself part of the movement, but he changed his terminology to "activist" instead of "enactive" in his book (Noë, 2004). I am not philosopher enough to know whether I am "enactivist." I suspect I am not, since I can accept the usefulness of representations. I also don't think that an explanation of the mysteries of phenomenal consciousness can be found by simply proclaiming that minds are embodied. More work needs to be done, and that is what I am trying to do in this book.
2. For a richly documented historical overview of the imagery debate and an argued account of Kosslyn's theory, see Kosslyn, Thompson, and Ganis (2006).
3. For a well-balanced account of the literature on mental imagery in history and philosophy, see Thomas (2010) in the *Stanford Encyclopedia of Philosophy*. This article also dissects and analyzes the decade-long and very heated debate between Stephen Kossylyn defending his "analog" or (quasi-)pictorial account and Zenon Pylyshyn defending his propositional account. See also the excellent article in Thomas (1999) and its ongoing development on Nigel Thomas's Web site: http://www.imagery-imagination.com/newsupa.htm.
4. There has been a big debate about the role of V1 in visual consciousness. In his book *The Quest for Consciousness: A Neurobiological Approach*, Christof Koch takes pains to counter the claim that V1 by itself should give rise to visual consciousness (Koch, 2004).

5. V. Lamme thinks it's *reverberation* (Lamme, 2006).
6. For a review of recent neurophysiological and imaging work related to consciousness, but which does not espouse my sensorimotor approach, see Tononi and Koch (2008).
7. As well as auditory and olfactory sensations and feelings of familiarity, and movements. All these may be more or less precise or coordinated depending on the cortical area. Penfield's article (Penfield, 1958) can be freely downloaded from PNAS on http://www.pnas.org/content/44/2/51.full.pdf+html. Among lurid pictures of exposed brains it is amusing to observe Penfield's florid, pretentious, and sometimes sexist style.
8. For very interesting recent work and references to previous work, see Stokes, Thompson, Cusack, and Duncan (2009).
9. Timo Järvilehto similarly mocks the idea that the brain should generate mental states by making the analogy with an artist painting: Clearly it makes no sense to ask where the painting occurs: in the brain, in the hands, in the paintbrush, or in the canvas (Järvilehto, 1998a)?
10. In dreaming, furthermore, the state would be particularly easy to maintain because what characterizes dreaming would seem to be a lack of attention to the absence of disconfirming evidence, which is quite unsurprising, since you are asleep. This lowering of standards of belief implies that, while dreaming, you are easily led into thinking you are perceiving, while—if only you were to pay attention—it would be obvious that you are not. Thus, you can remain convinced for the whole duration of your dream that you are experiencing reality. In point of fact there is evidence from "lucid dreaming" that the detail we think we see when we are dreaming is a kind of invention. It appears to be a characteristic of lucid dreams that every time we come back to contemplate some detail, like say a line of text, the detail changes. (I thank Erik Myin for helping me express these ideas.)
11. This is also the view of Nigel Thomas (Thomas, 1999, 2010).
12. The original paper is by O'Regan and Noë (2001). Also see Noë (2004) and, more recently, Noë (2009).
13. See Thomas (1999, 2010) and ongoing development on N. Thomas's Web site: http://www.imagery-imagination.com/newsupa.htm.
14. The experiments he refers to are developments of the original experiments on "scan paths" by Noton and Stark (1971), for example, Brandt and Stark (1997). Not many people believe in scan paths today.
15. Nick Humphrey (Humphrey, 1992) deals with the fact that sensation can occur without action by invoking "virtual" or "surrogate" action, in which the action that would usually occur at the surface of the organism becomes detached from the surface and is represented in higher levels of the nervous system. I think this is a suspicious step to take, since it raises the question of how neural loops inside the organism can replace real action. Furthermore, there are other issues that I have with Humphrey, in particular, he goes on in his theory to invoke additional concepts like affect, reverberation, and evolution, which I consider unnecessary.
16. Though my colleague Alva Noë does discuss the role of bodiliness without using that term, he does not stress this aspect of the role of action as much as I do (Noë, 2004).
17. To understand the substance of this claim, one could imagine a person who had spent his entire life without ever having been able to move his eyes or body. I would

predict that the person would still "see" in the sense that he would be able to extract information from the visual world. But because the person would not have action as a tool to distinguish real visual input from his own hallucinations or imaginings, his form of "vision" would not be so obviously different from such hallucinations and imaginings as it is to us. In confirmation of this prediction, it seems that people who are confined in sensory isolation chambers, and people suffering from locked-in syndrome, may indeed have the problem of confusing their own thoughts and imaginings with reality. This was the tragic fate of the editor-in-chief of French magazine *Elle*, Jean-Dominique Bauby, described in his book, *The Diving Bell and the Butterfly: A Memoir of Life in Death* (Bauby, 1998).

PART TWO

The Feel of Consciousness

Chapter 6

Toward Consciousness

When I was a child, my dream was to build a conscious robot. At that time in the 1960s, computers were just coming into existence, and they were where I hoped to find inspiration. I haunted technical bookstores and libraries and read all about "flipflops" and "core memories." I memorized complicated diagrams of binary "half-adders" and "full-adders" with "AND" and "OR gates." At school I astounded the Science Club with a demonstration of how you could build a simple computer that used water instead of electricity, making binary calculations at the same time as spraying jets of water all over the chemistry lab.[1]

I found an ad in a popular science magazine for a kit to construct a machine called Geniac that solved logical puzzles and played tic tac toe (see Fig. 6.1).[2] In the picture the machine looked impressive with complicated dials and lights. To the despair of my parents (who thought I was a bit too young), I insisted on ordering the machine. When it finally arrived from overseas, I spent a feverish week wiring it up after school every day. When I finished, I was disappointed. Admittedly the machine played good tic tac toe. But it was essentially just a sophisticated set of switches. There were hundreds of criss-crossing wires, but it didn't seem to be intelligent. It couldn't think. It wasn't conscious.

I kept wondering what was missing from the machine. Consulting a book in my parents' bookshelves on the anatomy of the nervous system, I saw diagrams showing complicated connections, leading from different parts of the body to the spinal cord, synapsing wildly with other nerve pathways, going up into the brain and spreading out all over the place. I spent hours poring over that book. How, I wondered, was the brain different from the tic tac toe machine? Was there more than just complicated wiring? What special principle or what additional module would I have to add into the tic tac toe machine so that it would be conscious?

How to build consciousness into a machine is a question that many people have been thinking about for several decades. If we could solve this question, we would make considerable headway in understanding how consciousness arises in humans, which in turn would shed light on the nature of feel.

In this chapter, I shall be looking at the progress that scientists have made so far in making machines that think, perceive, learn, use language, and that have the notion of self. Then, in the next two chapters, I shall discuss two different kinds of consciousness: access and phenomenal consciousness. I shall be arguing that thinking, perceiving, learning, the self, and access consciousness pose no logical problem to science and as such are achievable in these machines—if not now, then at some

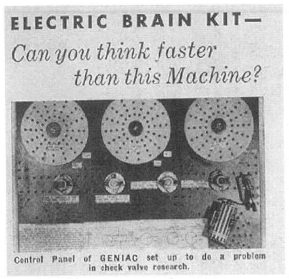

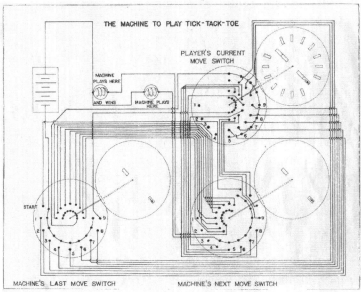

Figure 6.1 Ad for Geniac kit and circuit diagram for tic tac toe from
http://www.oldcomputermuseum.com. Used with permission of Old Computer
Museum.

point in the future. But we shall see that phenomenal consciousness—or what
I shall be calling "raw feel"—is going to need special treatment. The new view of
seeing will provide inspiration for how to solve this problem.

Machines That Think, Perceive, Use Language, and Learn

Artificial intelligence (AI) was born in the 1960s when "knowledge-based systems"
or "expert systems" were designed in computer laboratories to analyze information

contained in large, complicated databases. Such systems worked best in very specific domains. For example, they were used to find oil deposits, to give investment advice to banks, to diagnose blood diseases and recommend antibiotics, to optimize the way companies stock warehouses and organize deliveries, to play games like chess, checkers, and "go," and to solve mathematical problems. After a slow-growing period in the 1980s and 1990s, sometimes called the "AI winter," such systems have now matured into commercially viable products that are used daily across the world. For example, the spam filter in your e-mail program has been quietly analyzing the mails you have thrown away to fine tune the way it will work in the future. The ads that appear on your Web browser are selected by analyzing the information you have recently been obtaining.

Recent AI systems also use numerical methods based on statistical pattern recognition techniques, some of them modeled on the functioning of networks of neurons in the brain. Such approaches have given birth to active research domains like "connectionism" or "artificial neural networks" and "machine learning," which are proving successful in applications where pattern recognition is needed. For example, robot vision and control systems guide autonomous vehicles like surveillance drones or driverless cars. Speech recognition systems are used to understand simple telephone commands in airline reservation systems. Systems that recognize car license plate numbers can use "neural network" pattern recognition techniques. Other examples are search engines that ferret out information from the Web, or programs that analyze stock market trends or recognize handwritten addresses on envelopes in mail sorting.

Progress is also being made in language processing.[3] Useful devices operate today for specialized purposes like generating multilanguage lexicons and language-independent semantic representations, tagging parts of speech in text corpuses, correcting grammar and orthography, indexing, summarizing text, answering simple questions in help applications, subtitling speeches, and translating computer menus for different countries. One of the earliest automatic translation systems from the 1960s is today a successful commercial company,[4] SYSTRAN, which sells the translation technology used by Google, Yahoo!, and Alta Vista, as well as by the European Commission, which circulates documents in more than a hundred languages. There are also frivolous offshoots of early natural language processing research, like ELIZA the automated psychoanalyst, and like the admirable postmodern article generator, a Web site that you can use to generate amusing spoofs of postmodern articles on literary criticism.[5]

But for all these advances, it remains true that the goal of human-like thought, perception, and language understanding is still far from being attained in machines. To solve the problem, two promising ideas are currently being explored: One is to provide the systems with common-sense knowledge about the world and about human life.[6] The other is the idea that in order for machines to attain human cognitive performance their involvement in the world may have to replicate that of humans.[7] Humans have bodies and live, move, and interact in particular ways with the objects that they use and with other humans in the real world. Human language and thought are not just raw symbol manipulation: The concepts that are manipulated are constrained by the physical world and the particular way humans interact with it. People live in a shared social environment and have desires, emotions, and motivations that play an important role in conditioning thought and communication. Thus, it may be that to think and use language like humans, machines will have to have human-like immersion in the world.

For this reason a domain of robotics has emerged recently called "autonomous robotics," where the idea is to construct machines that possess sufficient intelligence to control their own behavior, and that move and explore their environments and act of their own accord. Such machines are beginning to be used in situations where communication with a human is impractical, for example, in space or in surveillance. Other examples are domestic robots that clean a swimming pool, mow the lawn, vacuum the living room,[8] or entertain grandma and the kids.

A related trend is "developmental robotics" (also called "epigenetic robotics"). This involves building autonomous robots that are initially provided with only basic capacities, but that, by interacting with their environments like a human infant, evolve to master more complex perceptual and cognitive behavior.[9] One early example was BabyBot, constructed at the Laboratory for Integrated Advanced Robotics (LIRAlab) in Genoa (see Fig. 6.2). Another baby robot, the icub, is a more recent project financed by the Robotcub consortium of the European Union.[10]

By constructing a robot that can interact with its environment and with humans and other robots, these projects aim to study how problems such as visual segmentation, tactile recognition, manual manipulation, and word meaning can emerge in a way similar to human infant development. For example, usually machines that visually recognize objects only make use of information extracted through video cameras. BabyBot, on the other hand, recognizes a toy car not only visually but also by poking it around and understanding that depending on which way the robot pushes it, the car will or will not roll. This information allows the robot to link visual information to manual "affordances," which may then help it to recognize other objects and understand what it can do with them.[11]

Even if progress has been much slower than some luminaries predicted in the past,[12] the AI and robotics communities remain confident that gradually but surely we will have machines that approach or surpass human thought, perception, and language skills. In this venture, it is clear that in order for machines to capture meaning in the same way as humans, engineers will have to take account of the essential involvement that humans have in the real world. Artificial systems may have to be provided with sensors and the ability to move, and to be embedded in the world and possibly even in a social system. With better hardware and closer attention to the way humans are physically and socially embedded, logically nothing should prevent us from understanding and replicating in these systems the mechanisms at work in human thought, perception, and language—even if in practice this may remain impractical for years to come.

But something still seems to be missing.

The Self

We as humans have the distinct impression that there is someone, namely ourselves, "behind the commands." We are not just automata milling around doing

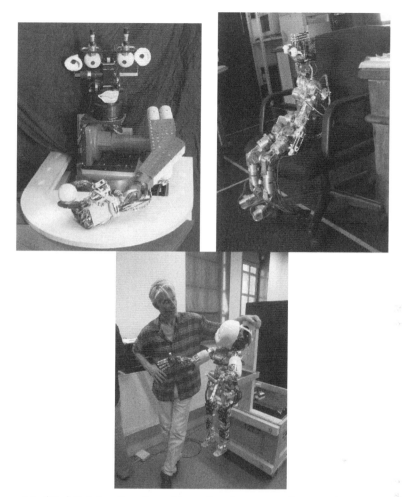

Figure 6.2 (*Top*) Babybot from http://www.lira.dist.unige.it/babybot/robot.htm. and icub from http://www.robotcub.org/index.php/robotcub/platform/images/icub_ sitting, and (*Bottom*) myself conversing with icub. Used with permission of Lira Lab in Geneva and G. Sandini.

intelligent things: There is a pilot in the system, so to speak, and that pilot is "I." It is I doing the thinking, acting, deciding, and feeling. The self is a central part of human thought, and it also plays a fundamental role in language.

So what is the self? The nature and origin of the notion of the self is an actively discussed subject today.[13] Philosophers are trying to decide what precise components the notion of self boils down to. Within psychoanalytical approaches, Freud's well-known distinction between the id, the ego, and the superego as components of the self, and Heinz Kohut's self psychology with its own tripartite theory of the self,[14] are just two examples within a very rich, diverse, and complex tradition. Very active work is also being done in cognitive psychology. Developmental psychologists and psycholinguists are trying to ascertain how the notion of self develops in the maturing child; cognitive anthropologists look at whether the notion is different in different human societies; cognitive ethologists study which species possess a self; and social psychologists investigate how the self is determined by an individual's social environment.

To get an idea of the complexity of the notion of self, we can begin by looking at how psychologists and philosophers have decomposed and refined the distinctions between different aspects of the self.[15] At the end of the 19th century, the philosopher William James[16] distinguished the physical self, the mental self, the spiritual self, and the ego. Further refinements were suggested in the 1980s by the cognitive scientist Ulrich Neisser[17] with his ecological, interpersonal, extended, private, and conceptual aspects of the self. Yet further concepts have been proposed more recently, such as the primary self, secondary self, cognitive self, conceptual self, and representational, semiotic, contextualized, embodied, social, extended, verbal, dialogic, fictional, narrative,[18] private, and minimal[19] selves, as well as the notion of self model,[20] the essential self, and the transparent self[21]!

How can we make sense of this plethora of different terms that have been invented to describe the self? In particular, is there anything hidden within the concept of self that somehow prevents it from being built into a robot or approached by the scientific method? To try to bring some order into this discussion, I would like to isolate two important dimensions along which different notions of self are defined[22]: a cognitive and a social dimension.

The Cognitive Self

The cognitive dimension concerns *self-cognizance*, namely the amount of knowledge an individual has about itself. We can mark off three tiers in a continuum of self-cognizance, going from "self-distinguishing" to "self-knowledge" to "knowledge of self-knowledge,"[23] and ask whether there would be any problem building these tiers into a robot.

Self-distinguishing is a precursor to the cognitive self: It is the fact that an organism acts differently with regard to parts of its own body as compared to the outside world. It is something very basic that doesn't require a brain or any form of cognitive capacity. For example, an animal's immune system must distinguish foreign cells from the host body's own cells. For any animal, moving around in the environment requires implicitly distinguishing itself from that environment. Clearly there is no problem building this into a robot. For example, the Humanoid Robotics Group at MIT's Computer Science and Artificial Intelligence Laboratory (CSAIL) has developed Domo, a robot constructed to investigate this stage of the self notion (see Fig. 6.3).

The robot is an upper torso equipped with moveable eyes, head, arms, and grippers. It uses vision-based movement detection algorithms to determine whether something is moving in its visual field. It checks whether by commanding movements of its own body, the movements it sees are correlated with the movements it commands. If such a correlation occurs, it assumes that what it is seeing is part of its own body. In this way it is able to figure out what its own hand looks like, and later, what its own fingers look like.[24]

Self-knowledge requires a system with cognitive capacities, that is, a system which is more than simply reactive and that can make choices between different courses of action, make judgments, and plan its behavior. Self-knowledge involves

Figure 6.3 Domo was constructed by Charles Kemp, now at Georgia Tech. Reprinted from Edsinger, A., & Kemp, C. (2006) with permission.

cognitive behavior that makes use of the fact that the system is a whole, with a body that separates it from its environment and other individuals. This allows the system to avoid bumping into other individuals, to find mates, and to avoid predators. It allows it to have the notion of ownership and to distinguish its possessions from the possessions of others. But note that under this definition of "self-knowledge," the system may not actually know that it has this self-knowledge. Thus, for example, a bird may function perfectly in its environment, choosing courses of action, finding food that it has hidden away, distinguishing itself from others, and separating its territory from other birds' territory; yet it may not in any sense know that it is an individual. To the extent that computers today can already be programmed to manipulate concepts and make inferences, there is nothing to prevent engineers in the future from programming a robot so that it reasons about itself as an entity that can be distinguished from its surroundings in order to make plans, judgments, and decisions about what to do next.

Knowledge of self-knowledge is the further stage where an individual may have various kinds of meta-knowledge about its self-knowledge. For example, the most basic meta-knowledge is for an individual to know that it exists as an individual. It may also know that other individuals know that they exist as individuals. It may also know that other individuals know that *it* knows that it exists and that *they* exist. . . Things can get complicated, leading to finely graded social strategies ranging from selfishness, through misleading other individuals, to cooperating with them. Such meta-knowledge is necessary for an individual to have embarrassment, shame, pride, and contempt. With this level of meta-knowledge of self-knowledge, the individual has a "Theory of Mind": It can empathize with others, and interpret other individuals' acts in terms of their beliefs, desires, and motivations. Knowledge of self-knowledge underlies what has been called the "intentional stance" that humans adopt in their interactions with other humans: They consider that other humans have *intentions and goals* just as they themselves do. As concerns robots, knowledge of self-knowledge requires a level of conceptualization in which the robot must make the link between its own plans, judgments, and decisions and those that can be attributed to other agents in a social context. Again, as a matter of concept manipulation, there is in principle no obstacle to building such a capacity into a robot. It would, of course, have to be immersed in a social context, either with other robots or with humans.

Many research teams are currently working on projects in this direction, and although, as compared to human self-knowledge or knowledge of self-knowledge, the robotic self is a pale imitation, progress is being made. Work on these higher notions of self is being done, for example, with the COG platform, also developed at CSAIL (see Fig. 6.4). COG is an upper-torso humanoid robot equipped with visual, auditory, tactile, vestibular, and kinesthetic sensors; it can move its waist, spine, eye(s), head, arms, and primitive hands. COG has been used by a variety of groups at CSAIL to do experiments in object recognition, tactile manipulation, and human–robot interaction. It was actually one of the first humanoid robotic platforms built at MIT, and it is approaching "retirement." It has provided the inspiration for more recent work.

The ideas being used to study the emergence of the self in COG are based on analyses of what psychologists consider to be the most basic capacities postulated to underlie the self in humans.[25] One such basic capacity is the ability to locate and follow an agent's gaze direction. For this, skin, face, and eye detection algorithms in

Figure 6.4 COG, from Scassellati, now at Yale (Scassellati, 2003). Reprinted from Scassellati, B. (2003) with permission from the author.

the robot's visual system allow it to locate eyes and infer where a human is looking. By extending this gaze-following capacity, the researchers hope to implement algorithms for joint attention, that is, algorithms that allow the robot to attend to an object that another agent or human is also attending to.

The COG, Domo, and many other projects are work in progress and at the moment represent only the very first steps toward implementation of different self notions in a robot. But the vitality of this and related research projects suggests that providing robots with a realistic notion of self and accompanying Theory of Mind is an achievable goal. Even if it takes many more years, as concerns the cognitive capacities involved, the problem of building a robot with a self seems in principle solvable.

The Societal Self

The cognitive dimension of the self concerns how an individual's cognitive capacities allow it to interact with the environment. There is already a social dimension to this, to the extent that the individual interacts with other individuals and can develop a Theory of Mind. But there is another social aspect to the self that concerns how an individual fits into a society and how each individual considers him- or herself within this society.[26]

Scientists studying this societal aspect of the self agree that even though each of us has the intimate conviction that individually we are just one person, "I" is essentially a melting pot of subselves, each manifesting itself in different conditions, and all having learned to cohabit under the single label: "I." The 18th-century philosopher David Hume proposed that contrary to the individual's impression of being a single self, "I" am in fact a composite bundle of different capacities and entities. "I" am like a republic or commonwealth, or like a nation or club whose structure may change over time, but it can nevertheless be usefully described as a single unit.[27] Under this view, "I" am a convenient abstraction that "I" use to describe (both to others and to "my" self) how the entity that composes "me" behaves, with "my" thoughts, attitudes, and opinions.[28] Daniel Dennett proposes that the self is a "center of narrative gravity," useful for describing to others and ourselves what we do, want, or believe.[29]

But how can "I" seem so *real* to myself, if "I" am merely a cognitive construct? An analogy that helps to understand this is *money*. Despite just being bits of metal or paper, money is perfectly real in our society. The reason is that money is self-validating: It requires a social consensus to function, but it also creates, through its functioning, a situation where it can continue to function effectively. The self might be a similar self-validating social construct.

Compared to money, however, there is something additional about the self: "I" have the intense conviction of my own self as really *existing*. Unlike money, which is used by *people* (and not by money), the *self* is a notion used by the very *selves* that the notion defines.[30] The concept of self is in that sense not only self-validating like money but also *self-referring*.

Thus, the reason I experience myself as being so real is that I am telling myself a self-consistent story about myself being real. Furthermore, this story is reinforced by my interactions with other people who have similar stories about themselves and about me, and they and I act in ways that cause the stories we are all telling to be true. Said in another way: "I" is part of its own story. The story has evolved so that what we mean by "I" includes being convinced that "I" is real. The story of "I" is precisely the story of a single entity that is the center of its own story. If you are part of the story, you must by definition be convinced that you are real.

Thus, the notion of a self is defined within a social context, from the outside. Yet it is a notion that the self in question must espouse on the inside.[31] And although it is only a social construct, it is a self-referring social construct that enables the self to perceive itself as being very real. This rather shocking idea has some interesting consequences. One concerns the question of who writes the story of "us." The other concerns how to escape from our story.

Social psychologists studying the unconscious influence of cultural prototypes on our behavior show that our everyday actions are more determined than we think by automatic, socially driven influences. We unconsciously espouse images of ourselves as having a certain personality, as belonging to a particular social category, and these cultural prototypes strongly influence the construction of our identity. Indeed, a person's gait, gestures, speech, taste, and dress are all exquisitely sensitive to their cultural or social context. You can tell a person's origins from the way he or she moves and talks. I've lived in France so long now that my mother (who is American) says she can't understand me anymore because when I talk, I move my hands like a Frenchman. Even something so primal as the expression of pain[32] is influenced by cultural pressures: When I'm among French people and I hurt myself, I exclaim "aïe." Among Anglo Saxons, I cry "ouch."[33]

But even if it is true that the main influence on the construction of our identities is unconscious and dependent on our social environment, do "I" not also play *some* conscious role in the construction of "I"? This would have to be the exception and not the rule, because if people constantly changed their stories to suit their momentary whims, they would never be the same and the effect would be destabilizing for society. It probably has to be part of "my" story that I should be convinced that I am an entity that cannot just switch to a dramatically different identity. There has to be something like a social taboo preventing us from consciously modifying ourselves.

There are, however, ways in which people can and do escape from their normal stories and change their identity—for example, through alcohol and soft drugs, through hypnosis,[34] or through channeling, possession trances, and culturally bound syndromes[35] like amok, zar, latah, and dissociative identity disorder (multiple personality disorder). Changes in identity also occur as a result of pathologies like schizophrenia, brain lesions, and traumatic head injury. Take, for example, my friend FP, who knocked his head in a skiing accident and completely lost his long-term memory. I only got to know FP a few months after the accident, but I had noticed that he had a hesitant, inquiring way of acting in social contexts, as though he were searching for approval. As he explained to me years later, he was actually reconstructing his self. He explained how even his slightest action was filled with questioning. He needed to search for his own self in the eyes of others. He would sit down at the table and pick up his knife and fork. But should he pick them up this way or that way? Of course, we all encounter such problems in new social situations where we are not sure how to behave. But FP had a much harder time because not only did he have to work out the social constraints, but much more important, he needed to find out what *he* was like. He would look around and try to judge from the way his friends looked at him whether he was behaving in the way they expected the real FP to behave. Was he the kind of person who sat upright or did he slouch relaxedly? Did he talk loudly or softly? I think this example is interesting because it is an exceptional case where a person has some degree of insight into the social construction process that constructs his own self.

The previous paragraphs only scratch the surface of the active research being done on the cognitive and social aspects of the self.[36] However, what they illustrate is that to give a scientific account of the self, at least as concerns the cognitive and social aspects, no magical, as yet unknown mechanism is likely to be needed. Making machines with cognitive and social selves is a task that may still take years to achieve, but it seems clear that once we have machines with sufficient cognitive capacities that are embedded in the real world and integrated into a social system, a notion similar to the "I" that humans use to refer to themselves is likely to become so useful that it is "real".

Notes

1. Doing calculations with fluids was a project in the Amateur Scientist section of *Scientific American*, May 1966 (p. 128).
2. The Geniac machine was conceived by Edmund C. Berkeley, a computer scientist and antinuclear activist, author of the book *Giant Brains or Machines That Think* (1949). See http://www.oldcomputermuseum.com/geniac.html and especially http://www.computercollector.com/archive/geniac/ for more information.
3. For machine translation, see the review by Hutchins (2003). Examples of the difficulty encountered in making a computer understand natural language are given in the Supplements to this book on http://whyred.kevin-oregan.net
4. In 2010 you could buy the SYSTRAN program for your own PC, starting at only 39 euros, and choose from the Professional Premium, the Professional Standard, the Personal, the Web, the Office Translator, and other versions of their software!
5. Weizenbaum's ELIZA program is on http://courses.cs.vt.edu/~cs3604/lib/Ethics/eliza.html, the postmodern generator on http://www.elsewhere.org/pomo. The generator was written by Andrew C. Bulhad using the Dada Engine.
6. The best known example of an attempt to compile "common sense" is Douglas Lenat's "CYC" project, which started in the 1980s at Atari corporation and has now become a company, Cycorp. Cyc is an ongoing effort to accumulate human consensual knowledge into a database of more than a million assertions which can be used to understand, for example, newspaper articles or encyclopedia entries. On http://www.cyc.com/ the company says: "Cycorp's vision is to create the world's first true artificial intelligence, having both common sense and the ability to reason with it."
7. This point was forcefully made in 1972 by Hubert Dreyfus in his influential book *What Computers Can't Do: A Critique of Artificial Intelligence*, updated in 1992 to *What Computers Still Can't Do: A Critique of Artificial Reason* (Dreyfus, 1972, 1992).
8. The company iRobot, inspired by the work of Rodney Brookes, has a Web site http://www.roombavac.com/. They say they deliver "... innovative robots that are

making a difference in people's lives. From cleaning floors to disarming explosives, we constantly strive to find better ways to tackle dull, dirty and dangerous missions—with better results." They say that if you have iRobot Scooba: "check mopping off your list." With iRobot Roomba: "check vacuuming off your list."

9. See http://www.epigenetic-robotics.org for ongoing activities in this field, with bibliographic references. For a survey of the related field of developmental robotics, see Lungarella, Metta, Pfeifer, and Sandini (2003).

10. See http://www.lira.dist.unige.it/ for BabyBot, created by Giorgio Metta when he was working in the COG project at MIT. It is now part of the larger, European RobotCub project (http://www.robotcub.org/). Videos can be seen on that site as well as on http://www.lira.dist.unige.it/babybotvideos.htm. An overview of some other current efforts in autonomous and developmental robotics can be found on the Web site for the supplements to this book: http://whyred.kevin-oregan.net

11. See Fitzpatrick and Metta (2003). The notion of "affordance" is due to the ecological psychologist J. J. Gibson.

12. For a very critical article in *The Skeptic* about the possibilities of AI, see Kassan (2006).

13. For a useful bibliography on different approaches to the self, see the Web site maintained by Shaun Gallagher: http://www.philosophy.ucf.edu/pi/ or his excellent review (Gallagher, 2000). See also the special issue of *Annals of the New York Academy of Sciences* in Vol. 1001, 2003.

14. Kohut, 2009.

15. I based this quick overview on Gallagher (2000).

16. James, 1890.

17. Neisser, 1988.

18. Dennett, 1991, 1992.

19. Gallagher, 2000.

20. Metzinger, 2004, 2005.

21. Part of this long list is taken from Strawson (1999); see the book by Gallagher and Shear (1999) for a recent interdisciplinary survey of many approaches to the self.

22. Here I am going to follow the two dimensions of classification proposed by Vierkant (2003).

23. This classification is based on that proposed by Bekoff and Sherman (2004). They use the umbrella term "self-cognizance" to designate the whole spectrum of ways that a system can have knowledge of itself. In their classification they use the three terms "self-referencing," "self-awareness," and "self-consciousness" instead of the terms "self-distinguishing," "self-knowledge," and "knowledge of self-knowledge." I prefer my terms because they are more neutral as regards the question of whether any phenomenal quality might be associated with the notion of self, and because they avoid the difficult terms "awareness" and "consciousness."

24. See Edsinger and Kemp (2006).

25. As suggested by cognitive psychologists Simon Baron-Cohen (Baron-Cohen, 1997; Leslie, 1994). For robots that imitate humans' social development, see Breazeal and Scassellati (2002) and Scassellati (2003). See Triesch, Teuscher, Deak, and Carlson (2006) for a discussion of how gaze following might be a learned faculty.

26. Because this social self is such an important concept in our society, it is discussed from a myriad of different points of view, in the popular press, in psychological counseling, in psychoanalysis and in academic psychology, sociology, and anthropology.

In these domains, a plethora of concepts have been defined, including for example self-actualization; self-awareness; the self-concept; self control; self development; self disclosure; self-efficacy; self-esteem; self harm; self help; self-identity; self image; self monitoring; self-perception; attitude change; self-realization; self-regulated learning; self talk.

27. The comparison Hume makes actually concerns what he calls the "soul" (Hume, 1793/2003, Book 2.i.vi). Derek Parfit also makes the comparison with a nation or club (Parfit, 1986).

28. Why does this abstraction exist and why is it so useful? To understand this, we can appeal to the concept of "meme," invented by the biologist Richard Dawkins. A meme is the social or cognitive equivalent of a gene. Just as there are genes corresponding to traits replicated in biological reproduction, there are "memes," which are ideas, skills, or behaviors that stick in the mind, serve a social purpose, and so become part of human society. Memes are "replicators"; they are adapted to human cognitive capacities. They are easy to remember and stable enough to be accurately propagated through social interactions and from one generation to the next. Furthermore, memes may have the self-validating property that they influence the structure of society so as to favor their own preservation and propagation. As suggested by writer Susan Blackmore, the self may be one of the most fundamental memes in human society. The self is a concept which each of us uses in order to understand the goals and desires not only of our own selves but of our fellow humans (Blackmore, 2000; Dawkins, 1976).

29. Dennett, 1992.

30. Martin Kusch cited by Vierkant (2003) mentions the doubly self-referring and self-validating roles of social constructs like money and selves, though there may be a difference in the way Kusch uses these terms.

31. It is hard to believe that this kind of circularity could provide something that seems so real to us. Surely I can sense my existence—I can perceive myself talking and thinking. If I am just a story, then how can this story perceive itself talking and thinking? It's as though it made sense to say that Sherlock Holmes, who we all know is just a fictional character, *really* considers himself to have an identity.

To make these ideas more plausible, consider another example of a self-referring and self-validating social construct, which is the notion of country or nation. A group of people can proclaim itself as a nation, and from that moment on, the nation takes on a real existence on the international scene. Furthermore there is a *real* sense in which nations have "selves." They have national identities, they build alliances, they make pacts and wage wars, they communicate and trade. They can be offended, envious of others' resources, aggressive, or peaceful. They have national memories and even what might be called split personalities when under stress (e.g., French Resistance under German World War II occupation).

Thus, judging from international events and talk in the media, and judging from the dramatic excesses that nations are willing to engage in to preserve and extend themselves, nations are real and really have identities. Because nations generally "express themselves" in different ways than humans, with no single "voice," the analogy with a human "self" is not perfect, but if we were somehow able to go out and actually interview a nation, and ask it if it *really* felt it had a self, an identity, and if it *really* felt it was real, it would reply "yes." (These ideas are presented admirably by Dennett, 1989.)

32. It may be that not just the expression of pain but also pain itself may be influenced by cultural factors, but the evidence is difficult to interpret (see Rollman, 1998).

33. Seminal experiments showing unconscious influence of social norms on behavior were done by the social psychologist John Bargh, now at Yale (see Bargh & Chartrand, 1999). In these experiments, participants were told that they were being tested on language proficiency in a sentence unscrambling task. They were given five words (e.g., "They her respect see usually") and were required to write down a sentence which made use of four of those words. Actually, however, this supposed language proficiency task was used to "prime" participants with different cultural stereotypes. For example, in one experiment, the words used in the sentence unscrambling task were those that were either associated with politeness (e.g., honor, considerate, appreciate, patiently, cordially), or with rudeness (e.g., brazen, impolitely, infringe, obnoxious). It was found that when the participants had been primed for rudeness, on leaving the experimental room they were more likely to interrupt the experimenter who was ostensibly talking to a colleague. In another experiment the sentence unscrambling task used words that primed for an "elderly" prototype (e.g., worried, Florida, old, lonely, gray) versus a neutral prototype (e.g., thirsty, clean, private). It was found that the time it took for the participants to cross the hall on leaving the experiment was longer when they were primed with "elderly" words. A different experiment showed that participants primed for the "elderly" prototype could also not remember as many details about the room in which they participated in the experiment.

34. Hypnosis is so easy to induce that any basic text on hypnosis will provide an induction technique that can be used by a complete novice to hypnotize someone else. The Web site http://www.hypnosis.com/ provides a wealth of information, including induction scripts and numerous scripts purported to cure anything from AIDS to constipation to procrastination. Some hypnotists claim to be able to hypnotize people (even people who have not previously been sensitized) in a matter of seconds.

   The ease with which hypnosis can be induced is consistent with the idea that hypnotic trance is a matter of choosing to play out a role that society has familiarized us with. The suggestion that hypnosis is such a culturally bound phenomenon comes from the very high correlation between hypnotizability and a person's belief that hypnosis works. Conversely, it may be impossible to hypnotize someone from a different culture, who has never heard of hypnosis. "Playing the part of being hypnotized" would seem to be a culturally accepted way of exploring a different story of "I." In this story, by simply choosing to do so, one allows one's "self" to be manipulated by others (or, in the case of self-hypnosis, by one's own self). A view similar to this as concerns reported involuntariness of hypnotic trance is suggested in Lynn, Rhue, and Weekes (1990). I have read that people who are hypnotized to think that an ice cube burns them will actually develop blisters. Paul (1963) concludes that there may be some effect of suggestion on the formation of blisters, but Benham and Younger (2008) agree with Paul that any effects will generally have causes other than hypnosis itself.

   This is not to say that the hypnotic state is a pretense. On the contrary, it is a convincing story to the hypnotized subject, just as convincing as the normal story of "I." Moreover, it produces measurable effects in physiology and on the brain, so much so that clinicians are using it more and more in their practices, for example, in complementing or replacing anesthesia in painful surgical operations.

For a recent review on hypnosis, including chapters on physiological and brain effects by Barabasz and Barabasz (2008) and by Oakley (2008), see *The Oxford Handbook of Hypnosis* (Nash & Barnier, 2008). See also the 2009 special issue of *Contemporary Hypnosis* on hypnotic analgesia introduced by Liossi, Santarcangelo, and Jensen (2009). For a review of the use of hypnosis in the treatment of acute and chronic pain, see Patterson and Jensen (2003). Hardcastle (1999) authoritatively devotes a chapter to expounding the extraordinary effectiveness of hypnosis, which she says surpasses all other methods of pain control. Marie-Elisabeth Faymonville (Faymonville et al., 1995) has performed thousands of heavy surgical procedures under only local anesthetic, using hypnosis. She told me that even though usually it is claimed that only a small percentage of people are sufficiently receptive to hypnosis for them to become insensitive to pain, in her own practice, among about 4,000 patients on whom she had operated, the hypnotic procedure had failed only in isolated cases.

As a sampling of mention of hypnosis in the press: In April 2008 a British hypnotist submitted to a painful orthopedic operation where bone was sawed from his hand, without any anesthetic: http://news.bbc.co.uk/2/hi/uk_news/england/sussex/7355523.stm. Referring to the Montgomery et al. (2007) study using hypnosis in breast cancer operations: http://news.bbc.co.uk/2/hi/health/6969298.stm. Dr. Christina Liossi, from University of Wales, Swansea, using hypnosis with local anesthetic in cancer operations in children: http://news.bbc.co.uk/2/hi/health/3642764.stm; also see Hawkins, Liossi, Ewart, Hatira, and Kosmidis (2006).

35. These are examples of culturally bound syndromes (Simons & Hughes, 1985; Somera, 2006) where an individual will temporarily change his or her identity. Here is a description of *latah*, found in Malaysia and Indonesia:

> A person exemplifying the Latah syndrome typically responds to a startling stimulus with an exaggerated startle, sometimes throwing or dropping a held object, and often uttering some improper word, usually "Puki!" ("Cunt!"), "Butol!" ("Prick!"), or "Buntut!" ("Ass!"), which may be embedded in a "silly" phrase. Further, he or she may, while flustered, obey the orders or match the orders or movements of persons nearby. Since spectators invariably find this funny, a known Latah may be intentionally startled many times each day for the amusement of others. (Simons, 1980)

Similar syndromes are found in Burma (yaun), Thailand (bah-tsche), Philippines (mali-mali, silok), Siberia (myriachit, ikota, amurakh), South-West Africa, Lapland (Lapp panic), Japan (Imu), and among French Canadians in Maine (jumping).

It has been suggested that the phenomenon may be related to the belief that fright or startle can cause people to lose their soul, leading then to the intrusion of evil spirits (Kenny, 1983). This is interesting because it shows how an innate human startle reaction can be profoundly modified to serve cultural purposes. When this happens, people can espouse the syndrome so completely that they claim it is involuntary and that they are powerless to prevent it.

There are more dramatic examples where one's self is involuntarily modified. Often these can be attributed to a person being subjected to strong social or psychological stress. The Malay phenomenon of amok may be such a case. Here, typically, an outsider to a local group is frustrated by his situation or by social pressures, and, after a period of brooding, suddenly grabs a weapon and wildly attempts to kill everyone around him, afterward falling into a state of exhaustion and completely forgetting what happened. Despite its extreme violence, this behavior may correspond to a historically sanctioned tradition among Malay warriors that people consider is the appropriate response to personally intolerable conditions (Carr, 1978). Similarly indiscriminate homicidal attack behaviors are observed in other societies, in particular recently in the United States, and they may be culturally determined in different ways.

Hypnosis, latah, and amok are just a few examples of short-lived changes in the self that can be observed in special circumstances, with other cases being possession trances, ecstasies, channeling provoked in religious cults, oracles, witchcraft, shamanism, or other mystical experiences. More permanent, highly dramatic involuntary modifications of the self can also be provoked by extreme psychological stress or physical abuse, as shown by Lifton (1986, 1989, 1991), for example, in the cases of people subjected to brainwashing by sects, in religious cults, and in war.

There is also the case of dissociative identity disorder (formerly called multiple personality disorder). A person with DID may hear the voices of different "alters" and may flip from "being" one or other of these people at any moment. The different alters may or may not know of each other's existence. The philosopher Ian Hacking, in a discussion of multiple personality disorder, Paris café garçons, and the gay community (Hacking, 1986), suggests that the surprising rise in incidence of DID/MPD over the past decades signals that this disorder is indeed a cultural phenomenon. This may be one explanation why the illness is considered by some to be very suspect. Under the view I am taking here, DID/MPD is a case where an individual resorts to splitting his or her identity in order to cope with extreme psychological stress. Each of these identities is as real as the other and as real as a normal person's identity—since all are stories. See Hartocollis (1998) for a review of different viewpoints of MPD as a social construction.

36. I have also not mentioned the ethical, moral, and legal problems that these ideas pose (see Greene & Cohen, 2004), and I have not discussed the fascinating related idea that what we call free will is a construction similar to that of the self. According to Daniel Wegner (Wegner, 2003a, 2003b), the impression of having willed an action is a cognitive construction that we assemble from evidence that we gather about what occurred.

Chapter 7

Types of Consciousness

Where are we now with respect to my dream of building a conscious robot? So far I've been trying, one by one, to lay aside aspects of consciousness that pose no logical problem for science and that could be—and to a degree, in a few instances, are now—attainable in robots. I started with thought, perception, and communication, and went on to the self. I hope to have shown that even if we are still a long way from attaining human levels of these capacities in a robot, there is no *logical* problem involved in doing so.

Now what about achieving full-blown consciousness? To answer this question, we first need to look at the various ways in which the term *consciousness* is used.[1] Then we will try to single out a way of talking about consciousness that lends itself to scientific pursuit.

Intransitive and Transitive Notions

There are some usages of the word *consciousness* that have been called "intransitive," that is, they are uses for which there is no grammatical object, as in the following examples:

- "Humans are conscious, whereas ants are probably not"[2] (consciousness as a general human capacity).
- "After an interval of consciousness, the injured soldier lapsed into unconsciousness" (consciousness as the alert, waking state).
- "The criminal was acting consciously when he stole the money" (consciousness as awareness of one's actions and their implications).
- "Mary was too self-conscious to be a good actress" (self-consciousness as a social personality trait involving excessive observation and judgment of the self).

All these intransitive notions of consciousness can be understood as being derived from an underlying "transitive" form of being "conscious of" something, a grammatical object. Thus, for example, saying that "humans are conscious" means that they have the potential to be conscious of things: for example, of their own existence, their own selves, their mental states, and the things around them. Saying "after an interval of consciousness, the injured soldier lapsed into unconsciousness" means that he lapsed from a state where he could be conscious of things, to a state where he was no longer able to be conscious of anything. Saying that "the criminal was acting consciously when he stole the money" means that as he did it, he was potentially conscious of the different things he was doing and their implications. Saying that Mary is self-conscious means that she is excessively conscious of herself.

So what we really need to explain is the transitive use of the word, as in "someone is conscious of something." Certainly one important aspect of this phrase is that the person is aware of that thing—that is, he or she has it in mind and is cognitively engaging with or mentally attending to it. The philosopher Ned Block calls this activity access consciousness, because it involves mentally "accessing" something. There is also another way of being "conscious of" something, according to Block, which is what he calls phenomenal consciousness.[3] This way corresponds to the *experience itself* or the "phenomenology" that one has when attending to the thing. So, for example, one is not only access conscious of a pain (in the sense of mentally attending to the fact that one was having the pain) but is also actually *experiencing* the pain.

I shall be looking at this latter kind of consciousness—again, I shall call it "raw feel"—in the following chapters. Here I'll look more closely at the first kind of consciousness of something.

Access Consciousness

Ned Block has a neat way of nailing down what is meant when we say we have access consciousness of something. He says it means that we are "poised" (i.e., "ready" or "prepared") to make use of that thing in our rational actions, decisions, planning, or linguistic or communicative behavior.

Still, I think that this definition is not quite satisfactory. I would say that what Block is referring to corresponds to what I would call having *cognitive* access to something, rather than *conscious* access. Conscious access, I would claim, requires more than just being poised to make use of something in rational actions and communicative behavior.

To illustrate why, imagine a machine that we might call the Mark I Chessplayer. This machine is a chess-playing automaton with a torso, a head with eyes, and an arm. It is designed to sit in front of you, look at the chessboard, note the position, do some processing, and then verbally announce and make its move in reply to yours. This seems reasonable with today's technology; in fact, without the head and eyes and arm there are already good chess-playing automata on the market, and it would be easy to link such a device to a speech production and comprehension system.

Surely, as it plays chess with you, the Mark I Chessplayer is "poised to make use of your chess moves in its current actions, decisions, planning, and rational, linguistic or communicative behavior." But I don't think we can say that the machine has "conscious access" to your moves. The reason is not so much that the machine's rational and communicative behavior is more limited than a human's. The main reason is that all the machine is doing is making a calculation and responding automatically to your moves. It has "cognitive access" rather than full-blown conscious access to them.

So how would we build a Mark II Chessplayer so that it had full-blown conscious access? Conscious access seems to fundamentally involve a wider realm of choice than simply the restricted set of possibilities involved in choosing a chess move. Having conscious access involves not only cognitively accessing something in order to exercise a choice about what to do with respect to that thing but also being aware of the whole context within which you are doing that cognitive accessing. Thus, it involves being ready to show, by choosing from a wider set of alternative actions, that you can make use of your awareness that the more restricted cognitive accessing is going on. For example, you would assume a chess-playing machine had this kind of higher order capacity if the machine sometimes bantered with you about the move you made, or if it mentioned that it was deliberating whether to invoke a classical defense, or even if it ventured a word about the weather during a boring phase of the game. In other words, not only would the machine have to have cognitive access to your move, but it would additionally have to be ready to reason or communicate about *the fact that* it had this cognitive access to your move.

This idea can be expressed succinctly by using the notion of cognitive access in a hierarchical way.[4] A necessary (but as discussed later, insufficient) condition for an agent to have conscious access to something is as follows: *The agent must have cognitive access to the fact that it has cognitive access to that something.*

Note that the wider context of awareness and choice that we require in conscious access is implicit in the definition of cognitive access. This is because the notion of cognitive access already contains the notion of choice among a range of possibilities. We already see this in a limited way for the Mark I machine. Its first, lower order cognitive access to your move means that it is poised to make use of your move in its rational behavior. But what does that mean? It means that there are a *variety* of possible moves you might have made and a *variety* of possible rational behaviors the machine could undertake (like moving this piece or that). Thus, having cognitive access implies choice on two accounts: with regard to the situation, and with regard to the possibilities for action.

This two-fold context of possibilities applies also to the second, higher level of cognitive access in the Mark II machine. With regard to the first context, the situation, the machine is poised to make use of the fact that it is poised to make use of your moves. This carries the implicit assumption that there are a variety of possible other things that the machine could have been poised to make use of, like the expression on your face, for example, or the fact that it's playing chess and not dominoes. The second context, possibilities for action, derives from the variety of things the machine could do about the fact that it is poised to make use of your moves. (It could carry on playing, but it can also do other things, like talk about your move or ignore your move and talk about the weather.)

Thus, using the simple notion of cognitive access in a hierarchical fashion allows us to capture a condition that seems necessary for conscious access, namely that it requires the machine's chess-playing capacities to be embedded in a wider field of possible activities than just responding to moves on a blow-by-blow basis. To have conscious access to chess playing, the Mark II Chessplayer must have richer cognitive capacities than just playing chess.

There is also another condition that is implicit in conscious access. Take again the Mark I Chessplayer. Saying that "it" had cognitive access to your moves was a way of describing what the machine does. It takes in the current situation, does some calculations, and comes out with the riposte. But who is the "it"? In the case of Mark I Chessplayer, the machine itself does not know there is this "it." Its cognitive faculties are limited to inputting and outputting chess moves. The "it" is only what we use to describe the machine *as seen by us, from the outside*.

But for the Mark II Chessplayer, the situation is different. The machine is not only poised to apply its cognitive abilities, but it also knows that *it* is in this way poised. It thus has to additionally possess the notion of *itself*. It has to know that *it* exists as an independent entity in its environment. Furthermore, if its self is well developed, it might also know that this entity can be considered by others, and by itself, as having desires, motivations, purposes, plans, reasons, and intentions. Such a self is socially defined, in the sense that it knows the social presuppositions and implications of the situation (the fact that it is supposedly good for it to win the game, that presumably you yourself also want to win, that you and it have come together and agree to obey the rules. . .). Depending on the degree of sophistication of the machine, it can have more or less of a notion of self. But some notion of self is implicit in the idea of conscious access.

In sum, the notion of access consciousness can be captured by using the idea of cognitive access in a hierarchical way.[5] This automatically implies that the agent will have to be situated in a context which is sufficiently rich for it to make sense to say that there are a variety of behaviors which the agent can choose from and a variety of situations that it can be cognitively accessing. Additionally, the agent must have at least a rudimentary form of "self."

The notions I've considered of cognitive access, conscious access, and the self are complicated. There are many aspects of mental life we can be access conscious of, and the extent to which these are developed in an agent can be different. With regard to cognitive and conscious access, I have taken the example of a chess-playing machine, but the same notions can apply to insects, animals, and humans, albeit to differing degrees. With regard to the notion of self, as described in the previous chapter, there are many notions of the self.

But what is important is that scientists have hopes of successfully coming to grips with the different aspects of access consciousness and the self. These topics are being approached today in artificial intelligence, robotics, psychology,[6] and cognitive ethology. There is faith that they are amenable to science.

Notes

1. A useful classification from a neurologist's point of view, which I have broadly used here, is due to Zeman (2004). Many other authors have also provided interesting classifications from the psychologist's or the philosopher's point of view (e.g., Baars,

1988; Chalmers, 1997). A review of nine neurocognitive views is to be found in Morin (2006). The distinction between "transitive" and "intransitive" types of consciousness is used by Armstrong and Malcolm (1984) and Rosenthal (1997). It's worth pointing out that many philosophers start off by distinguishing "creature consciousness" from "state consciousness" before then distinguishing transitive and intransitive forms (see, for example, Carruthers, 2009). I have difficulty understanding the notion of state consciousness, because I think it is unnatural to say that a mental state can be conscious. For me it only makes sense to say that people (or perhaps some animals and future artificial agents) can be conscious. In any case, I think that the creature/state distinction should be considered subsidiary to the transitive/intransitive distinction, since both creature and state consciousness can be found in transitive and intransitive forms. Self-consciousness and reflexive consciousness are other subclasses of consciousness that are often mentioned, but that, again, I think can be considered as varieties of consciousness of something.

2. The word *self-conscious* is sometimes used here also, as when we say "mice do not have self-consciousness."

3. Block's distinction (Block, 1996) has been seriously criticized, notably by Rosenthal (2002). I have preferred my own term of *raw feel*, which I shall be defining in a more precise way.

4. There is a large literature in philosophy on "higher order thought" theories of consciousness—for a review, see Carruthers (2009). From my nonphilosophical point of view, the debates concerning possible such theories are difficult to understand because they refer to the idea that mental "states" might somehow themselves be conscious. To me it is hard to understand what it would mean to say that a state is conscious.

5. This account of access consciousness is strongly related to what the philosophers call the higher order representational (HOR), higher order thought (HOT) (Rosenthal, 1997, 2005), and higher order experience (HOE) or higher order perception theories (Armstrong, 1968; Armstrong & Malcolm, 1984; Lycan, 1987, 1996; for reviews, see Gennaro, 2004 and Carruthers, 2009). But I venture to say that what I am suggesting is a form of what has been called a dispositional HOT theory, with the added constraints of the notion of choice that I have emphasized, and additionally the fact that the agent in question has the notion of self. I consider the notion of self to be a cognitive and social construct that poses no problem for a scientific approach. This applies insofar as access consciousness is concerned. But with regard to phenomenal consciousness, we shall see later that there is an important difference in my approach. Contrary to Rosenthal or Carruthers, who claim that phenomenality emerges (magically?) through having a thought about a thought, I say that phenomenality is a quality of certain sensorimotor interactions that the agent engages in, namely interactions that possess richness, bodiliness, insubordinateness, and grabbiness. (For a discussion of Carruthers' approach and his comments on Rosenthal, see ch. 9 in his book [Carruthers, 2000a; see also Carruthers, 2000b].)

6. In psychology it is worth noting the influential "global workspace" model of (access) consciousness developed first by Bernard Baars (Baars, 1988, 1997, 2002) and its recent connections with neuroanatomical data proposed by Stanislas Dehaene (Dehaene, Changeux, Naccache, Sackur, & Sergent, 2006). This model attempts to show how the occurrence of access consciousness corresponds to the brain having simultaneous "global access" to information from a variety of processing modules.

Chapter 8

Phenomenal Consciousness, or Raw Feel, and Why They're "Hard"

Imagine that we had, many years from now, succeeded in constructing a robot that had a more fully developed, human-like capacity to think, perceive, and communicate in ordinary language than is achievable now, and that had a sophisticated notion of self. The machine would be something like the highly evolved robot played by Arnold Schwarzenegger in the film *Terminator*. But take the moment in the film when Terminator has its arm chopped off. Most people have the intuition that Terminator *knows* this is a bad thing, but that it doesn't actually feel or experience the pain in the way humans would.

Another example would be the "replicants" in Ridley Scott's brilliant 1982 film *Blade Runner*: these androids are genetically engineered to look identical to normal humans (apart from often being much more beautiful, perfect, and intelligent!) and to have human-like memories. It is so difficult to tell the difference between them and humans that some of Tyrell Corporation's most advanced "Nexus-6" replicants themselves do not know that they are replicants.

Yet most people think that it would be impossible for a machine like Terminator or the Nexus-6 replicants, no matter how complex or advanced, to actually feel anything like pain. It might be possible to program the machines to *act* as though they were having pain: We could make the machines wince or scream, and we could even program them so they are convinced that they feel, but most people think that this would have to be a simple pretense. It seems inconceivable that a robot could in any way really feel pain.

And similarly for other sensations. For instance, robots might give all the right answers when asked about whether they feel the sweet smell of the rose and the beauty of the sunset, but most people have the strong conviction that these sensations would have to be artificially programmed into the machines, and would have to be a kind of playacting.

On the other hand, when you and I experience a pain, when we smell a rose, listen to a symphony, see a sunset, or touch a feather, when we humans (and presumably animals too) have sensations, it feels like something to us. There is a specific felt quality to sensations.

How can this come about? Why is there "something it's like" for humans to have a feel? What special mechanism in the brain could convert the neural activity provoked by an injury, the rose, or the symphony into the real feel of hurting, the smell of the rose, the sensation of a beautiful sound?

"Extra" Components of Feel and "Raw Feel"

To understand the problem, let's analyze more closely what "feel" really is. Take the example of the color red. One aspect of the feel of red is the *cognitive states* that red puts me into. There are mental associations such as, among other things, roses, ketchup, blood, red traffic lights, anger, and translucent red cough drops. Additional mental associations may be determined by knowledge I have about how red is related to other colors, for example, that it is quite similar to pink and quite different from green. There are other cognitive states that are connected with having an experience of red, namely the thoughts and linguistic utterances that seeing redness at this moment might be provoking in me, or changes in my knowledge, my plans, opinions, or desires. But all these cognitive states are extra things *in addition to* the raw sensation. They are not themselves experiences. They are mental connections or "add-ons" to what happens when I have the experience of red.[1]

Another aspect of the feel of red is the *learned bodily reactions* that redness may engender, caused by any *habits* that I have established and that are associated with red, for example, pressing on the brake when I see the red brake lights of a car ahead of me. Perhaps when I see red I also have a tiny tendency to make the swallowing movements that I make when I suck those nice translucent red cough drops. But again, all these bodily reactions are add-ons to the actual raw experience of red.[2]

Yet another aspect of the feel of red may be the *physiological states or tendencies* it creates. Certainly this is the case for feels like jealousy, love, and hate, which involve certain, often ill-defined, urges to modify the present situation. Similarly, emotions like fear, anger, and shame, and states like hunger and thirst, would appear to involve specific bodily manifestations such as changes in heartbeat, flushing, or other reactions of the autonomic nervous system, and to be accompanied by drives to engage in certain activities. Even color sensations may produce physiological effects; for example, it may be that your state of excitement is greater in a red room than in a blue room.[3] But if such effects do exist, they are *in addition to* the actual raw feel of the redness of red itself.

In short, all these extras may provide additional experiences that may *come with* the feel of red. But at the root of the feel of red is a *"raw feel"* of red itself, which is at the core of what happens when we look at a red patch of color.

Another example is the pain of an injection. I hate injections. I have a host of mental associations that make me start sweating and feel anxious as soon as (or even before) the needle goes into my arm. There are also automatic physical reactions to the injection: My arm jerks when the needle goes in; my body reacts to the alien fluid; and I feel faint. But again, these effects are over and above the raw feel that constitutes the pain of the injection itself. When all the theatrics caused by my imaginations and by the physical effects of the injection are taken away, then presumably what is left is the "raw feel" of the pain of the injection. "Raw feel" is whatever people are referring to when they talk about the most basic aspects of their experience.[4]

But is anything actually left once all the add-ons are stripped away? Most people will say that there *is* something left, since it is this that they think *causes* all the theatrics of their experience. Raw feels really must exist, people will say, since how else can we identify and distinguish one feel from another? Taking the example of red again: Surely two very slightly different shades of red would be clearly seen as different even if all the mental associations or bodily changes they produce were identical. Even if we can't pin down and say exactly what is different, we can see *that* they are different. Something at the core of feel must be providing this difference.

Another reason why people think raw feel must exist is because otherwise there would be "nothing it's like" to have sensations. We would be mere machines, empty vessels making movements and reacting with our outside environments, but there would be no inside "feel" to anything. There would only be the cognitive states, the learned reactions and the physiological states, but there would be no raw feel itself.

What I have been calling raw feel is related to what philosophers call "qualia," the basic quality or "what-it's like" of experience. Qualia are an extremely contentious topic in philosophy.[5] Some philosophers believe that qualia are a misguided and confused notion, and that in fact there is nothing more to experience than cognitive states, bodily reactions, and physiological states or tendencies. My own position is that regardless of whether qualia are a misguided notion, there's no denying that a lot of people talk about their experiences as though there are raw feels causing them. We need a scientific explanation for what people say about them, independently of whether qualia make sense.

Before trying to account for what people say about raw feel, I want to look at why the problem of raw feel is difficult.[6]

Why Raw Feel Can't Be Generated in the Brain

Take the example of color. At the very first level of processing in the retina, information about color is coded in three so-called opponent channels.[7] A first light-dark opponent channel measures the equilibrium between light and dark. This corresponds to luminance (or lightness) of a color as it would appear if seen on a black/white television monitor, for example. A second red-green opponent channel is sensitive to the equilibrium of hue between red and green, and a third blue-yellow opponent channel is sensitive to the equilibrium between blue and yellow.

The existence of these opponent channels in the visual system is generally assumed to explain certain facts about which colors seem "pure" or "unique" to people, and which colors are perceived as being composed of other colors.[8] For example, pink is perceived as containing red and white, orange is perceived as containing red and yellow, but red, green, blue, and yellow are perceived as "pure," that is, as not contain-ing other colors. Another fact taken to be a consequence of opponent channels is that you cannot have hues that are both red and green or both blue and yellow.[9] Color opponency also explains the well-known phenomenon of afterimages. If you look steadily at a red patch for 10–20 seconds, the red-green opponent channel gets tired of responding in the red direction and for a while things that are actually white appear tinged in the opposite direction, namely green.

But whereas scientists believe firmly in such mechanisms, there is currently no answer to the question: What is it exactly about (for example) the red-green channel that gives you those raw red and green sensations? Information in the opponent channels gets transmitted via the optic nerve into the brain, through the lateral geniculate nucleus up into area V1, where it then gets relayed to a multitude of other brain areas, and in particular to area V4, which is sometimes thought to be particularly concerned with color sensation.[10] What is it in these pathways or in the higher areas that explains the difference between the raw feel of red and green?

It is not hard to imagine how differences in the activity of certain brain areas could create differences related to what I have called the "extra" aspects of the feel of red and green. We can easily imagine direct stimulus–response reactions that link the sensory input to the systems controlling the appropriate muscular output. We can further imagine that more indirect effects related to physiological states are caused by red and green stimulation, and that such states affect our tendencies to act in different ways. Finally we can also imagine that computations about the use of linguistic concepts, about knowledge and opinions, might be determined by the incoming information about red and green. For example, we can envisage that the neuronal circuits responsible for the feel of red activate those responsible for the memory of strawberries and red cough drops and red traffic lights.

But what about the "core" aspect of the sensations of red and green: the "raw feel"? How could brain mechanisms generate these? And here I want to make a logical point. Suppose that we actually had localized the brain system that provided the *raw feel* of red and green. And suppose that we had found something different about how the circuit responded when it was generating the red feel, as compared to the green feel. It could be something about the different neurons involved, something about their firing rates or the way they are connected, for example.

For the sake of argument, suppose it was two different populations of neurons that coded the raw feel of red and the raw feel of green. What could it be about these different groups of neurons that generated the different feels? Their connections to other brain areas could certainly determine the *extra* components of the feel, for example, any immediate bodily reactions or tendencies to act or changes in cognitive state that are produced by feels of red and green. But what precise aspect of these neurons might be generating the differences in the actual raw feel *itself*?

There can be no way of answering this question satisfactorily. For imagine we had actually hit upon what we thought was an explanation. Suppose that it was, say, the fact that the red-producing group of neurons generated one particular frequency of oscillations in wide-ranging cortical areas, and that the green-producing neurons generated a different frequency. Then we could ask: Why does *this* frequency of oscillation produce the raw feel of red, and *that* frequency the raw feel of green? Couldn't it be the other way round? We could go in and look at what was special about these frequencies. Perhaps we would find that the red producing frequencies favored metabolism of a certain neurotransmitter, whereas the green producing frequencies favored metabolism of a different neurotransmitter. But then we would be back to having to explain why these particular neurotransmitters generated the particular raw feels that they do.

We would not have any logical difficulty if we were simply interested in understanding how the neurotransmitters determined the *extra* components associated with red and green by influencing brain states and potential behaviors and bodily states. But how could we explain the way they determined the raw feel *itself*?

Appealing to the idea that it was different cell populations that generated the red and green feels was just an example. I could have made the same argument if I had claimed that the red and green channels excite other brain regions differently, or are connected differently, or have differently shaped dendrites, or whatever. Clearly no matter how far we go in the search for mechanisms that generate raw feel we will always end up being forced to ask an additional question about *why* things are this way rather than that way.[11]

Isomorphic Brain Structures

A possible way out of this situation has been proposed by some scientists and philosophers.[12] The idea is to give up trying to explain why raw feels are the way they are, and instead just concentrate on explaining why the *differences and similarities* between the raw feels are the way they are. For example, some scientists suggest that we might find a set of brain states corresponding to color sensations, and that the *structure* of the similarities and differences between the different states could be mapped onto the similarities and differences between color sensations. They suggest that such an *isomorphism* between the structure of brain states and the structure of color sensations is the best we can do as an explanation of color sensations, even though of course, for all the reasons explained earlier, there would still be lacking an explanation of what individual colors themselves feel like.

But actually even this isomorphic mapping of brain states onto color sensations leaves some unanswered questions. To see this, take the following example. Suppose it turned out that some brain state, call it B2, produces the raw feel of red, but furthermore, brain states near B2 produce feels that are near to red; and as you move further and further away from B2 you get further and further away from red. This could happen in a lawful way that actually corresponds to people's judgments about the proximity of red to other colors. So if brain state B1 is blue and B3 is yellow, then as you move from B2 in the direction of B1 you would get feelings that go from red through purple to blue, whereas as you move from B2 to B3 your feeling would go gradually from red through orange to yellow.

Wouldn't that be at least the start of an explanation of color? The trouble is, what is meant by saying "move from B2 in the direction of B1"? Brain states are activities of millions of neurons, and there is no single way of saying one brain state is "more in the direction" of another brain state. Furthermore, even if we do find some way of ordering the brain states so that their similarities correspond to perceptual judgments about similarities between colors, or if we find that they lie in an ordered way on some cortical map, then we can always ask, Why is it this way of ordering the brain states, rather than that, which predicts sensory judgments?

My argument here shows that even having an isomorphic neural structure actually does not live up to the claim of providing an explanation of the similarities and differences between color sensations. The reason is that a justification still needs to be given for the choice of metric used to compare brain states.

Finding brain structures that are necessary and sufficient to generate a particular raw feel would no doubt be very interesting, but it would still not explain what we would really like to know about the feel, namely why it is the way it is. The underlying problem is that there is no way of making a link between feel and physical mechanisms. Neural firing rates, or any physically definable phenomena in the brain, are incommensurate with raw feels. Even discovering an isomorphism between perceptual judgments and certain associated brain states, though interesting (and for that matter, necessary in any scientific explanation of how the brain determines feel), is no help as an explanation of raw feel.

Atoms of Experience

Let's consider the following last resort. Scientists have the right to postulate the existence of "basic units" of consciousness if these are necessary to explain the mysteries of feel.[13] After all, this is the approach used in physics where there are a small number of basic concepts like mass, space, time, gravity, and electric charge. Nobody is supposed to ask why these entities are the way they are. They are taken to be elementary building blocks of the universe, and scientists politely refrain from asking what they "really are." Scientists feel entitled to do this, because there are only a few such building blocks, and because the theories made with these building blocks work really well. They build bridges, cure diseases, send men to the moon, make computers and airplanes.

So with regard to color, for example, it could be that two neurotransmitters determine perceived hue along the red/green and blue/yellow opponent axis, and *this is just a fact about nature.* Just as electric charge and gravity are basic building blocks of the physical universe, the two neurotransmitters are part of the basic building blocks of the mental world; they are the "atoms" of color sensation. We could call them "color sensatoms."

But unfortuately adding red/green and blue/yellow "sensatoms" to the basic building blocks of the mental universe is going to lead us down a very slippery slope. For a start, what about mixtures? Even if we have postulated a particular "feel" to a given sensatom, what happens when we have a mixture in different proportions of two sensatoms? What does the result exactly look like and why? And then what about animals like bees and birds and snakes and fish that have very different color vision from ours—Will we need to find other sensatoms to capture their ultraviolet or infrared color sensations? And what about other raw feels? Are we going to have to postulate *sound* sensatoms that determine the pitch and intensity and timbre of sounds, and yet other sensatoms for touch and smells and taste, not to mention the (to us) more bizarre sensations experienced by bats and dolphins and electric fish? The resulting theory about the origin of raw feel in the animal kingdom is quickly going to get out of hand and populated with a myriad of supposed basic entities of sensation. In effect, there will be too many types of sensatoms to make for a good theory.

Is there really no way out of this situation?

Ned Block and Daniel Dennett's Views

Several years ago, the well-known philosopher of consciousness, Ned Block, came for a sabbatical in Paris. I was excited to have this influential thinker so close at hand. I was happy when he agreed to my proposal to meet every week at a different "gastronomic" restaurant and talk about consciousness. I have fond memories of our friendly discussions despite the dent they put in my bank account.

The problem of explaining sensations is something that Ned Block is very concerned with. As mentioned, it was he who stressed the distinction between access consciousness and phenomenal consciousness.[14] He is also is very impressed by recent research on the brain, and he valiantly (for a philosopher!) keeps abreast of current developments in neuroscience. He does not accept the argument I have just put forward about the impossibility that raw feel is generated by some neural mechanism. He says the history of science is "strewn with the corpses" of theories about the supposed impossibility of certain mechanisms. Science will find a way, he says; we just have to steadfastly keep looking at how the brain works, locating mechanisms that correlate with conscious feel, and one day we will find the solution. This idea is shared by the majority of scientists thinking about consciousness today. One of the most outspoken proponents of this view is the neuroscientist Christof Koch, who in his work with the discoverer of DNA, the late Sir Francis Crick, explicitly argues that searching for "neural correlates of consciousness" will ultimately allow science to crack the problem.[15]

But my point is that whereas neural correlates will undoubtedly crack the problem of explaining what I have called the *extra* components of feel, the problem of *raw feel*, or what the philosophers call phenomenal consciousness or "qualia," is different. As I have been suggesting in the preceding paragraphs, there is a logical impossibility that prevents us from finding an explanation of how *raw feel* is generated. The problem arises because of the way raw feel is defined: What we *mean* by raw feel is precisely that part of experience that remains after we have taken away all the extra components that can be described in terms of bodily or mental reactions or states. But since a science of human mental life or behavior can only be about what can be described in terms of bodily or mental reactions or states, what is left, namely what cannot be described in these terms, is *by definition* going to be excluded from scientific study. If we ever had a mechanism that we thought generated raw feel, then because by definition it can have no repercussions on bodily or mental reactions or states, we have no way of knowing whether it is working.

And it's no good trying to deftly cover up this logical impossibility by cloaking one's ignorance with some arcane mechanism that sounds obscure and so distracts people's attention from the real problem. There are hundreds of articles in the literature on consciousness, proposing impressive-sounding machinery like "cortico-thalamic reverberation," widespread "phaselocking of synchronous oscillations," "quantum gravity phenomena in neuron microtubules," among many others.[16] All or any such mechanism could conceivably contribute to what I have called the *extra* components of feel. But the situation is quite different for raw feel. By the very definition of raw feel, any such mechanism, no matter how impressive sounding, will always leave open another question: Why does the mechanism produce this feel rather than that feel? And how does it account for the multiplicity and different natures of all the different feels we can experience?

The philosopher Daniel Dennett in his well-known book *Consciousness Explained* is not so concerned with distinguishing "raw feel" from other forms of consciousness, but he has made a very similar argument about consciousness to the one I have made here about raw feel. He says once we have found a mechanism that supposedly conjures up consciousness, we can always ask, after the mechanism comes into action: "And then what happens?" What aspect of the mechanism conjures up the magic of consciousness? Dennett's approach to consciousness involves dismissing the whole question of "qualia," or what I am calling raw feel, on the grounds that it makes no sense. For that reason he has been criticized as trying to "explain qualia away" instead of actually explaining them.

In the following chapters, I will be suggesting an alternative to Dennett's tactic. My own tactic involves slightly modifying how we conceive of raw feel so that it becomes amenable to science, yet still corresponds relatively well to our everyday notions about what raw feels are supposed to be like. My approach agrees with Dennett's in saying that there is a sense in which qualia do not really exist. But on the other hand my approach accepts that people find it useful to talk about raw feels, and it goes on to try to explain in a scientific way what people say about them—why they have a feel rather than no feel, why and how they are different, and why they are ultimately impossible to describe.

With this new way of thinking about raw feel we can actually say scientifically testable things about raw feel. Furthermore, the new view generates interesting experiments and predictions that turn out to be confirmed.

Four Mysteries of Raw Feel

Before I put forward this new view, let me elaborate very precisely on the essential aspects of raw feel that I want the new view to explain. These are the aspects that make raw feel special; it is they that make it impossible to envisage how raw feel might be generated by physical or biological mechanisms.[17]

Mystery 1: Raw Feel Feels Like Something
In the philosophy of consciousness, people say that "there's something it's like" to have a feel[18]: it "feels like something," rather than feeling like nothing. Other words to capture the particular nature of sensory feel are perceptual "presence"[19] and "phenomenality,"[20] meaning the fact that a feel presents itself to us, or imposes itself on us, in a special "phenomenal" way. While all this somehow rings true, the concept still remains elusive. Clearly we are in need of an operational definition. Perhaps a way to proceed is by contradiction.

Consider the fact that your brain is continually monitoring the level of oxygen, carbon dioxide, and sugar in your blood. It is keeping your heartbeat steady and controlling other bodily functions such as those of your liver and kidneys. All these so-called autonomic functions of the nervous system involve biological sensors that register the levels of various chemicals in your body. These sensors signal their measurements via neural circuits and are processed by the brain. And yet this neural processing has a very different status than the experience of the pain of a needle prick or the redness of the light: Essentially whereas you *feel* the pain and the redness, you do not in the same way feel any of the goings-on that determine internal functions like the oxygen level in your blood. A lack of oxygen may make you want to take a deep breath, or ultimately make you dizzy, but the feels of taking a breath or being dizzy are not oxygen feels in the same way as redness is a feel of *red*. The needle prick and the redness of the light are perceptually present to you, whereas states measured by other sensors in your body also cause brain activity but do not generate the same kind of sensory presence.

Why should brain processes involved in processing input from certain sensors (namely the eyes, the ears, etc.) give rise to a felt sensation, whereas other brain processes, deriving from other senses (namely those measuring blood oxygen levels, etc.), do not give rise to this kind of felt sensation? The answer that comes to mind is that autonomic systems like those that detect and control blood oxygen are simply not connected to the areas that govern conscious sensation.

At first this seems to make sense, but it is not a satisfactory explanation, because it merely pushes the question one step deeper: Why do those areas that govern conscious sensation produce the conscious sensation? Any argument based on brain functions is going to encounter this problem of infinite regress. We need a different way of looking at the question of why some neural processes are accompanied by sensory "presence" and others are not.

A similar problem occurs for mental activities like thinking, imagining, remembering, and deciding—I will call all these "thoughts." Thus, as in the situation for sensory inputs, you are *aware* of your thoughts, in the sense that you know that you are thinking about or imagining something, and you can, to a large degree, control your thoughts. But being *aware* of something in this sense of "aware" does not imply that that thing has a feel. Indeed I suggest that as concerns what they feel like, thoughts are more like blood oxygen levels than like sensory inputs: Thoughts are not associated with any kind of sensory presence. Your thoughts do not present themselves to you as having a particular sensory quality. A thought is a thought, and it does not come in different sensory shades in the way that a color does (e.g., red and pink and blue), nor does it come in different intensities like a light or a smell or a touch or a sound might.

Of course, thoughts are *about* things (they have "intentionality," as the philosophers say) and so come with mental associations with these things; for instance, the thought of red might be associated with blood and red traffic lights and red cough drops. But the thought of red does not *itself* have a red quality or indeed any sensory quality at all. Thoughts may also come with physical manifestations; for example, the thought of an injection makes me almost feel the pain and almost makes me pass out. But any such pain is the sensory pain of the injection, not the sensory quality of thinking about it. People sometimes claim they have painful or pleasing thoughts, but what they mean by this is that the content of the thoughts is painful or pleasing. The thoughts *themselves* have no sensory quality. Some people find this claim unsatisfactory. They say that they really do feel a quality to their thoughts. I actually am not adamant about not wanting thoughts to have a quality. All I wish to claim is that if thoughts have a quality, then the quality is quite different from what I call "sensory presence." If thoughts have a "presence," or "phenomenality," the presence is not of a "sensory" nature.

Why? What is it about the thought-producing brain mechanisms that makes thoughts fail to have the sensory presence that is associated with sensory feel? As was the case for autonomic functions, any explanation in terms of particular properties of such brain mechanisms will lead to an infinite regress.

To conclude on Mystery 1: Raw feel "feels like something" in ways that other brain processes, such as autonomic processes and thoughts, do not. Neither of these impose themselves on us or have the "phenomenality" of sensory feel, which really does seem "present." We can take this difference as an operational way to distinguish what it means to "have a feel" rather than no feel. It is the existence of this difference that constitutes the first mystery about raw feel.

Mystery 2: Raw Feel Has Different Qualities

Not only does raw feel feel like something, but whatever it feels like is different from one feel to another. There is the redness of red, the sound of a violin, the smell of lemon, the taste of onion, the touch of a feather, the cold of ice, among innumerable others.

If miraculously we found the answer to the first mystery of why certain brain mechanism generate a feel whereas others don't, we would then still need to find out why those mechanisms that generate feel can actually generate a large variety of different feels. Any explanation for such differences runs into a logical problem. As I explained when talking about the color red, raw feel is incommensurate with physical phenomena like neural activations. Neural mechanisms, isomorphic brain structures, or atoms of experience cannot provide a satisfactory way of explaining why there are differences between raw feels.

Another way of expressing this point is in terms of the testability of any hypothesized link between feel and a physical mechanism. Suppose we postulated that certain modes of functioning of the brain's feel mechanism gave rise to certain different feels. How would we test this?

Any test would require the mechanism to have some measurable effect, and yet anything that has a measurable effect is affecting what I called the *extra* components of feel. What we mean by *raw* feel is precisely what is left after we have taken away all the measurable effects. Thus, any theory to explain the differences cannot be tested.

The existence of differences between the feels is therefore a second mystery about raw feel.

Mystery 3: There Is Structure in the Differences

Not only are feels different from each other, but there is structure in the differences, in the sense that certain feels can be compared, but others cannot; and when they can be compared, the comparisons can be organized along different types of dimensions.

Let's start with feels that cannot be compared. For example, how is red different from middle C? Or how is cold different from onion flavor? It seems to make no sense to try and compare red and middle C, since they have nothing to do with each other. The same goes for cold and onion flavor. For these reasons we classify red and middle C in different sensory modalities (namely the visual modality and the auditory modality). Similarly coldness and onion flavor are in different sensory modalities (namely the modalities of tactile and taste sensations).

On the other hand, there are many cases where feels can be compared. In fact, the essential pleasures of life derive from contemplating and comparing our experiences. Furthermore, when such comparisons are possible, they can often be described in terms of what could be called *dimensions.*

Intensity is a dimension along which many sensations can be compared. Sometimes the dimension of intensity is considered to go from nothing to very strong (the intensity of sound, for example, or the brightness of light), but sometimes intensity operates in two opposite directions, like the sensation of temperature, which goes from neutral to either intense cold or intense hot.

Color is more complex. In addition to having one dimension of intensity, which we call brightness, color has a second dimension called "saturation," which depends inversely on the amount of white a color contains. So, for example, you can have a pink and red that have the same hue, but the pink is less saturated because it contains more white than the red. More interesting is a third dimension that can be used to classify the color itself (or "hue"). It is a circular dimension: You can arrange colors in a closed circle of similarity going from red to orange to yellow to green to blue to purple and back to red again.

Sound is also complicated. Like many sensations, sounds can vary in intensity; they can also vary in pitch: for example, middle A is higher in pitch than middle C. But things get tricky when you start considering timbre. What is the difference between "A" played by a violin, by a flute, or by a piano? We can *identify* the different instruments, but we are at a loss to describe clearly the relations between their different timbres. We can use terms like "rough" or "pure" or "harmonic," but the simple notion of a dimension seems not to work so well here. Another point about sound is that it is analytic rather than synthetic. If you mix several notes together, providing there are not too many, the mixture forms a chord; you can hear each note individually. This is a different situation from color. If you mix two colors together, the result is a single new color, and it does not have the appearance of containing the two original colors in the way a musical chord does.

Smells are even more complicated than color or sound. Sometimes it seems there are dimensions along which smells can be classified—for example, Linnaeus[21] proposed aromatic, fragrant, ambrosial, alliaceous (garlicky), hircine (goaty), foul, and nauseating—but sometimes it seems difficult to come up with any such description. For example, think of the smell of lemon and the smell of lime. They are obviously different. But *how* exactly are they different? Is one more fruity, more acid, or softer? We are hard put to describe the difference, even though we can easily distinguish the two smells. A recent study[22] suggests that a minimum of 30 independent dimensions would be needed to account for smell comparisons.

Thus, once you have taken away all the extra components of sensory feel, that is, those that involve cognitive states and bodily reactions or dispositions, and once all that is left is the qualities of a set of raw feels, then these qualities can sometimes be compared and contrasted, and sometimes not. The exact way in which the possible comparisons are structured may be more or less complex.

Why are things like that? Presumably the answer depends on the physics of the world, on the nature of our sensory organs, and on the way the brain processes incoming information.[23] But note the important point that brain processes by themselves can never explain why feels are organized the way they are. For, as explained earlier for the case of color, suppose we found an isomorphism between the structure of feels and the structure of certain brain processes. Finding such an isomorphism requires defining a way of ordering brain states so that their similarities and differences correspond to similarities and differences in feel. But even if we found such a correspondence, we would still be left with the problem of explaining why *this* way of ordering brain states works, whereas others don't. And we would also have to explain why the particular brain codes involved provide the particular feels that they do.

So the structure of feels is a third mystery that we need to explain.

Mystery 4: Raw Feel Is Ineffable

Ineffable is a wonderful word, laden with associations about mysterious medieval cults and obscure magical practices. Something that is "ineffable" cannot or should not, for deep, fundamental reasons, be spoken of.

In the philosophy of consciousness, raw feel is said to be ineffable because it is impossible to communicate to someone else what a raw feel is fundamentally like. Even though you may be able to compare and contrast feels within a sensory modality, the actual basic raw feel itself is something that you are at a loss to describe. You can describe the taste of caviar to someone as much as you like, but only when you actually taste caviar will you be able to say, "Oh, *that's* what caviar tastes like."

Note that even when we can describe the *relation* between two sensations by appealing to their dimensions, the exact relation still cannot be transmitted to someone who does not possess certain common knowledge about these dimensions. Saying that a sound is louder, or that pink has more white in it than red, or that the bath water is hotter is comprehensible only to someone who actually knows what happens to one's sensation when a sound gets louder, white is added into a color, or when the bath water is made hotter. And even then, communicating the experience precisely is difficult. Pinning down exactly what feels are like and communicating their nature to other people are difficulties usually taken to be very specific to experiences. This leads many people to conclude that an extra kind of theoretical apparatus will be needed to solve the problem of the "what it is like" of experience.

Thus, the ineffability of raw feels is the fourth mystery of raw feels that that we need to explain.

Notes

1. It might nevertheless be the case that having these cognitive states produces *additional* experiences. For example, the association with anger may put me in a particular mood or make me more likely to get angry. But such effects, regardless of whether we want to call them experiences, are *in addition* to the basic, core, raw experience of red itself.

2. Note that the behaviorists would say that in fact the feeling of red is precisely the sum total of all those fleeting, bodily tendencies associated with red. However, that is certainly not the subjective impression one has. Here I will try to analyze more closely the nature of our subjective impressions. Later we will see that one can give a more plausible account of feel than the behaviorists and still eschew dualism.

3. There may be genetically inbuilt links that cause people to move faster or be more agitated or aggressive in red rooms and to be calm and cool in blue rooms. The literature showing effects of color on mental or physical functioning is controversial. There are a variety of experiments investigating the effect of putting subjects—be they men, women, children, prisoners, office workers, depressed or mentally deficient people, or monkeys—in rooms of different colors to see how this affects their state of arousal, their heart rate and blood pressure, their grip strength, their work efficiency, their cognitive capacities, their score on the Scholarship Aptitude Test (SAT), their score on the Depression, Anxiety, and Stress Scale (DASS), their estimation of time, and their tendency to hit, kick, and spit. Nakshian (1964) studied adults, and Hamid and Newport (1989) studied children and found increased motor activity in red (and yellow) or pink environments as compared to green and blue. Pellegrini, Schauss, and Miller (1981) found that pink rooms decreased hitting but not spitting and yelling in mentally deficient patients. Etnier and Hardy (1997) and Hatta, Yoshida, Kawakami, and Okamoto (2002) found effects of color on systolic blood pressure, heart rate, and reaction time.

4. Feigl (1967) has also used the term *raw feel*.

5. An overview of the debates about qualia can be found in Tye (2009).

6. A very succinct and sensible vignette explaining why the problem of feel is problematical is given in Chapter 1 of Austen Clark's excellent book *Sensory Qualities* (Clark, 1993).

7. To show the weakness of arguments based on neurophysiological correlates, I am pretending there really is neurophysiological evidence for opponent channels. In fact, current research suggests that such evidence only exists at the very first levels of processing. For a review, see Gegenfurtner and Kiper (2003).

8. Actually, closer examination of judgments of purity of colors shows that so-called unique hues cannot be explained simply in terms of opponent neural pathways, Nonlinear combinations of cone signals are necessary (for an overview of recent evidence, see Jameson, D'Andrade, Hardin, & Maffi, 1997; Wuerger, Atkinson, & Cropper, 2005). This does not affect the argument here, which claims that whatever neural mechanisms underlie color experience, something more will be needed to explain why colors feel the way they do.

9. Note that the question of what colors people perceive to contain different lights is quite a different question from what happens when you mix different paints. It is, of course true, that if you mix blue and yellow paint, you get green. The point here concerns lights: Whereas you can get lights that seem to contain colors from two different opponent channels (e.g., purple is seen to contain both red and blue; orange seems to contain both red and yellow), there are no lights that seem to contain colors from opposite ends of a single opponent channel; that is, there is no light that seems to contain both red and green or both blue and yellow.

10. See Gegenfurtner and Kiper (2003) for a review and a critique of this claim.

11. This is the so-called explanatory gap argument made by Levine (1983).

12. Notably, Clark (1993), Hardin (1988), and Palmer (1999).

13. This approach might be advocated by philosopher David Chalmers (Chalmers, 1996).

14. Block, 1996.

15. Crick & Koch, 1995, 2003.

16. In his excellent book, Chalmers discusses a long list of such mechanisms (Chalmers, 1996).

17. The aspects I have chosen here as being problematic are those that seem to me to preclude a scientific theory. Philosophers, on the other hand, are sometimes concerned with other critical questions. For example, P. Carruthers in his book (Carruthers, 2000a) puts forward the desiderata for an account of phenomenal consciousness. See the précis of the book on http://www.swif.uniba.it/lei/mind/forums/carruthers.htm, where he says: "Such an account should (1) explain how phenomenally conscious states have a subjective dimension; how they have feel; why there is something which it is like to undergo them; (2) why the properties involved in phenomenal consciousness should seem to their subjects to be intrinsic and non-relationally individuated; (3) why the properties distinctive of phenomenal consciousness can seem to their subjects to be ineffable or indescribable; (4) why those properties can seem in some way private to their possessors; and (5) how it can seem to subjects that we have infallible (as opposed to merely privileged) knowledge of phenomenally conscious properties."

18. Nagel (1974) probably originated the expression "what it's like" to refer to the phenomenal aspect of consciousness.

19. The notion of "presence" is fundamental in the philosophical tradition of phenomenology and is to be found in different forms in Bergson, Heidegger, Husserl, and Merleau-Ponty. Examples of recent work on phenomenological presence in psychology are in Natsoulas (1997). More recently the notion of "presence" has become a key concept in virtual reality (see, for example, IJsselsteijn, 2002; Sanchez-Vives & Slater, 2005). I'm not sure whether my usage of the term *perceptual presence* is identical to the usage in these different traditions. I wish to emphasize the "presence" of raw sensory feels, whereas it may also make sense to speak of the presence of more complex perceptual phenomena.

20. To me this term seems apt to denote the "what it's like" of sensory phenomenology. I'm not sure whether in the phenomenological literature such as Husserl, Heidegger, and Merleau-Ponty, the term is used in this way.

21. According to Austen Clark (Clark, 1993), who cites a number of other authors on this issue.

22. Using multidimensional scaling on a corpus of 851 stimuli described each by 278 descriptors (Mamlouk, 2004).

23. Austen Clark's book *Sensory Qualities* (Clark, 1993) is a masterpiece introducing multidimensional scaling as a way to describe the structure of sensory qualities. Another classic originally published in 1953 is by Hayek (1999). However, Hayek is more concerned with the theoretical question of how a system like the brain could make discriminations and classifications of the kind that are observed.

Chapter 9

Squeeze a Sponge, Drive a Porsche

A Sensorimotor Approach to Feel

Now I shall suggest a solution to the four mysteries of feel. Imagine you are squeezing a sponge and experiencing the feel of softness.[1] What brain mechanism might generate the softness feel? This seems to be a stupid question. The word *generate* seems inapplicable here, and so this seems to be the wrong kind of question to ask about softness. Softness is a quality of the *interaction* you have with a soft object like a sponge. Feeling softness consists in the fact of your currently being in the process of noting that as you press the sponge, it squishes under your pressure (see Fig. 9.1). Having the feeling of softness does not occur *in your brain*; rather, it resides in your noting that you are currently *interacting in a particular way with the sponge*.

Of course, there will be brain processes involved when you feel softness. They are processes that correspond to the different motor commands your brain emits and to the resulting sensory inputs that occur when you are involved in the squishiness testing interaction. There are also the brain mechanisms related to your paying attention and cognitively making use of the laws that currently link motor commands and resultant sensory inputs. But note that all these brain mechanisms are not *generating* the softness feel. They are enabling the different processes that correspond to the sensorimotor interaction that constitutes the experiencing of softness.

It might be possible to artificially stimulate bits of the brain and to put it in the same state as when you are testing the squishiness of the sponge, but without you actually doing anything. You would then be hallucinating the interaction you have with the world when you are experiencing softness. But notice that even if brain stimulation might be able to engender a feel in this way, this does not mean that the brain is then generating the feel. The brain is simply put in the same state as when it is involved in the particular type of interaction with the environment that constitutes experiencing softness. The feel of softness should be considered a quality of the ongoing interaction, and not some kind of "essence" that is generated by the brain.[2]

Take another example. Most people would agree that there is something it's like to drive a car, and that different cars can have different "feels." What is the distinctive feel of driving a Porsche? Is it an accumulation of Porsche-specific sensations like

Figure 9.1 The feel of softness lies in the squishing.

the smell of the leather seats or lowness of the bucket seats or the whistling wind as you speed down the Autobahn? No, each of these is an individual experience in itself—an experience of *smell* or *touch* that can be obtained in other situations. The "feel of Porsche driving" is the critical aspect that concerns how, compared to other cars, Porsches *handle* when you drive them. You have the Porsche driving feel when, while driving, you implicitly know that if you press the accelerator, the car will whoosh forward, whereas if you are driving a Volkswagen nothing particularly noteworthy about its acceleration happens. In a Porsche, if you just lightly touch the steering wheel, the car swerves around, whereas in a Volkswagen nothing much happens.

Thus, the essence of experiencing the Porsche driving feel derives from—no, it is *constituted by*—your noting that you are currently engaged in the manipulations typical of driving the Porsche rather than some other vehicle; it derives from—no, it *consists in*—your noting that you are currently putting to use your Porsche-specific driving skills rather than some other skill.[3] The Porsche-driving skills consist in your implicit, practical knowledge of all the Porsche-specific things that would happen now if you performed certain actions, such as pressing the accelerator or touching the steering wheel in Porsche-specific ways.

Though these two examples are not prototypical feels like the feel of red or of the sound of a bell, they serve to show that there are feels where it makes little sense to search for a mechanism that generates them. In the cases of sponge squishing and Porsche driving, it seems clear that their accompanying feels are qualities of *what we do* when we squish the sponge and drive the Porsche. They are not localized or generated anywhere. They are aspects of the laws that describe what happens when we interact in certain ways with sponges and Porsches.

In the next sections I shall suggest that, like sponge squishing and Porsche driving, feels in general are simply not the kinds of thing that can be generated.

Instead, feels should be conceived of as qualities of our *mode of interaction with the world*. Taking this view will provide a way of overcoming the four mysteries of feel defined in the last chapter.

Mystery 1: Raw Feel Feels Like Something

Interacting with the world has something quite special about it as compared to thinking and autonomic functioning. I listed what was special when discussing the experienced "presence" of vision in Chapter 2, namely *richness, bodiliness, insubordinateness, and grabbiness*. I shall now test the applicability of these aspects to other sensory modalities.

Richness
Try to imagine an entirely new sound or smell which is unrelated to any known ones. It is impossible. On the other hand, it is a fact that every day we encounter new sounds or smells, and thereby have completely new experiences. The richness provided by the outside world outweighs what your mind can invent.[4] Richness distinguishes real-world sensory interactions from thinking and imagining.

However, richness is not a criterion that is completely sufficient to distinguish real-world sensory interactions from autonomic functions of the body. The variety of possible levels of blood sugar or oxygen present in the blood, coupled with all the myriad chemical and physical processes going on in the body, is enormous. Thus, though richness of interaction is clearly a quality of real-world sensory interactions and therefore a characteristic of what it is to have a sensory feel, richness is not unique to sensory feels, because it is shared by other bodily functions.

Bodiliness
In Chapter 2 I had described bodiliness for vision as the fact that when you move your body (in particular, your eyes), sensory input coming into the visual system is dramatically modified. The same dependence between body motion and sensory input also applies in the other sense modalities.

The sense of touch is obviously an exploratory sense, since only by moving our hand, for example, can we accurately recognize an object. Even when someone touches you (passive touch), you could still voluntarily remove or shift the body part being touched and there would be a change in sensory input. A similar observation applies to taste and movements of the mouth and tongue, though to a lesser extent.

For hearing, moving the body modifies auditory input by changing the amplitude of the sound impinging on the ears and, in the case of rotation of the head, by changing the relative delay between signals coming into the two ears. The complicated shape of the earlobes creates microreflections that change with head orientation, thereby helping in sound localization and identification. When you have a ringing in your ears or when you listen to music through headphones[5], you identify the sensation as being inside your head because turning your head doesn't change the sound.

Recent research on smell[6] has also shown that like other animals, humans can use sniffing and body and head movements to monitor the delays and differences between the smells coming into our two nostrils and to follow scents. We know that we are really smelling and not just imagining it when we can confirm that sniffing and moving our body (in particular our head) change the signal coming from our olfactory receptors. Perhaps the reason we don't usually smell our own odors is that there is very little change in the incoming signal from our own odors when we move our heads or our bodies.

The susceptibility of sensory input from vision, touch, taste, hearing, and smell to voluntary body motion is not shared either by autonomic processes in the nervous system or by thoughts. Voluntarily moving your body only has an indirect effect on autonomic body parameters like blood oxygen, carbon dioxide and sugar levels, and on the functioning of internal organs. Moving your body has no systematic effect on thought or imaginings.

Thus, moving your body is a way of checking whether neural activity derives from the outside world. If no change in activity occurs when you move, then it probably corresponds to autonomic neural processes in the body, or to thoughts or imaginings. In other words, bodiliness is a distinguishing feature of neural activity deriving from external-world stimulation.[7]

(Partial) Insubordinateness

Whereas dependence on voluntary body motion is an essential feature of sensory input originating in the outside world, not all changes in sensory input from the outside world are caused by our voluntary body motions. The outside world has a life of its own: Objects move, sounds change, and smells appear and disappear. As a consequence, we are not complete masters of the changes that the world causes in our sensory input. This partial insubordinateness of the world is another factor that characterizes "real" sensory inputs and distinguishes them from our own thoughts and imaginings. Thoughts and imaginings are entirely the property of our own minds; they are under our voluntary control. Autonomic body functions are on the opposite extreme. They are completely insubordinate to us, since we have essentially no direct voluntary control over them.

What characterizes real-world interactions, therefore, is the fact that they have an intermediate status. They are subordinate to our voluntary body motions, but they are not completely subordinate, since they can cause changes in sensory input without us moving.

Grabbiness

Grabbiness was another quality of visual interactions that I talked about in Chapter 2 to explain the realness of visual perception. It consists in the fact that our visual apparatus is wired up so as to be able to incontrovertibly grab our cognitive resources in certain circumstances. In particular, in vision, sudden changes in the sensory input ("transients") immediately and automatically trigger an orienting reflex.

The other sense modalities also have this capability of grabbing our cognitive processing. In hearing, transients like sudden noises cause our cognitive processing to be deviated toward the source of the change. Interestingly, in hearing, certain nontransient signals also can grab attention: Very loud continuous sounds can prevent one from thinking properly. In touch, transients in stimulation, such as anything from a tickle to a poke or punch, clearly capture our attention. But certain types of continuing, nontransient stimulation involving tissue damage to the body can also grab our attention. In smell, it would seem that it is not so much transients but certain pungent or obnoxious odors that grab our attention.

All these are cases where a sensory input channel has the power to deflect our cognitive resources and grab them incontrovertibly so that it is difficult for us to voluntarily concentrate on anything else. I suggest that, like bodiliness, grabbiness is a general property of sensory systems and is not shared by other brain systems.

In particular, consider the brain systems that deal with autonomic functions that keep blood pressure stable, hold blood-sugar levels constant, adjust breathing and digestion, and keep a host of other body functions working properly. These systems do not have the faculty of interrupting cognitive processing. If something goes wrong in such systems, you may faint, become short of breath, or lose balance, but your attention is not grabbed directly; it is grabbed only indirectly by the *consequences* that ensue. For example, you fall over, thereby provoking grabby visual flows and sudden tactile stimulation as you hit the floor.

Or consider thoughts. Thoughts do not grab your attention like loud noises, pungent smells, or intolerable pain. Except in pathological cases, you are not possessed by thoughts; you possess *them*.

Grabbiness then is another reason (in addition to bodiliness and partial insubordinateness) that explains why we feel our sensory experiences, but we do not so acutely feel our thoughts and imaginings or our internal vital functions. It would be interesting to know if there is a special class of nerve projections from sensory areas in the brain to areas of the cortex involved in cognitive processing. These special circuits could provide a kind of "interrupt" command that causes normal cognitive functioning to stop and orient us toward the source of the interrupting signal. Such circuits would only be wired in for sensory channels, and not for systems in the brain that control our autonomic functions.

In summary, experiencing a raw feel involves engaging with the real world. Doing so provides us with a *richness* of sensory input that we do not get from within our minds. But richness is not a sufficient condition to characterize sensory stimulation, since autonomic processes in the nervous system could be argued to be rich. Three other concepts, however, allow a sufficient characterization of what it is to have a sensory feel. These concepts concern the degree of control we have over our sensory interactions. Specifically, engaging with the real world involves having control, but not complete control, of this engagement. Control derives from *bodiliness*, that is, the fact that voluntary bodily changes provoke systematic variations in sensory input. But control is not complete because our sensory input is not only determined by these bodily motions: The real world is *partially insubordinate*. It has a life of its own that creates variations in our sensory input that we cannot cause through our voluntary body motion. A final way in which our engagement with the real world escapes our control derives from *grabbiness*—the fact that our sensory input systems are wired up to be able to grab our cognitive resources incontrovertibly in certain circumstances, making us tributary to the outside world.

When they all occur together, these aspects of engaging with the real world are specific to what we call feels or sensory experiences. Together, these attributes of the sensorimotor interaction that we have with our environments provide the quality of sensory "presence" or "phenomenality" possessed by sensory inputs and make them "feel like something." Such presence is not possessed by mental activities like thoughts or imaginings (where control is complete), nor by autonomic control systems that keep our body functioning normally (where we have no voluntary control). In Chapter 14, I shall look more closely at how different mental and neural processes differ in the amount of sensory presence they are perceived to have.

Mystery 2: Raw Feels Have Different Qualities

The laws that describe sponge squishing and Porsche driving are clearly quite different. There is a difference between what it is like to feel softness and what it is like to drive a Porsche. Furthermore, *within* each of these activities there are many possible differences. There are many ways of squishing sponges and many ways of driving Porsches.

These differences are not generated anywhere; they are objective facts about the different ways you can interact with sponges and Porsches. Note that if we thought the feels of sponge squishing and Porsche driving were generated in the brain, we would have to find brain mechanisms that corresponded to the different qualities of softness and Porsche driving, and we would have to explain what made these mechanisms generate those particular feels rather than others like, say, the sound of a bell.

Taking the view that feels are modes of interaction relieves us of this burden. The reason is that under this view we would consider the feels to be constituted by different modes of interaction whose objective differences in turn constitute, by their very nature, objective differences in the feels. There is no problem of trying to make a link between brain processes and feel, because now we consider that it is not the brain process that generates the feel, but the mode of interaction that *constitutes* the feel.

Now apply the analogies of sponge squishing and Porsche driving to all feels. There are many ways of interacting with the environment. The accompanying laws will be as different as the sensory systems and ways of acting with them are different. The fact that raw feels can have different qualities is thus a natural consequence of the definition of feel as a sensorimotor interaction.

Mystery 3: There Is Structure in the Differences

Many things can be objectively said about the different ways to squish sponges or drive Porsches. One thing to note is that there is structure *within* the gamut of variations of sponge squishing. Some things are easy to squish, and other things are hard to squish. There is a continuous dimension of softness, allowing comparisons of degrees of softness. Furthermore, it is an objective fact that "hardness" is the opposite concept from "softness." So one can establish a continuous bipolar dimension going from very soft to very hard. In contrast, there is little objectively in common between the modes of interaction constituted by sponge squishing and by Porsche driving. (You do, of course, press on the accelerator like you press on the sponge, so you might say that the Porsche's accelerator felt soft, but that is not the feel of Porsche driving *itself*; rather, it's the feel of pushing the Porsche's accelerator.)

But here again, if we take raw feels to be modes of interaction with the environment, we will be able to apply this same idea to the question of structural differences between feels. We will be able to understand why sometimes comparisons between raw feels will be possible, with dimensions along which feels can be compared and contrasted; but sometimes comparisons will be difficult to make.

Philosopher and former psychologist Nick Humphrey had, prior to my own work, already been thinking along very similar lines. He says: ". . . consider the differences between eating, dancing, speaking, and digging the garden: while it is easy to imagine a string of intermediate activities within each category, such as from dancing the tango to dancing the mazurka or from eating figs to eating turkey, there is arguably an absolute disjunction between dancing the tango and eating figs."[8]

Again note the advantage of the view that feels are modes of interaction. The existence of differences and the structure of the differences in the skills involved in perceptual activities are objective facts concerning the modes of interaction involved. If we considered that the differences in structure were caused by neural circuitry or mechanisms, we would have to explain why the neurons involved generate the particular structure of feels that they do. Even if we managed to find some brain mechanisms that were isomorphic to the observed structure in feels, then we would have to explain the particular choice of classification scheme or metric that we used in order to make the isomorphism apparent.

In the account of feel in terms of an interaction with the environment, brain mechanisms do of course play a role: They enable the particular interactions that are taking place when we are experiencing something. Furthermore, it will necessarily be the case that we will be able to define an isomorphism between the brain mechanisms and the quality of the feel, because we can characterize the brain mechanisms in terms of the categories and concepts that we use in describing the interactions to which the feel corresponds. But the quality of the feel involved is not caused by the activity of the brain mechanism; it is *constituted* by the quality of the interaction that is taking place and that the brain mechanism has enabled. We no longer need to attempt a description of the similarities and differences between feels in terms of neural similarities and differences for which we have no natural, justifiable way of choosing a classification or metric. We no longer need to ask whether we should take this similarity measure or that among the many possible ways of comparing neural states, or whether we should take neural firing rate or its logarithm or inverse. Instead, similarities and differences in feels are described in terms of the metrics or classifications that humans already use every day to describe the way they interact with the world (e.g., an object is softer when it cedes more under your pressure).

Mystery 4: Raw Feels Are Ineffable

Ultimately, the feels of sponge squishing and Porsche driving are ineffable; that is, you don't have complete cognitive access to what you do when you squish a sponge or drive a Porsche. Exactly at what angle do you put your fingers when you squish the sponge? Exactly what is the pressure on each finger? Exactly how does the accelerating Porsche throw you back into the seat? You can describe these things approximately, but there always remain details to which you yourself don't have access. If you try to communicate them to someone else, you'll have difficulties.[9]

Applying this idea to feels in general, we can understand that the ineffability of feels is a natural consequence of thinking about them in terms of ways of interacting with the environment. Feels are qualities of sensorimotor interactions in which we are currently engaged. We do not have cognitive access to each and every aspect of these interactions. As an example, the particular muscle bundles we use to sniff a smell or move our head are part of the feels of smelling or hearing, but usually (barring, perhaps, the use of biofeedback to make them apparent to us) we cannot know what they are, even though they are involved in feeling the feel.

Summary: Why the New Approach Overcomes the Four Mysteries

If we abandon the idea that feels are the kind of things that are generated, and instead take the view that they are constituted by skilled modes of interaction with the environment, then the four mysteries about feel dissipate. Indeed, we can explain why feels have these mysterious characteristics.

Conversely, if we take the view that feels are generated by brain mechanisms, then we have to find ways of linking the physics and chemistry of neural firings to the experiences we have when we have sensations. But there is no natural way of making such a link. If we thought feel was generated in the brain, we would have to go looking in the brain for something special about the neural mechanisms involved that generate the feel. We would have to postulate some kind of special neurons, special circuitry, or chemical basis that provides the feeling of "presence" or "what it's like." And then we would be led into an infinite regress, because once we had found the special neurons, we could always then wonder *what exactly it was* that made them special.

Even something so simple as the intensity of a sensation suffers from this problem. Suppose you told me that the perceived degree of softness of an object is explained by the increased firing rate of a particular set of neurons. Then I could ask you: "Why does increased rather than decreased firing rate give you increased softness?" Suppose it turns out that the relation between firing rate and softness is, say, logarithmic. Then I can always ask: "Why? Why is it not linear or a power function? Why is it *this* way rather than *that* way?" To give an explanation, you will always need to hypothesize some particular "linking" mechanism[10] that links physical mechanisms in the brain with the different phenomenal experiences. Again, you will inevitably come up against the infinite regress involved in bridging this "explanatory gap."

On the other hand, if we take feel to be a quality of our interaction with the world, then we escape this difficulty. This is because the concepts and language we can use to describe the modes of interaction we have are now the same concepts and language that people use in everyday life to describe the feels themselves. We perceive an object to be softer when the mode of interaction we have allows our fingers to penetrate further into the sponge when we press it. There will, of course, be brain mechanisms that code this—indeed, further penetration into the sponge may be coded by a higher firing rate of some neurons. But it could just as well be coded in some other way, and that would not change the fact that we feel the sponge as soft, since the origin of the softness is not in the brain or in the code used by the neurons, but in the quality of the interaction we have with the sponge.

In conclusion, if we generalize from sponge squishing and Porsche driving to feels like color, sound, and smell, we are able to circumvent the four mysteries of feel. Even the biggest mystery of why there is something it's like to have a feel becomes soluble because the sensory presence or what it's like of feel can be seen to correspond to certain qualities of the interaction, namely richness, bodiliness, partial insubordinateness, and grabbiness. We are on the way to providing an explanation for why raw feels are the way they are.

A Note on Other Authors

The views of certain other authors are partially in line with what I have been suggesting, and I would like here to briefly point out similarities and differences. Timo Järvilehto is a Finnish psychologist and psychophysiologist with wide interests and a philosophical bent. He has an important series of articles, in which he talks about the "organism–environment system" and espouses a similar view to mine concerning the role of the brain, but in relation to all mental processes and not just sensation, and attempting to point out the ramifications of this view for cognitive science in general, rather than specifically targeting the problem of consciousness or "raw feel."[11]

Nigel Thomas is a philosopher, cognitive scientist, and historian of science who has written authoritatively on mental imagery and imagination. More specifically in relation to vision, Nigel Thomas makes a similar proposal in his theory of mental imagery with his "perceptual activity" approach.[12]

Philosopher and ex-psychologist Nick Humphrey has a theory of feel or "sentition," as he calls it, which starts off in a similar way to the one I'm suggesting here.[13] Humphrey takes as his starting point the idea that a sensation is "an activity that reaches out to do something at the very place where the sensation is felt. In fact every distinguishable sensation in human beings must correspond to a physically different form of bodily activity (either at the real body surface or at a surrogate location on an inner model)—and what it is for someone to feel a particular sensation is just for him to issue whatever 'instructions' are required to bring about the appropriate activity."[14] The similarity between my approach and that of Humphrey's is thus that we both take the stance that sensing should be considered to be an activity on the part of the observer, and not a form of passive reception of information.

Both Humphrey and I have realized that taking this stance (dis)solves the mysteries about the nature of sensation and the mind–body problem. Humphrey's list of mysteries is somewhat different from mine, and more in line with a philosopher's preoccupations, but they are brilliantly presented in his different works.

On the other hand, there are important disagreements that I have with Humphrey. They concern the idea that action is "virtual" or "surrogate" in the case of higher organisms, the role of affect, the role of evolution, of perceptual representations or "internal copies" of the physical stimulus as it is occurring at the body surface, and, most important, the role of reverberatory loops, in making a feel "felt" or "conscious." In my opinion, all these are simply not necessary and obfuscate the essential idea of taking the qualities of interaction to constitute the quality of feel.

With regard to the important issue of reverberatory loops, Humphrey's view is that for a primitive animal like an amoeba, having a sensation is a loop: responding by an action to a stimulus at the surface of the organism. In higher organisms like humans, Humphrey says that sensation is also a loop linking stimulation to action, but the loop no longer need extend all the way to the body surface. Referring to responses to a stimulation, Humphrey says: "instead of carrying through into overt behaviour, they have become closed off within internal circuits in the brain; in fact the efferent signals now project only as far as sensory cortex, where they interact with the incoming signals from the sense organs to create, momentarily, a self-entangling, recursive, loop. The theory is that the person's sensation arises in the act of making the response—as extended, by this recursion, into the 'thick moment' of the conscious present; moreover, that the way he represents what's happening to him comes through monitoring how he is responding."[15]

Thus, whereas there is indeed the idea of a sensorimotor loop in Humphrey's theory, he does not capture the explanation for why sensations have a feel rather than no feel. His need to appeal to evolution and to self-entangling recursive loops suggests that he thinks that it is these that somehow provide the "magic" which provides sensation with its "presence" or phenomenality, as well as its other sensory qualities. My view, on the contrary, is that recursion and entanglement and evolution are never going to solve the problem, and they will always leave open an explanatory gap. The sensorimotor approach solves the problem by showing that the particular quality of sensory presence or "what it's like" can be accounted for in terms of the four objective qualities that are possessed by those sensorimotor interactions that people actually say have sensory presence, namely richness, bodiliness, insubordinateness, and grabbiness. We shall see in Chapter 10 how the sensorimotor approach additionally invokes (the scientifically nonmagical) notions of conscious access and the self in order to account for how the quality of a feel can be experienced consciously. In contrast, as a sample of how Humphrey's view requires some kind of magical, or difficult-to-comprehend extra, here is a quote from him:

"The real-world brain activity is the activity that I call 'sentition.' In response to sensory stimulation, we react with an evolutionarily ancient form of internalized bodily expression (something like an inner grimace or smile). We then experience this as sensation when we form an inner picture—by monitoring the command signals—of just what we are doing. Sentition has been subtly shaped in the course of evolution so as to instill our picture of it with those added dimensions of phenomenality. Sentition has, in short, become what I call a 'phenomenous object'—defined as 'something that when monitored by introspection seems to have phenomenal properties.' I do not pretend to know yet how this is done, or what the neural correlate of phenomenous sentition is. My hunch is that feedback loops in the sensory areas of the brain are creating complex attractor states that require more than the usual four dimensions to describe—and that this makes these 'states of mind' seem to have immaterial qualities. But you do not need to understand what I have just said to get the message. Creating a thing that gives the illusion of having weird and wonderful properties need be no great feat, and is certainly much easier than creating something that actually has them, especially when it is possible to restrict the point of view.[16]"

Notes

1. I thank Erik Myin for coming up with this excellent example.
2. Timo Järvilehto gives the example of "painting," which cannot be said to be generated anywhere (Järvilehto, 1998a). Alva Noë gives the example of the speed of a car. He points out that though the speed is correlated with how fast the engine is running, you could not say that the speed was generated by the engine, since if the car were hoisted up in the air by a crane, it would have no speed despite the engine revving. The speed of the car lies in the interaction between the car and the environment (Noë, 2004).
3. There is a subtlety about my use of the word *noting* here. When you experience a feel, do you necessarily need to be *conscious* of the fact that you are experiencing it? For example, if you're driving the Porsche and yet are fully engrossed in a conversation with someone at the same time, you are certainly engaging in all the Porsche-driving activities, but are you experiencing the Porsche driving feel? I think this is a matter of definition. Although some philosophers say it makes sense to have an unconscious experience, I think that everyday usage of the term *experience* goes against this. It is for that reason that here I don't simply say that to experience the feel you are engaged in the Porsche-driving activities; rather, I say that to experience the feel you must be *noting* that you are engaging in the Porsche-driving activities. I shall return to this point in Chapter 10.
4. One should not really compare sensory input to thoughts, because sensory input is just uncategorized measurements provided by our sensors, whereas thoughts are concepts. What I mean by this statement is that the concepts potentially provided by the world far outnumber those we can provide by pure thought.
5. This is particularly true if the music is in mono, not stereo.
6. I once read an article in *New Scientist* that mentions that this implies that one should not fart in public, since people will be able to tell which direction it came from. . . . I have been unable to find the article again, however. Schneider and Schmidt (1967) discuss the role of head movements in improving odor localization. For sniffing, see Porter et al. (2007) and for neurophysiological correlates see Sobel et al. (1998). For a recent discussion of the active nature of the smell modality, see Cooke and Myin (in press).

7. It could be claimed that we *mean* by the outside world is related to what can be affected by our voluntary body motions.
8. Humphrey, 1992, p. 168.
9. To elaborate on the reasons you lack access to the details of what characterizes sponge squishing or Porsche driving: One reason is that you do not generally pay attention to all the details, even those that are potentially accessible to you. You could attend to precisely which fingers you use to squish with, or to how your back is pressed against the seat when you accelerate the Porsche, but generally you don't bother. A second reason is that even if you did pay attention to such details, you might not have the conceptual resources necessary to differentiate the details. For example, subtle differences in the pressures between the fingers might exist, but you may not have learned to distinguish them, although you might be able to if you tried. A third reason is that some of the details are inherently inaccessible. The exact muscle groups that you use, for example, or the number of times per second that particular neurons discharge in order to contract the muscles are aspects of the body's inner functioning which make no difference to what you as a person can observe about the way you can behave. For this reason, these inner functionings are not cognitively accessible to you. On the other hand, it might be possible, using some biofeedback device, for you to learn to control individual muscles or nerve firing rates.
10. Schall, 2004; Teller, 1984.
11. Järvilehto, 1998a, 1998b, 2009.
12. Thomas, 1999. Thomas' Web site (http://www.imagery-imagination.com/) is full of useful information and arguments for this approach.
13. Humphrey, 1992, 2000, 2006a, 2006b, 2008. In fact, in a letter to *New Scientist*, Humphrey complains that my sensorimotor approach is simply a reincarnation of his theory (Humphrey, 2005).
14. Humphrey, 1992, p. 192.
15. Humphrey, 2006b, p. 3.
16. Humphrey, 2008.

Chapter 10

Consciously Experiencing a Feel

There still is one thing missing in this account of what it is like to feel. If we accept that experiencing a feel just consists in interacting with the world (albeit in a special way involving richness, bodiliness, insubordinateness, and grabbiness), then why do we as persons have the impression of *consciously* feeling? After all, a thermostat interacts with the world, and a river interacts with its environment. Many complex systems can be said to obey sensorimotor laws. We could certainly arrange things so that such laws possess the hallmarks of sensory feel by ensuring that they are characterized by richness, bodiliness, insubordinateness, and grabbiness. But surely such systems do not consciously feel. We need a way to account for the fact that only certain organisms that interact with the world, in particular humans, experience these interactions *consciously*.

Access Consciousness Redux

To deal with this problem, I have in previous chapters assembled the necessary ingredients, namely the concept of "access consciousness," with its prerequisite, the notion of "self." Taking these concepts, we can simply say that an organism consciously feels something when it has at least a rudimentary self which has access consciousness to the fact that it is engaged in a particular type of sensorimotor interaction with the world, namely one that possesses richness, bodiliness, insubordinateness, and grabbiness.

Take the example of an agent (I say "agent" instead of "person" so as to potentially include animals and machines) experiencing the redness of a red surface. For this experience to come about, first, the agent must be currently interacting with the red surface in a particular way. The interaction must have those properties that make this mode of interaction a typically sensory interaction, namely richness, bodiliness, insubordinateness, and grabbiness. In the next chapter we shall look in greater detail at the sensorimotor interaction that characterizes redness, but broadly, to correspond to redness, there will be specificities of the interaction that typify *visual* sensations, and even more specifically, *red* sensations. For example, it will be the case that when the eye moves on and off the red surface, or when the agent moves the surface around, certain laws will apply concerning the changes registered by the retina that are typical of red surfaces and that are not shared by surfaces having other colors.

Second, the agent must have a *self* to have the experience. As discussed in Chapter 6, the self is certainly a complicated thing requiring the agent to have knowledge about its own body, mind, and social context. There are different levels of self; it is not an all-or-none concept, and it may be present to different degrees in machines, animals, babies, children, and adults. But having the notion of self involves nothing magical. It can be understood in terms of the same basic computational capacities that we build into computers every day.

Finally, *third*, the agent must have conscious access to the red quality. As we have seen, having conscious access means having two levels of cognitive access. At the lowest level, cognitive access to the redness, the agent is poised to make use of the quality of redness in its current rational behavior. For example, it is ready to press on the brake. Second, at the higher level, the agent has cognitive access to this first level of cognitive access, that is, for example, it *knows* it is ready to press on the brake and is making use of that fact (for instance, by saying, "I'm going to have to slow down now"). In other words, the agent is poised not only to make use of the red quality of the light in its planning, decisions, or other rational behavior, but also it is poised to make use, in its rational behavior, of the fact that it is so poised.

To summarize: The experienced quality of a sensory feel derives from a sensorimotor interaction that involves the particular "what it's like" aspects of richness, bodiliness, insubordinateness, and grabbiness. The extent to which an agent is conscious of such an experience is determined by the degree of access the agent has to this quality. If the agent only has first-order cognitive access, then it cannot be said to be consciously experiencing the feel. If it has cognitive access to cognitive access, with a number of choices of action available to the agent, then it is coming closer to conscious experience. Finally, if the agent has some sort of

Figure 10.1 Consciously experiencing a feel consists in the self consciously accessing the quality of a sensorimotor interaction. Consciously accessing means cognitively accessing the fact that the agent is cognitively accessing something.

notion of self, then it begins to make sense to say[1] that the agent is really consciously experiencing (see Fig. 10.1).

Do Animals and Babies Consciously Experience Feel?

I have been suggesting that what we call "conscious feel" involves an agent with a self having conscious access to a sensory interaction with the environment. As concerns beings like animals and newborn babies, depending on their cognitive capacities, and depending on the degree of development of their notion of self, their ability to have conscious access will be more or less developed. Does this mean that some animals and babies actually consciously feel nothing?

To go over the argument in detail[2], recall the Mark I Chessplayer, the hypothetical future robot with a head, torso, and arm, and with the ability to play chess with you. Is the machine *consciously experiencing* anything as it goes about its activities?

By my definition of conscious feel, in order to consciously experience a feel, an agent has to have sufficient cognitive capacities to have constituted at least a rudimentary notion of itself, and it has to have the ability to have cognitive access to the quality of the interaction that it is engaged in. I argued that the machine has cognitive access to your moves, but not cognitive access to what "it" is doing; worse, it has no notion of "it" at all. The answer, therefore, is that Mark I Chessplayer does not consciously experience feels.

The same would be true for an animal like, say, a gnat, which is essentially a biological machine that goes about its everyday activities in an entirely automatic way (albeit making use of sophisticated mechanisms that a roboticist would dearly like to fathom). It has no cognitive access to the quality of its interactions with the environment, and it has no self. It cannot consciously experience feels, under my definition.

Presumably if we made the chess-playing machine progressively more sophisticated, or if we considered animals higher on the phylogenetic scale, the degree to which it makes sense to say that they have a "self" increases. In parallel, the degree to which the agent has the cognitive capacity to mentally "stand back" and cognitively access the fact that it is cognitively accessing some quality of its current interaction with the environment, will also increase, and consequently so will the degree to which it makes sense to say that the agent consciously feels the experience.

Thus, as we go up the scale in cognitive capacity, in social insertion, in the variety of choice that an agent has within its environment, and to the extent that the agent can stand back from its immediate perceptions and make use of them in its rational behavior, the degree to which it makes sense to talk about "conscious" experience increases.[3]

There seems to be something deeply problematic with this claim. It suggests that sufficiently primitive animals and sufficiently young fetuses or even newborns, *because their cognitive capacities and notion of self are very limited, should consciously feel only in a correspondingly limited way, and possibly in some cases not all.* Dogs and cats and babies, then, would only consciously feel in a very limited way.

But the point is really just a matter of definition. I am suggesting that the way adult humans use the concept of conscious feel really implies having the notion of self.

In the case of an animal or baby, its *organism* is undoubtedly reacting in response to sensory stimulation, but there is not very much of a self for the organism to feel it, at least not in the way adult humans feel. The animal's or baby's body is reacting appropriately. For example, in the case of pain, the organism is providing an avoidance reaction, registering a stress response, signaling by its crying that it requires help from its conspecifics.[4] But since there is no structured "I" to know and cognitively use the fact that these things are going on in the body, we logically cannot say, under the definition I'm proposing, that the animal or baby, considered as a "self," feels anything in the same way as adult humans feel it. With pain, perhaps there is suffering that is somehow "taking place," and even if it can be shown that this suffering may affect the animal or baby in its future personality,[5] there's no conscious animal-self or baby-self *now* to feel that suffering. This is a logical point—it is a consequence of adopting the definition I'm proposing of what we mean by conscious feel.

Now you may not want to adopt this definition. But it really does seem to correspond to how we usually apply the word *feel* to human adults. Normally when we say we feel something, what we mean is that "we" feel it! Unless "I" pay attention to exactly how I am sitting right now, I am not aware of the little movements that I make to adjust my posture. My breathing goes on automatically without "me" generally being aware of it; that is, I do not consciously feel it unless I pay attention to it.

Or imagine you are playing rugby, and in the heat of the action, you injure your leg. It can happen that you don't become aware of the injury until later. Only later do you realize that there is a bruise on your leg and that your running has become less smooth. "You" as a self were not consciously aware of any pain when the injury took place. At that time, your body reacted appropriately, dodging the people running behind you, hugging the ball, and sprinting forward. But "you" were momentarily "out of your office," so to speak, as far as the injury was concerned; "you" were paying attention to running after the ball or to the strategy of the game.[6]

In other words, when your self is off paying attention to something else, you do not consciously feel your posture, your breathing, or your injury. When "you" are not at the helm (or rather when "you" are away at a different helm), "you" consciously feel nothing about what's happening at your original helm. So if what we mean by "conscious feel" is what conscious human adults usually call feel, then since primitive animals and newborns do not have much of a "you" to be at the helm at all, "they" will be in the same situation as you when you are away from the helm: They will feel nothing.

An Unconscious, Organism-Based Kind of Feel?

To safeguard our intuitions that while newborns and animals perhaps don't *consciously* feel very much, they nevertheless do feel things, perhaps we could conceive that there might be some *unconscious* kind of feel that happens in organisms that don't have selves. Such an "organism-based" kind of feel would not require "someone at the helm." It would be some kind of holistic life process going on in the organism that could be said to be experiencing something. Under this view, even though "I" don't feel my breathing or the injury to my leg, my body somehow does.

And in the case of primitive animals and babies, independently of whether they have fully developed selves, their *organisms* still could in some sense be said to experience feels. In the case of pain, it would be this organism-based suffering that would be occurring.

The trouble with defining such a kind of unconscious feel is that it's difficult to know exactly what we mean by it, and how to define the limits of its application as a term. What exactly distinguishes an organism-based process that experiences feel from one to which the notion of feel does not apply? Please note that this is a question of trying to pin down a definition of exactly *what we mean* by the notion of unconscious organism-based feel. I'm not asking which organisms have it and which organisms do not. I'm not asking what types of nervous system or biological systems are necessary for having organism-based feel. I'm asking how we want to *define* the notion.

So let me devote a few lines to thinking about how we might want to define organism-based feel.[7] Perhaps the term refers to an organism that is reacting to outside influences in an appropriate and adaptive way so as to preserve its normal existence and functioning within its ecological niche. This would certainly apply to animals, and clearly to fetuses and newborns. But it would also apply to plants, which after all, adapt to environmental conditions, for example, by turning to the light. They also can "suffer": They register stress by wilting when deprived of water and modify their metabolism when injured, and they can even signal their stress to nearby plants and affect them by emitting chemicals into the air.

In fact, this definition of organism-based feel as involving an adaptive reaction could also be applied to bacteria, single-cell organisms, and why not even . . . rocks. Forces inside the rock hold it together in its global form, and stresses and strains inside it modify the way electric fields, heat, and vibrations spread through the rock. When you tap on a rock, vibrations echo within it in a way specific to that rock. When you apply heat at one spot, expansion takes place and propagates across the rock. There are also slow chemical reactions going on inside the rock, as bits of the rock with different chemical composition diffuse molecules gradually through its interior and mix and react with other bits. Thus, seen on a geological timescale, there are various holistic, global processes that characterize the way the rock adapts to outside influences, and one might want to say that when they are interfered with and modified by things happening at the surface of the rock, the rock feels something and adapts.

Perhaps there is another way of defining organism-based feel that makes the notion correspond better to our intuition that fairly advanced living creatures have it, and that bacteria and rocks don't have it. But much more important is the following point: Even if we did end up finding a satisfactory definition of organism-based feel, this kind of feel is completely different from what conscious adult humans usually mean by feel. Indeed, it is a very odd kind of feel. Precisely because it is organism based and not felt by the self, a conscious adult human would actually say that he or she (as a self) *doesn't feel it*. In short, this organism-based type of a feel is one that you don't feel! What could that mean? I think the notion is not of much use. At any rate it is an arbitrary exercise to try to define it in a way so that it is possessed only by creatures that we empathize with.

This discussion on feel in animals and babies brings home the great responsibility we have as humans in deciding upon our ethical codes with regard to pain. Since science provides us with no nonarbitrary divide in the animal kingdom between animals that feel and animals (or other entities) that don't feel, or some precise moment in the fetus's or newborn's development after which it suddenly becomes able to feel, we are left with the acute difficulty of finding some other rationale to establish the lines of conduct that define our humanitarian ethic. It may be that it is more important to evaluate the stressful effects of pain on the development, (future) personality, and social integration of a fetus, neonate, or animal, rather than to assess whether it "feels" at the moment the pain is inflicted.

Notes

1. Note that I said "it begins to makes sense to *say* that . . ." The implication is that conscious access is not something in the agent. It is a way that an outside person (and consequently also the agent itself) can *describe* the state of the agent.
2. There is an expanded version of this section, including ethical considerations, on the supplements Web site: http://whyred.kevin-oregan.net.
3. There is an immense and very contentious literature on the question of which animals have which level of meta-cognitive capacities (for discussion, see, e.g., Carruthers, 2008; Heyes, 1998), and what degree of notion of self (for a discussion, see Morin, 2006). I think it is senseless to try to draw a line somewhere through the animal kingdom and say these animals have conscious feel and these do not.
4. For a review on fetal pain, see Lee, Ralston, Drey, Partridge, and Rosen (2005). There was an acrimonious debate in *British Medical Journal* in 1996 about whether fetuses feel pain, with its accompanying ethical question of the justification for abortion, following the article by Derbyshire and Furedi (1996). The minimum necessary condition for pain that everybody agrees on is that an agent should manifest a stress reaction and avoidance behavior. This is assumed to require a working connection between sensors, thalamus, and muscles. Some people think that some kind of "conscious" perception of the pain is additionally necessary. Conscious perception is generally thought to occur in the cortex, so to have this, connections between thalamus and cortex are thought to be additionally necessary. But all these are just necessary conditions, not sufficient ones, so in fact none of these arguments guarantees that neonates feel pain (Derbyshire, 2008). Hardcastle (1999) devotes a section of her chapter 8 to the question of whether babies feel pain, and she concludes that even though their bodies may register the stress of pain, they would not be able to *consciously* feel pain, at least not in the way adults do.
5. Hardcastle (1999, p. 199), in a discussion similar to what I am giving here, refers to a number of studies on babies showing changes in future personality or susceptibility to chronic pain following infliction of pain in infancy.
6. Though part of this effect may be accounted for by physiological reduction in pain sensitivity caused by the excitement of the game, a significant portion is due to the fact that "you" are not paying attention to the injury. A review of the attention and emotional effects on pain is provided by Villemure and Bushnell (2002). A review of the brain effects of attention-demanding tasks on pain perception is provided by

Petrovic and Ingvar (2002). A careful review of controlled experiments on hypnotic reduction of pain, showing that hypnosis really works, is provided by Patterson and Jensen (2003).

7. Relevant to such a "preconscious" kind of feel, Shaun Gallagher has an article discussing various ways of defining what he calls the "minimal self" (Gallagher, 2000).

Chapter 11

The Sensorimotor
Approach to Color

The previous chapters have sketched a "sensorimotor" theory of feel in which consciously feeling something involves a self having conscious access to the fact that it is currently engaged in interacting with the environment in a way that obeys certain sensorimotor laws. The particular quality of a given feel is determined by the laws that characterize the sensorimotor interaction involved. To illustrate the idea, I used the examples of sponge squishing and Porsche driving.

Let's now see how the approach can deal with what philosophers consider to be the prototypical feel, namely the feel of color.

Color as a Mode of Interaction

At first it seems peculiar to conceive of the feel of color as being constituted by our *doing* something or *manipulating* something. One usually has the impression that seeing a color consists in *receiving* or *absorbing* some kind of stimulation that comes into us. But consider what happens when you go into a shop and buy a sweater. You're not sure whether it's black or dark blue. To get a good idea of what color it is, you move it around, you hold it this way and that, and perhaps you go out of the shop into the street to check its color under daylight. This is an example of how seeing color involves actively manipulating.

Or look at an object and move it around. Depending on how you place the object and which way you orient it, a particular part of it may reflect back more light from the yellowish sun, the bluish sky, or a nearby lightbulb or other surface. Despite these changes in the light reflected off it, you see that part of the object as having the same color.

In these examples you are experiencing the surface color of an object by observing how the object changes incoming light. It is possible (e.g., by looking through a tube) to estimate the color of the light *itself* that is reflected off the object—but this is not what we generally perceive. Primarily, when we see color, it is the color of surfaces, that is, a property of the material that they are made of. We hardly ever see light itself. We almost always see surfaces illuminated by light. You cannot see the passing beam of light from a flashlight: You have to put your hand in the way and see your hand light up. In a discothèque you may think you see beams of laser light, but actually what you are seeing is the dust particles that the laser beam illuminates along its path.

Let us therefore start with the idea that basically color is not something about lights, but something about surfaces: It is the *way surfaces change incoming light*.[1] Taking this stance is somewhat unconventional, because usually scientists think about color in terms of *light* and consider the color of surfaces to be conceptually of secondary importance. But it makes sense from an ecological point of view: The brain should be built to extract, not the changing color of light coming off the object, but the color of the object *itself*. We need to perceive whether the cherry is ripe or the meat is rotten, not whether the light reflected off the cherry or the meat is red or green—since the reflected light can be quite different depending on what light is illuminating the cherry or the meat.[2]

This way of thinking about color, as fundamentally being something about surface material, provides the possibility of treating color in a way similar to how I treated softness and Porsche driving: in terms of a form of "manipulation"—a sensorimotor skill. We saw, for example, that what we mean by softness is an abstract property of our interaction with certain objects, namely the fact that they squish when we press on them. In a similar way, we could say that what we mean by red is an *abstraction* from our active (visual) interaction with surfaces (see Fig. 11.1). Color could be described as an aspect of the laws that govern the changing responses of our photoreceptors as we move surfaces around under changing illumination.

Figure 11.1 The experience of color is constituted by the way colored surfaces change incoming light as you "visually manipulate" them. As you tilt the red surface, it reflects more of the yellowish sunlight, the bluish sky light, or the reddish incandescent light. The fact that these changes can occur constitutes our perception of red.

The Laws of Manipulating Color

In my laboratory we attempted to see where this view of color leads. We first needed a way of describing how a surface of a given color modifies the responses of human photoreceptors when the surface is moved around under different lights. We showed that, as far as the response of the eye is concerned, the chromatic "behavior" of any surface can be accurately characterized by nine numbers.[3] The nine numbers define a 3 x 3 matrix that specifies the function determining how, for any arbitrary light shining on a surface, the light reflected off the surface will excite the three human photoreceptor types.[4]

When we calculated the matrices for a wide variety of different colored surfaces, we found something very interesting. Some of the matrices were "singular." What this means is that their behavior is simpler than normal, in the following way. Usually variations in photoreceptor activations caused by light coming off a surface will need three numbers to describe them. This is because there are three types of photoreceptors in the human visual system, and each of their activations can vary independently of the others. But singular surfaces have the property that they transform incoming light in a more restricted way: Whatever the variations in the incoming light, the photoreceptor activations for the reflected light need only two numbers or one number to describe them. We say they are restricted to a two- or one-dimensional space of the three-dimensional space of photoreceptor activations. The surfaces that we found to be strongly singular were red and yellow. Two more surface colors were less strongly singular: blue and green. And this reminded us of something.

In the mid 1960s, Brent Berlin and Paul Kay, two anthropologists at the University of California at Berkeley, sent their graduate students on a curious quest: to scour the San Francisco Bay Area for native speakers of exotic foreign languages. The students found 27. They showed speakers of each language a palette of about 300 colored surfaces and asked them to mark the colors that were "focal," in the sense that people considered them to be the best examples of the most basic color terms in their language.[5] To complement that study, Berlin and Kay subsequently contacted missionaries and other collaborators in foreign countries throughout the world and established what is now called the "World Color Survey." The survey compiles data about color names in a total of 110 languages, ranging from Abidjii in the Ivory Coast through Ifugao in the Philippines to Zapoteco in Mexico.

The survey showed that there are two colors that are all-out favorites: red and yellow. They are the same shades of red and yellow as we found in our analysis of the singularity of the matrices. There were two more colors that were quite popular: green and blue. They were the same shades of green and blue as our singularity analysis indicated. Then, depending on the culture, there were more colors for which people had a name, such as brown, orange, pink, purple, and gray, but their popularity was much less than the four basic colors.[6]

Thus, our singularity analysis of surface colors, suggesting that red and yellow were very simple colors, and green and blue were not-quite-so-simple colors, coincides astonishingly well with the anthropological data on color naming. This almost perfect correspondence is a major victory for the sensorimotor approach. Color scientists and anthropologists have up until now failed to find either cultural, ecological,[7] or neurophysiological[8] arguments[9] to satisfactorily explain why certain colors are more basic in the sense that people tend to give them names. On the other hand, the idea suggested by our singularity analysis is appealing: namely that these colors are simpler, as far as their behavior under different lights is concerned.

Another point is that theoretical models used to explain behavioral data often require various parameters to be adjusted so that the data fit the predictions as well as possible. But in our account *there are no parameters.* The account relies on a calculation from existing biological measurements (the sensitivities of the three photoreceptor types) and existing physical measurements (the spectra of natural light sources and the reflectance functions of colored surfaces). There has been no fiddling with parameters.

In addition to color naming, we also applied the approach to the perception of colored lights. Just as for colored surfaces where we have "focal" colors, color scientists refer to what they call "unique hues" as consisting of those particular wavelengths of monochromatic light that seem to observers to be "pure" red, yellow, blue, or green; that is, they seem to contain no other colors.[10] We have shown that observers' wavelength choices and their variability correspond very well with what is predicted from the sensorimotor approach. Indeed, our predictions are more accurate than those obtained from what is known about the red/green and blue/yellow opponent channels.[11]

It seems, therefore, that the sensorimotor approach to color registers surprising successes. By taking a philosophical stance about what color really is (a law governing our interactions with colored surfaces), we have been able to account for classical phenomena in color science that have until now not been satisfactorily explained.

Of course, more work needs to be done. Berlin and Kay's data are considered controversial because the procedures used to question participants may have caused biases. The experimenters were missionaries and other helpers not trained in psychophysics. But still, the fact that from first principles and simple mathematics we have found such a surprising coincidence surely is worth noting.

Another point is that we would like to identify a learning mechanism that explains *why* singular surface colors should be expected to acquire names, whereas other colors would not. A start in this direction would be to suggest that the simpler behavior of singular surfaces under changing lights makes them stand out from other colors. But even though we haven't yet identified a mechanism, both the coincidence between naming and singularity and the success of our predictions for unique hues are so compelling that they suggest there is something right about the sensorimotor approach.

What Red Is Like

How has the sensorimotor approach gone further in explaining the raw feel of color than approaches based on the "neural correlate" approach? Consider the answers to the four mysteries of feel, as applied to color.

Mystery 1: Colors Feel Like Something Rather Than Feeling Like Nothing

The sensorimotor approach suggests that what people mean by saying that something has a feel is that the associated sensorimotor interaction has four distinctive properties. Sensory interactions have *richness*, in the sense that they can take a wide variety of possible states. Sensory interactions (in contrast to other brain processes) have the property that sensory input changes systematically when you move your body (*bodiliness*), and that it can additionally change of its own accord (*partial insubordinateness*). Sensory interactions also have *grabbiness*: They can grab your attention under certain circumstances (in vision: when sensory input changes suddenly).

These four properties are clearly possessed by color sensations. Color experiences are rich, since they are very variable. They involve bodiliness: The responses of the photoreceptors change as you move your eyes or your body with respect to a colored surface. This is because as the angle between you and the surface changes, different mixtures of light are reflected, thereby changing the spectral composition of the light coming into your eyes, even though the surface color is constant. Such changes can also occur by themselves without you moving, implying that color also possesses partial insubordinateness. And color has grabbiness: When a color changes suddenly, it attracts your attention. Thus, we have the essence of what we *mean* when we say that color experiences have a feel rather than having no feel at all.

Mysteries 2 and 3: Different Colors Look Different; There Is Structure in the Differences

Red and green surfaces *behave differently* when you move them around under different lights. We have seen that red (or at least a certain red) is a color that has a high degree of singularity, behaving in a "simpler" fashion than orange or coral or peach. Red really is a special color, and it makes sense that it should be given a name in most cultures across the world. Sensorimotor laws give us leverage to characterize different colors (e.g., in this case their stability under changing illumination) in terms that are meaningful in everyday language. No arbitrary hypotheses need to be made about links with neural activation.

There are also other sensorimotor laws that characterize colors which I have not yet described. One law concerns the yellowish film called the macular pigment, which protects the particularly delicate central portion of our retinas from high-energy blue and ultraviolet light. Because of this protection, light sampled by the photoreceptors in central vision contains less short wavelength energy than light sampled in peripheral vision. The particular way sampled light changes as a function of its position in the visual field, and thus also as a function of eye position, will be different for different colored surfaces. This is just one of many sensorimotor laws that distinguish different colors. These differences are among those that the sensorimotor approach could appeal to in order to describe the way color experiences are structured.

Neurophysiological constraints do of course determine what kinds of light we can and cannot see. For example, the simple fact that we have no photoreceptors sensitive to the ultraviolet part of the light spectrum means that we cannot see patterns that birds and bees see, like ultraviolet sunlight that gets through clouds and that they use to orient themselves. Another important constraint is imposed by the fact that our photoreceptors are very broadly tuned. This means that physically completely different light spectra can all look identical to us.[12] Further constraints may be imposed by the wiring of the human color system if it introduces transformations in which information about the incoming light is lost.

Why does the feel of color have a visual nature rather than being like, say, touch or hearing or smell? Color is a visual-like feel because the laws that describe our interactions with colored surfaces are laws that are shared with other visual experiences. In particular, when you close your eyes, the stimulation changes drastically (it goes away!). This is one of many facts that govern those interactions with our environment which we call visual. It is a fact that is not shared by, say, auditory interactions, which do not depend on whether you have your eyes open or closed. Other laws that characterize visual interactions concern the way sensory input changes when you move your eyes, or when you move your head and body, or when you move objects in such a way as to occlude other objects from view. All these facts are shared by the interactions involved when we experience color.

Mystery 4: Colors Are Ineffable
The sensorimotor approach cannot account for all the aspects of the experience of color, because sensory experiences are by nature ineffable—their aspects cannot be completely apprehended within our cognitive structures because we do not have cognitive access to every detail of the skills we exercise when we interact with the world. But this is not a mysterious thing, no more than it is mysterious that we cannot completely describe everything we do, every muscle involved, when we squish a sponge or drive a Porsche.

In conclusion for the four mysteries: The sensorimotor approach has the advantage of providing ways to ground descriptions of the experienced quality of color sensations that are accessible to ordinary language and thinking. In contrast, excitation in neural channels must be described in terms of neural activity, for which there is no natural link to descriptions that are used every day to qualify experiences.

A Test of the Sensorimotor Approach to Color

The sensorimotor approach suggests that the raw feel of a particular color is constituted by the abstract laws that govern the way surfaces of that color behave when we interact with them. If this is true, then there is an interesting prediction we could make. We could predict that if we were able to artificially change the laws, then the quality of the perceived color should change.[13]

With my PhD student Aline Bompas we decided we would try to change the hue of perceived color.[14] We started by trying to replicate an old experiment done by Ivo Kohler[15] as part of his extensive work on perceptual adaptation. (I discussed his experiments with inverting goggles in Chapter 3.) We constructed a pair of glasses with lenses that we dyed half blue, half yellow. When Aline looked at something and turned her head one way or the other, she could make the thing she was looking at become tinged with yellow or with blue, depending on the angle of her head. We predicted that after wearing the glasses for a while, Aline's brain would adapt to these laws so that she would come to see things as no longer changing color when she moved. Furthermore, we expected that when, after adaptation, she took off the glasses, there would be an aftereffect such that now, a particular patch of color, when looked at directly, would appear to change color when she moved her head back and forth. In other words, we expected that the sensory experience of the patch would be more bluish or more yellowish, even though exactly the same area of the retina was being stimulated, and even though exactly the same light spectrum was being sampled by the eye.

Aline wore the glasses for 3 weeks without ever taking them off except to go to bed (see Fig. 11.2). She braved the Paris streets and cafés, and she patiently explained to curious passersby why she looked like she harked back to the psychedelic era of the 1960s. After 3 weeks, when she came to the lab, she looked at a gray patch of light on the computer screen. She took off the glasses and turned her head this way and that. For a few seconds she had the impression that the color of the gray patch was tinged differently, blue or yellow, depending on which way she turned her head. But within a minute or two the effect went away. Three weeks of effort for very little effect, if any.

We went back to the drawing board and thought some more about sensorimotor laws. We realized that what we had been doing was to associate an orientation of the eyes in the head with a particular blue or yellow tint. If what is important in providing the feel of color is really sensori*motor* laws, then we needed to design an experiment in which it was the eye *movement* which was coupled with the change in tint, and not the orientation of the eyes in the head.

Figure 11.2 Aline Bompas wearing her psychedelic half-field (left, blue; right, yellow) spectacles to test for adaptation of color perception to eye movements.

We managed to create this kind of dependency in a series of experiments that constituted the subject of Aline's PhD thesis, and in which observers moved their eyes back and forth on a computer screen. We arranged things so that the hue of what they saw was altered in a systematic way as a function of the direction of the eye movements. We now easily obtained a reliable effect, even after only 40 minutes of moving the eyes back and forth.

Our experiments have now been replicated by another group of researchers, who have more carefully quantified the color changes.[16] They confirm the existence of the effect, even though it is small. They have also tried an interesting additional experiment, in which they correlate the hue change on the screen with a tone that the observer hears, instead of with an eye movement. In this case they find no effect. This suggests that a correlation between two types of sensory input is not sufficient for the brain to adapt. What is important in determining the perceived sensory adaptation seems specifically to be a dependency between sensory changes and movement of the body. In sum, taken together with our own results, we have here a striking confirmation of the predictions of the sensorimotor theory according to which it should be possible to change color experience by changing sensorimotor laws.

Notes

1. Under this view, the color of *light* (as what you see when looking through the tube) is a *derivative* of what you see when you look at surfaces. The brain could interpret the color of *light* as being the color of an equivalent *surface* illuminated by white light. The philosopher Justin Broackes has been developing a very similar idea, starting in Broackes (1992).

2. In other words, the brain must be able to extract something invariant from objects, namely a property of surface material, despite the changing lighting conditions. Specialists in human color perception call this "color constancy." The extreme case would be to take a piece of white paper into a room lit mainly with red light. The light reflected into the eye from the paper would be red, and yet the paper would still look white. A related case is sunglasses. At first when you put them on, everything looks brownish. But soon colors go back to normal. How is color constancy achieved? Researchers are working on this question actively, but what is known is that obtaining information about surface reflectance requires more than just registering the spectrum of incoming light; it is an operation of abstraction that can be helped by sampling the surface under different lighting conditions by moving it around, and by comparing it to other surfaces in the surroundings.

3. This work was done by David Philipona for his PhD (see http://www.kevin-oregan.net/~philipona), and it is only the beginnings of a possible sensorimotor approach to color. However, it has provided some very exciting insights.

4. Calculating the nine numbers for a surface is a simple mathematical exercise if you have the surface's reflectance function, the spectrum of different types of natural and artificial illumination, and if you know how the three human photoreceptor types absorb light at different wavelengths—all these data have been measured by physicists and are readily available.

5. See Berlin and Kay (1991); Regier, Kay, and Cook (2005). Berlin and Kay paid particular attention to defining what they meant by "basic" color terms. They are words in the language upon which most speakers agree, and which apply to a variety of different objects. They are terms like "red" and "yellow" as distinct from terms like "blond" (restricted to hair), "crimson" (a type of red), "turquoise" (you can't say "turquoisish"), and "ash" (also the name of a thing). The stimuli, instructions, and results are publicly accessible on http://www.icsi.berkeley.edu/wcs/data.html

6. This aspect of the Berlin and Kay's study and later studies is not the one that is usually mentioned. The most frequently mentioned result concerns the fact that colors become encoded in the history of a language in a fixed order: white, black, red, green/yellow, yellow/green, blue, brown, purple, pink, orange, and gray. Thus, if a language contains only two color terms, these will always be black and white. The next color term to appear is red, which is usually followed by green or yellow, and so on.

7. One possibility for red is that focal red is the color of blood, which is presumably the same across all cultures. Perhaps focal yellow, blue, and green are related to the natural colors of the sun, the sky, the sea, or of foliage (Wierzbicka, 1996). But up until now no unifying theory has been proposed to explain these facts in terms of the colors encountered in nature. As concerns blue, a recent paper makes the suggestion that unique blue corresponds to the color of the sky (Mollon, 2006). There may then be a link between unique blue (for lights) and focal blue (for surface colors).

8. Even vision scientists often think it is the case that the opponent black-white, red-green, and blue-yellow channels explains why black, red, green, blue, and yellow should in some way be "special" colors. However, explanation in terms of the opponent process theory has not been successful (Knoblauch, Sirovich, & Wooten, 1985; Kuehni, 2004; Valberg, 2001; Webster, Miyahara, Malkoc, & Raker, 2000), and even if it had been, this wouldn't easily explain why the popularity of choices in the anthropological naming data of the World Color Survey are in the order of red, yellow, and green/blue.

9. Up until recently, the conception of color naming has been in terms of a double mechanism. First, the boundaries between color categories have been considered to be determined by social and linguistic mechanisms within each culture. Second, however, the focal colors that best represent each category have been thought to be determined by natural constraints, that is, either by facts about the external world or by facts about the nervous system. A critical discussion of this two-mechanism view can be found in Ratner (1989). Contrary to the classic view, Regier, Kay, and Khetarpal (2007) have recently proposed a way of accounting for the boundaries of color categories in terms of a perceptually optimal way of dividing up color space, but this does not explain precisely which colors will be considered the prototypical instances within each category.

10. For example, people will choose a wavelength of between about 570 to 580 nm as being pure yellow, with no trace of green, blue, or red. They will choose a wavelength of between about 510 to 560 nm for their choice of unique green, between 450 and 480 for unique blue, and something beyond 590 nm, generally at about 625, for unique red.

11. The predictions for unique hues also provide a more accurate account of hue cancellation than is provided by classical opponent mechanism approaches. See Philipona and O'Regan (2006).

12. This phenomenon is called "metamerism." The light from a computer picture of a rose is a sum of spectra deriving from three pixel colors. The light coming off a real

rose will have a totally different spectrum, even though to humans it looks exactly the same as the picture. But to a bird or bee, which has more than three photoreceptors, the picture and the real rose would not look the same color.

13. In a way, you could say that color quality changes depending on whether a surface is shiny or matte. When you look at one point on a matte surface while you tilt the surface, there is not very much change in the spectrum of the light coming into your eye. This is because a matte surface scatters light fairly uniformly in all directions. But in the case of shiny surfaces there is an additional, so-called specular component of the light coming off the surface, which behaves like light coming off a mirror. This light, because it is essentially constituted by reflections of nearby objects, changes strongly when you tilt the surface. Thus, if we consider the qualities of matteness and shininess to be aspects of color, then these aspects are already an example of how perceived color quality is constituted by sensorimotor laws.

14. Bompas & O'Regan (2006a,b).

15. Kohler (1962).

16. Richters & Eskew (2009).

Chapter 12

Sensory Substitution

If the feel of a sense modality is determined by the laws that characterize the mode of interaction we have with the environment when we use that modality, then, among many other possibilities, we should, for example, be able to *see with our ears* or *through the sense of touch*, providing we arrange things to obey the same laws of interaction as when we see with our eyes. Such *sensory substitution* is a challenge that has been investigated in different ways, as we shall see in this chapter.

The Tactile Visual Substitution System

In the 1970s Paul Bach y Rita, a medical doctor and specialist in visual physiology at the Smith Kettlewell Institute of Visual Sciences in San Francisco, was working extensively with blind people. Bach y Rita became convinced that the adult human brain had much greater plasticity, that is, could adapt its functioning, more than was normally envisioned at the time. Because of this belief, he thought it should be possible to train people so that they could use a different sense modality in order to see. In a fascinating book,[1] he described his experiments with what he called his tactile visual substitution system (TVSS).

The first versions of the TVSS consisted of a dentist's chair equipped with a 20 x 20 array of vibrators that would stimulate the back of a person sitting in the chair. The pattern of vibration in this tactile array was a kind of "vibratory image" of the signal coming from a video camera mounted on a nearby tripod. Bach y Rita spent much time training blind people and normal sighted people wearing blindfolds to recognize simple vibrator-generated image signals of objects in his office, like a telephone or a cup, with relatively little success at first.

Bach y Rita recounts in his book how one day he made an accidental discovery: A person who had grown impatient with the strenuous training grabbed the video camera on the tripod and started waving it around. Within moments he was able to recognize objects by "scanning" them with characteristic hand movements. He rapidly came to feel the stimulation he was receiving on the skin of his back as not being on the skin, but "out there" in front of him. Further research over the following decades and with wearable equipment (see Fig. 12.1) confirmed the importance of allowing observers to control their own camera motion. Bach y Rita reasoned that this control compensated for the very low resolution of the image (only 400 pixels in all!) and for

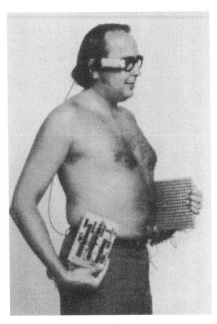

Figure 12.1 A later, portable, version of Bach y Rita's Tactile Visual Substitution System, with an array of vibrators to be worn on the abdomen, and with portable electronics and a camera mounted on a pair of spectacles. Using such a system, a person is able to navigate around the room within seconds of putting on the device, and he or she is able to recognize simple objects with minimal training by "scanning" them using head movements. © The estate of Paul Bach y Rita.

the fact that at this low resolution, the skin of the back is probably unable to distinguish the individual pixels.

Bach y Rita was certainly right that camera motion can improve the ability to distinguish detail. But I suggest that something else is happening here. Normal seeing involves checking the changes in visual flow as the eye and body move; it involves jumping with the eye from one part of an object to another and observing the accompanying changes in retinal input. When camera motion is allowed, the experience with the TVSS becomes closer to the normal experience of seeing, in which eye and body motion are an essential component. This explains why it is only when they can manipulate the camera that people experience the information they are obtaining as coming from the outside world, instead of coming from the tactile stimulation on their skin.

In recent years a strong current of research has developed from Bach y Rita's initial work,[2] and the credo of this work is his claim that "we see with our brains, not with our eyes," and that brains have more plasticity than previously thought.

I suggest something different. First, although the sensorimotor approach recognizes that the brain provides the neural machinery for seeing, the emphasis is not on the brain, but on the fact that we see by interacting with the environment. Second, as regards plasticity, if the same laws of sensorimotor dependency in normal seeing apply to the TVSS, then *essentially no adaptation or plasticity should be required* to see with the device. All that would be required is the same kind of familiarization as

when you come to feel a car's wheels against the curb via the sensations you get sitting in the driver's seat. Such learning happens in a matter of days. It would be misleading to call this "brain plasticity," where the implication is that the structure of
the brain is radically changing. Indeed, the speed, within hours if not minutes, with
which the TVSS sensation transfers from the skin to the outside world suggests a
much faster mechanism than "brain plasticity."

Another indication of the difference in my point of view from Bach y Rita's concerns two findings that he mentions as surprising in his book. One finding is related
to the fact that in the chair-based version of the apparatus, for practical reasons, the
array of vibrators was divided into two strips of 10 x 20 vibrators, separated by a gap
to accommodate the observer's spine. Yet people did not "see" such a gap in the
objects they recognized using the apparatus. The second finding is the following:
On one occasion, Bach y Rita accidently bumped into the zoom control of the
camera, creating a sudden expansion of the tactile "image." The observer jumped
backwards, expecting that something was approaching him from the front. Bach
y Rita is surprised that the observer did not jump *forwards*, since the vibrators were
stimulating the observer's *back* and so should have caused him to see something
approaching him from *in back.*

The fact that Bach y Rita finds both these findings surprising shows that his view
of what is happening with his apparatus involves the observer "seeing" a picture,
namely a mental translation of the vibrotactile image projected on his back by the
vibrators. His view would be that since the picture has a gap, why do people not see
the gap? Since the picture is on the back, why do people not physically perceive the
picture as being *behind them* in space?

I would interpret what is happening quite differently and say that neither of these
findings is a surprise. Seeing does not involve perceiving a "picture" that is projected
somewhere (be it in the brain or on the back). We do *not* see with our brains. Rather,
seeing is *visual manipulation.* In the case of the TVSS, visual manipulation involves
controlling the camera. The location of the sensors on the body is irrelevant, and
their spatial organization is also irrelevant.[3] What count are the *laws* that describe
how certain motions of the camera affect the stimulation provided by the vibrators.
The finding that people do not notice the gap in the vibrator array is expected: The
perceived distance in the outside world that is represented by two pixels on the skin
does not depend on the distance between them on the skin. It depends on the distance
that the person has to move in order to go from one pixel to the other. Thus, pixels
that straddle the gap in the vibrator array can represent the same distance in the
outside world as pixels that do not straddle the gap, if *the same motion* has to be
made to move between them.

Also expected is the finding that the observer jumped forward and not backward
when the zoom control was accidently bumped. This is because what the observer
perceives as *in front of him* is determined by the particular pattern of change (namely
an expanding flow-field) in the vibrations that occurs when moving the body
forward. The location of the tactile array on the body is irrelevant. Indeed, the basic
fact that observers felt the stimulation as *out in the world* and not on their skin is
expected: The felt location of a sensation is not determined by where the sensors
are, but by the laws that link body motion to changes in sensory input.

I agree that the brain is the neurophysiological mechanism that enables seeing, but I stress that the experienced quality of vision derives from the mode of interaction that we engage in with the environment when we see. Putting too much emphasis on the role of the brain leads one to make errors like expecting that one should be able to get the impression of seeing without controlling the camera, or that one should see a gap in the visual field when there is a gap in the vibrator array.

Do people really see with the TVSS?[4] This is the critical question for the sensorimotor approach, to which one would like to be able to answer "yes." But the sensorimotor approach would only predict this to be true if the laws governing the sensorimotor dependencies in the TVSS really are identical to those for normal seeing. And this is patently not the case, and indeed even logically impossible, since for the laws to be strictly identical, all aspects of the input-output loop would have to be identical. Consider the fact that the TVSS's camera resolution is so much poorer than the eye (400 pixels instead of the eye's 7 million cones and 120 million rods), that it has no color sensitivity, that it is moved by the hand or (in a later version) the head rather than by the extraocular muscles, that this movement is much slower than eye movements, that there is no blinking, and that the spatial and temporal resolution of the skin is incomparably worse than that of the retina. Each of these differences is a little difference from what is involved in the normal interaction with the environment that we have when we are seeing. The more we have of such differences, the greater the difference will be from normal seeing.

But if subjective reports are anything to go by, there is evidence that using the TVSS is nevertheless a bit like seeing. The evidence comes from the report of a congenitally blind person who used the apparatus extensively. Like Bach y Rita's early patients, he said that although at first he felt the tactile vibrations where they touched his skin, very quickly he came to sense objects in front of him. Further, he said: ". . . the experienced quality of the sensations was nothing like touch. Rather than coining a new word or using 'touch' or 'feel,' I shall use the word 'see' to describe what I experienced."[5]

Going against the idea that people "see" with the TVSS is Bach y Rita's own report[6] that congenitally blind people who, after learning to use the TVSS, are shown erotic pictures or pictures of their loved ones do not get the same emotional charge as sighted people. But I would claim that their lack of emotional response could come from the fact that sighted people have developed their vision over time, through childhood and adolescence and in a social context when emotional attachments and erotic reactions develop, whereas those who are congenitally blind have not gone through such a critical period while using the TVSS. Furthermore, it might be that emotional reactions depend on cues that are difficult to extract using the very low-resolution TVSS. Thus, the lack of emotional quality reported by users of the TVSS is not an argument against the idea that ultimately visual-like quality should be possible with more extensive practice and with improved devices.[7]

More Recent Work on Visual Substitution

The work I have been describing started in the 1970s. What is the situation now with tactile vision? One might expect that, from its promising beginnings, technical progress would have today brought the TVSS into everyday use. But curiously this has not happened.[8] One reason may be that for a long time research on the TVSS was not in the scientific mainstream and was not considered seriously. Another factor may be that the device has had little support from the blind community, some of whom consider that using prosthetic devices labels them as disabled. Finally, and perhaps the main reason for the slow development of the TVSS, was and remains the technical problem of creating a very dense array of vibrators with reliable contact with the skin in a body area where the skin has sufficient tactile acuity.

For this reason in recent years Bach y Rita and collaborators have turned to a different way of delivering stimulation, namely through an array of electrodes held on the tongue.[9] Unfortunately, the Tongue Display Unit or "Brain port" has its own challenges, the main one being that recognition of forms is still limited by the poor resolution of the device, which generally has not exceeded 12 x 12 electrodes, although prototypes are being developed with up to 600 electrodes in all.[10]

Alongside tactile (or tongue) stimulation, auditory stimulation is another possibility that has been investigated for replacing vision. Several devices have been tried, all relying on the idea that one can recode an image by translating each pixel into a tone whose loudness depends on the pixel's brightness and whose pitch is higher when the pixel is higher in the image. Horizontal position in the image can also be coded via frequency, by using stereo sound, or by scanning the image repetitively and coding horizontal position by time relative to the beginning of each scan.[11]

In my laboratory we have extensively tested such a scanning device, namely one developed by Peter Meijer, in Eindhoven in the Netherlands. Meijer is an independent researcher whose "The vOICe" (for "Oh I see!") is an inexpensive substitution system that can be freely downloaded to run on a laptop with a Webcam (see Fig. 12.2)

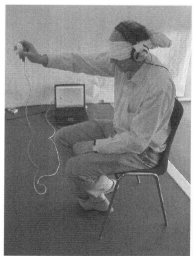

Figure 12.2 (*Left*) **Sensory substitution researcher and philosopher Charles Lenay trying out Peter Meijer's The vOICe in my laboratory in Paris. Blindfolded, he is holding a Webcam connected to a laptop which is converting the image into a "soundscape" that is scanned once per second, and which he is listening to through headphones. (*Right*) Malika Auvray "showing" Jim Clark a simple object.**

or on a java-equipped mobile phone with a built-in camera. Meijer's Web site is well worth visiting for up-to-date information on all aspects of sensory substitution.[12]

Work done by Malika Auvray in my laboratory with The vOICe shows that after about 15 hours of training, people are able to distinguish about 20 objects (flower-pot, book, various bottles, spoons, shoes, etc.) and navigate around the room. The background must be uniform so that the sound is not too complex. We have a video showing how people's ability to recognize develops through a first stage in which they learn how to actively maintain contact with an outside source of information, a second and third stage where they come to experience this information as being located outside their bodies in a spatial array, and a fourth stage where they come to comprehend how to link the information with outside objects.[13] What is impressive is that in a final, fifth stage, users become fully immersed in the environment via the device, and naturally use the word *see* to describe their experience. Reports by one regular user of The vOICe also suggest that it is possible to attain a sufficient degree of automaticity with the device so that it can be used in everyday tasks. For example, whereas this user found it impossible to "see" when there was other auditory infor-mation to attend to, now, after years of practice, she reports being able to listen to the radio at the same time as she washes the dishes using the device.[14] Even though both dishes and radio are delivered as sounds, the two sources of information are not confused and remain independent. She hears the radio, but "sees" the dishes.

While The vOICe does have a small community of enthusiastic users, it is far from being a realistic visual-to-auditory substitution system. Apart from its very low resolution as compared to vision, its essential drawback lies in the fact that the image is scanned repetitively rather than being present all at once. This means that when a user moves the camera, the effect on the input is only available once every scan, that is, in our experiment, every second. This is much too slow to resemble the visual flow that occurs when sighted persons move their body, and it also does not allow smooth tracking, even of slow-moving objects.[15]

To overcome this problem, we have experimented with a device that we call The Vibe, in which horizontal position in the camera image is coded exclusively by stereo sound location. That way, the "soundscape" that users hear at any moment contains the whole visual scene, making scanning unnecessary and thereby allow-ing for sensorimotor dependencies more similar to those that occur in normal vision, where the whole scene is visible at any moment. An interesting finding that we discovered when experimenting with this device concerned an aspect of the sen-sorimotor interaction that is important for giving the impression of vision. This is the ability to interrupt the stream of sensory information by interposing an occluder (like a piece of cardboard or the users' hands) between the object and the camera attached to their head. Said in another way, one condition for people to interpret, in a vision-like way, a sensation as coming from outside of them is that they can cause the sensation to cease by putting, say, their hands between the object and their eyes.[16] However, even if spatial resolution can be improved by using three-dimensional stereo sound to code horizontal position, The Vibe will require more research before it can be useful as a visual prosthesis.

To conclude, current techniques of visual-to-tactile and visual-to-auditory sub-stitution are a long way from the goal of achieving a real sense of vision. Using tactile or auditory stimulation, it is possible only to provide a few aspects of normal visual impressions, like the quality of being "out there" in the world, and of conveying information about spatial layout and object form. But the "image-like" quality of vision still seems far away. Indeed, because the eye is such a high-resolution sensor, it will probably never be possible to attain true substitution of the image-like quality of vision.

Other Substitution Devices and Means for Perceiving Space

If we are merely interested in providing information about spatial layout, there are much simpler methods available than the technically sophisticated substitution systems I have been discussing. The blind man's cane is the simplest of all, and philosopher and sensory substitution researcher Charles Lenay, using a minimalist electronic version, has been studying how such devices allow space to be apprehended.[17] Commercial devices like the Sonic Guide, UltraSonic Torch, Sonic Glasses, or the Sonic Pathfinder also exist that, in addition to providing a touch sensation when pointed at a nearby object, can use ultrasound or laser to give information about the object's texture, size, and distance.[18] Another system called "Tactos" allows blind people to explore drawings or Web pages by stimulation of their fingers.[19] As just one more example, a device is being investigated not so much as a prosthesis but as a way of augmenting awareness of one's surroundings. It is a kind of "haptic radar" consisting of half a dozen vibrators mounted on a headband. When the user approaches an object in a given direction, the vibrators on that side of the head vibrate.[20] This can give the user a global impression of the size of the space surrounding the object.

And one should not forget that a sense of space can be obtained without any technology at all, that is, through echolocation. Many blind people use the echos of their cane on the ground or of clicks they make with their mouth to estimate the size, distance, and the texture of nearby surfaces.[21] One 17-year-old boy was such an expert at this that he was able to roller skate in the street and avoid obstacles.[22] Another expert is Daniel Kish, a specialist in orientation and mobility who teaches the method and has founded a nonprofit organization to help in training blind people to use echolocation.[23]

Perhaps we do not want to call the blind man's cane and human echolocation "sensory substitution" systems. But what is important is that, consistent with the sensorimotor approach, the user of a cane feels the touch of the cane on the outside object, not as pressure in the hand. The user of echolocation is aware of objects in the environment, not of auditory echos, although these carry the information. It is spatial information about the environment that is perceived, not pressure on the hand or auditory information.

Another interesting phenomenon concerns spatial information about the environment that is provided through audition, but felt as having a tactile nature. This is the phenomenon called "facial vision," "obstacle sense," or "pressure sense." In approaching large objects at a distance of about 30–80 cm, blind people sometimes have the impression of feeling a slight touch on their forehead, cheeks, and chest, as though they were being touched by a fine veil or cobweb.[24] Psychologist William James at the turn of the 20th century, and others since then, have demonstrated that blind people obtain facial vision by making use of the subtle changes in intensity, direction, and frequency of reflected sounds.[25] What is particularly interesting for the question of sensory substitution is the fact that this form of object perception is experienced as having a tactile rather than an auditory quality. This makes sense for objects very close to the face, which can provoke slight disturbances of the air as well as changes in heat radiation that could be detected by receptors on the face. But we need to explain why the sensation is perceived as tactile when objects are further away. A possibility is that certain information received through the auditory modality depends on head and body motion in a way that tactile stimuli do. In particular, moving a few centimeters forward or backward may create a radical change in certain aspects of the auditory signal, which are analogous to moving a few centimeters forward or backward and bringing the head into and out of contact with a veil. Similarly, it may be that when the head is facing the object that is being sensed, slight lateral shifts of the head might create systematic changes analogous to the rubbing that occurs when one is touching a piece of cloth with the head.

What we can conclude from this discussion of visual substitution is that whereas there is little hope of finding a way of completely substituting all aspects of vision, different subaspects of vision, most easily the sense of external space that it provides, may not be hard to substitute via other modalities (in particular either tactile or auditory). More important, the research described here is consistent with the predictions of the sensorimotor approach: The experienced quality of a sensation, and in particular the location where it is felt, is not determined by the brain areas that are activated, but by the laws of dependence linking body motions to changes in sensory input.

Substituting Other Senses

Efforts to make an auditory-to-tactile device started in the 1960s at about the same time as the development of the TVSS. Since then several devices for those with hearing impairments have been produced that decompose sound, and in particular speech, into anything up to 32 frequency bands, and that use the energy in each band to stimulate different skin locations, either mechanically (as in the "Tactaid" and the "Teletactor" devices) or electrically (the "Tickle Talker").[26] The idea behind such devices is to approximate the way the cochlea decomposes sound into bands. Although such systems can improve people's sound discrimination and speech comprehension abilities, there remains great resistance to adopting this technology. Part of the reason may be that deaf people do not want to depend on such devices. Also there is a lobby in the deaf community claiming that hearing impairment should not be considered a disability to be corrected.[27]

Another factor may be the fact that the medical profession is strongly invested in cochlear implants, which would seem the obvious first choice for auditory rehabilitation. Indeed, one argument that has been made in favor of cochlear implants is that since they transmit information via the normal auditory channel, they should provide the normal impression of hearing—whereas vibrotactile prostheses, working through the skin, could never give the phenomenology of normal hearing. I would claim that this argument is fallacious: What provides the phenomenology of hearing is not the neural channel through which the information travels, but the laws of dependency between body motions and the incoming sensory information. There may be issues of how the auditory information is preprocessed before it is provided to the auditory nerve, in the case of cochlear implants, or before it is provided to the skin, in the case of tactile devices. But with appropriate preprocessing, vibrotactile prostheses should be just as able to provide true auditory sensations as cochlear implants. Note that in both cases we would expect that long familiarization, preferably from birth, would be necessary. It would thus be worth expending more effort on devices for auditory substitution, which might be easier to implement than those for visual substitution.[28]

Although visual and auditory substitution has received most interest, some efforts have been made to create other forms of sensory substitution. Compensation of vestibular deficits—that is, deficits in the system that controls our sense of balance—is one domain where sensory substitution really proves feasible and useful, be it with Bach y Rita's tongue display unit or through vibrator devices that can be worn on the body or on the soles of the feet.[29] Bach y Rita describes how by using such a device a person who previously wavers "like a noodle" can suddenly, within seconds, stand with good stability.

Loss of tactile sensation, for example, due to leprosy or injury, can also be remedied successfully through a glove that substitutes touch with hearing (see, for example, Fig. 12.3).[30] Bach y Rita and his colleagues report on patients with leprosy who wear a different type of glove that sends tactile stimulation on their leprous hand to

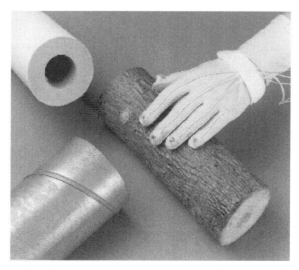

Figure 12.3 A tactile glove equipped with miniature condenser microphones on the fingertips. Transmitted to earphones worn by the user, the sound from these can be used to allow an observer to distinguish between different textures—in this case, wood, paper, and metal. (From Lundborg et al., 1999.) Reprinted with permission of Elsevier.

another body part. Within minutes they come to feel sensation in the hand, despite stimulation being relayed to a different body part.

Substitution of vestibular and of tactile senses are among the most successful sensory substitution systems, possibly because the sensorimotor laws involved in these senses are simpler than other senses, and so can more easily be instantiated in other sense modalities. Certainly the success of such systems convincingly confirms the notion that the felt quality of a sensation is determined by the laws of sensorimotor dependency involved, rather than by the particular sensory input channels.

Substitution of taste and smell is something that does not seem to have been tried, and for good reason. Taste, considered very strictly, might not be too difficult to substitute, since it seems to be a fairly simple modality with only five types of taste buds present on the tongue (bitter, salty, sour, sweet, and the more recently discovered "umami"—something like savory). But in addition to taste buds, other types of receptors participate in the taste sensation, namely somatosensory mechanosensors and chemosensors that register wetness/dryness, metallicness, pungentness, hot/cold sensations, and texture. Finally, an important component of taste is smell. One rarely if at all tastes something without it also stimulating the olfactory sense. Even when one blocks one's nose, vapors from the back of the mouth rise into the nasal cavity and stimulate olfactory receptors, of which there are about 1,000 different types.[31]

Thus, to make a taste substitution system, we would first have to substitute these different input channels. We would then also have to deal with the motor components, namely the chewing motions of the mouth and the various different forms of tongue motion that are associated with tasting. We would have to include the automatic salivation that is caused by tart substances and the changes in tongue exploration caused by the wetness, dryness, stickiness, or texture of foodstuffs. We would also have to include the automatic tendency to swallow that we have when we have chewed something for a while and it is well mixed with our saliva.

Thinking about these various challenges shows that the "what it's like" of tasting involves a rich repertoire of interactions. For example, part of the taste of vinegar is constituted by the salivation that it induces. Part of the taste of sugar perhaps involves automatic reactions of our digestive systems and the effects on blood sugar that it produces. It would be difficult to accurately re-create this complex set of interrelationships through another sense modality.

Substitution, Extension, or New Modality?

The discussion up to now shows that sensory substitution already exists to a limited extent. We can design systems that stimulate one sensory modality (e.g., touch, audition) but that give rise to sensations of a different nature, for example, visual sensation of space, of object identity. In a way, these systems are disappointing in that they do not provide the complete gamut of sensations that characterize the sensory modality to be substituted. Progress may yet be made, in particular as concerns the forms of preprocessing that are used in visual-to-auditory and auditory-to-tactile substitution. But when we think more deeply about what substitution of a sensory modality really is, we realize that a sensory modality involves such complex and idiosyncratic modes of interaction that it is unrealistic to try to simulate it completely with alternative sensors and effectors.

The practical difficulty of creating realistic sensory substitution does not weaken the sensorimotor approach. On the contrary, by realizing that having a sensory impression consists in engaging with the environment, the approach predicts that it becomes possible to add modes of interaction that, in a limited way, augment old modalities or provide new ones. Instead of thinking simply in terms of sensory *substitution*, we can think in terms of sensory *enhancement* or sensory *supplementation*.

Going in this direction is an interesting experiment performed by neuroscientist Peter König and his collaborators at Osnabrück. His idea was to try to create a new "magnetic" sense by providing observers with information about the direction of north.[32] He equipped users with a belt with 13 vibrators connected to an electronic compass. The vibrator closest to the direction of north vibrated continuously, with this sensation coming from a different vibrator as the observer turned. Four people wore the belt for 6 weeks in their everyday activities and additionally participated in weekly outdoor training sessions. After training it was found that the device improved users' outdoor navigation ability. This improvement seemed to consist in an improved spatial sense, in which people perceived things in a more map-like fashion than previously. In three observers, the effect of the belt was integrated into unconscious eye movement control loops, as shown by changes in the way their eyes moved automatically when they were subjected to rotations in a chair. It therefore seems that with practice it was possible to start creating a kind of "sixth," magnetic sense, which may sometimes be integrated into automatic, unconscious behaviors, and which (in two of the four observers) profoundly modified the "feel" that they had of spatial layout.

The idea of sensory enhancement is closely related to a current of thought that is gaining ground in philosophy and in virtual reality. It is the idea that any tools or artifacts that humans use, like pen and paper, spectacles, hammers, knives and forks, cars and bicycles, cellphones and computers, constitute part of our sensory experience and are part of our selves. The idea is thus to conceive the use of our five "natural" senses as no more basic or natural than the use of the tools and instruments that society has developed to enable us to probe or interact with our environments. Instead of thinking that we need brain plasticity to accommodate our cars into our body schemas when driving or to "feel" the paper at the tip of our pens when writing, we can realize that these experiences are as natural to constituting our sensory environment as is seeing it with our eyes or feeling it with our fingers. The idea even goes beyond merely extending *sensory* capacities and can apply also to one's cognitive processes and way of thinking, which can be enhanced and modified by the instruments that civilization has invented.[33]

Brain Plasticity

It is interesting to ask whether the change that sensory substitution induces in the way information is processed is accompanied by corresponding changes in the brain. The question has been answered for experienced users of Braille, whose *visual* cortex becomes activated despite Braille providing only tactile stimulation.[34] An experiment performed specifically with the frequent user of the The vOICe also shows that in her case visual cortex is involved in processing the purely auditory information provided by the device.[35]

Many neuroscientists nowadays marvel at what looks like a surprising degree of brain plasticity in these cases. The tendency is to suppose that it is because visual cortex becomes involved that the sensations experienced by the Braille readers and by the vOICe user are of a visual nature. But to think this, would be to make the error of thinking that somehow visual cortex could "generate" visual-type sensations. The reason a stimulation seems visual is not causally related to the cortical area involved, but to the modes of interaction we have with the environment when we use visual sensors.[36]

Indeed, there is another case of plasticity that confirms the view that it is not the cortex that determines the nature of sensation. In a series of experiments done by neuroscientist Mriganka Sur and his group at MIT,[37] newborn ferrets underwent a procedure in which part of their brains was surgically altered so that, during further development, the usual pathways connecting their eyes to the visual cortex were rerouted to the auditory cortex. Sur and his collaborators were able to show that after maturation, the structure of auditory cortex changed to resemble the very particular, columnar "pinwheel" structure of visual cortex. Additional behavioral studies showed that this restructured auditory cortex gave rise to visual-type reactions on the part of the ferrets. The way the researchers showed this was clever. They performed the surgical procedure only on one brain hemisphere, leaving the wiring in the other hemisphere with its normal connections. They then trained the ferrets to react differently to a light and a sound stimulation presented to the normal, unmodified hemisphere. When a light was then delivered to a part of the visual field that was processed only by the rewired hemisphere, they found that even though this light stimulated the auditory cortex, the ferrets responded in a way that showed that they perceived the stimulation as visual.

These results and recent replications with other animals and other sense modalities[38] further confirm that what counts in determining the experienced nature of a sensation is not the part of the brain that is stimulated, but the mode of interaction that is involved with the environment. In the case of the ferrets, if during maturation it is their auditory cortex that processes visual information, and they learn to interact with the environment in an appropriate way using this information, then they will end up having visual sensations even though they are using the auditory cortex. The role of the brain in all this is to serve as the substrate that learns the appropriate modes of sensorimotor interaction. Different cortical areas may be more or less specialized in this task, and so may do the learning more or less efficiently. But so long as the learning is done, the sensation will correspond to the mode of interaction involved.

Retinal and Brain Implants

As is the case for cochlear implants, in recent years many laboratories have become interested in the challenge of making the link between electronics and biology by finding ways to implant artificial retinae in the eye or to implant dense microelectrode arrays in the optic nerve or the visual cortex.[39] Some of the difficulties inherent in these ventures have been discussed in recent review articles,[40] and it is clear that there is still a considerable way to go before we can hope for a useful system. Still, with the large effort involved across the world, and with the burgeoning field of neural prosthetics and neural interfaces supported by many grant agencies, the next years will undoubtedly show great progress as far as the technical problems of neurobiological interfacing are concerned.

But even though restoring vision via retinal or brain implants is not strictly a form of sensory substitution, there is still a lesson to be learned from the sensorimotor approach. It is that we should not expect that stimulating the cortex or parts of the visual system will allow people suddenly to "see," as if turning the TV set on again. Seeing is not simply activating the visual system. Seeing is a way of interacting with the world. Thus, not very much true vision can be expected from retinal or cortical implants unless people use them in an active, exploratory fashion. The situation is, I suggest, similar to Bach y Rita's TVSS: Before he let the users actively manipulate the video camera, they felt vibrations on their back. People with implants will not have the impression of "seeing" unless the dynamic relation between their eye and body motions and the stimulation they receive obeys laws similar to those that apply in normal vision.

Indeed, that message seems to be gaining some traction. Scientists are now miniaturizing the implants so that they can be used in an exploratory way, at least by using head movements. Recent prototypes even use miniature cameras inside the eye, thereby allowing eye movements to create sensory changes that mimic more closely the types of change we have in normal vision.

Notes

1. Bach-y-Rita, 1972. An excellent documentary on PBS Wired Science contains historic sequences with interviews of Bach y Rita dating as far back as 1976, and images of his original apparatus as well as descriptions of the last work he did: http://www.pbs.org/kcet/wiredscience/video/286-mixed_feelings.html.
2. See, for example, Sampaio and Dufier (1988) and Segond, Weiss, and Sampaio (2007).
3. Strictly this is true only from a theoretical point of view: With David Philipona we have developed a very general theoretical method that extracts (through an algebraic rather than statistical approach) the spatial structure of outside space from the sensorimotor laws, with no a priori knowledge of sensor or effector properties (Philipona et al., 2003; Philipona et al., 2004). See also Maloney and Ahumada (1989) and Pierce and Kuipers (1997) for methods using statistical correlation to calibrate an unordered retina or robotic sensor array. From a practical point of view, however, if the vibrators were arranged in a disordered fashion so that local topology (i.e., the structure of proximity relations) in the video image no longer corresponded to topology in the tactile representations, then I suspect people would not easily learn to "see" with the device. The reason is that it may be very difficult for an adult brain to recuperate the local topology lost in a disordered tactile representation.

This is a situation similar to amblyopia in vision, where the local metric of the retina seems to be disturbed (Koenderink, 1990).

4. The Irish physicist and philosopher William Molyneux, in a letter in 1688, asked the philosopher John Locke whether a congenitally blind person suddenly given vision would be able to visually distinguish a cube from a sphere. "Molyneux's question" has since then been hotly debated (see the brilliant account by Morgan, 1977). It is related to the question of whether people really could see with the TVSS.

5. Guarniero, 1974, 1977.

6. Bach-y-Rita, 1997, 2002.

7. For further discussion of the emotional quality in sensory substitution, and of the question of whether sensory substitution systems can really substitute one modality for another, see Auvray and Myin (2009).

8. For recent reviews, see Auvray and Myin (2009) and Bach-y-Rita and W. Kercel (2003).

9. Bach-y-Rita, Danilov, Tyler, & Grimm, 2005; Sampaio, Maris, & Bach-y-Rita, 2001.

10. Brainport Technologies, Wicab Inc. See http://vision.wicab.com

11. For reference to these devices, see, for example, Auvray and Myin (2009).

12. http://www.seeingwithsound.com/ See also the work using The vOICe by neuro-scientist Amir Amedi at the Hebrew University (http://brain.huji.ac.il/press.asp).

13. The video shows excerpts from the progress of a French observer, over approxi-mately 15 hours of practice extended over several days. It was made in my laboratory by Malika Auvray during the course of her doctoral studies. See http://www.malika-auvray.com and http://www.kevin-oregan.net. The study itself is described in Auvray, Hanneton, and O'Regan (2007). A similar study with a head-mounted camera was performed by Petra Stoerig and her team in Düsseldorf (Proulx, Stoerig, Ludowig, Knoll, & Auvray, 2008).

14. Fletcher, 2002. See also extensive anecdotal observations by Fletcher and others who have used the system on http://www.seeingwithsound.com/users.htm, includ-ing this youtube exerpt: http://www.youtube.com/watch?v=I0lmSYP7OcM. And see the interview of her and neuroscientist Alvaro Pascual-Leone on CBC: http://www.seeingwithsound.com/cbc2008.html.

15. Interestingly, Peter Meijer informs me that experienced users like Pat Fletcher are no longer aware of the temporal gap in the scan. This may be analogous to the fact that users of the TVSS do not perceive the gap in the two halves of the tactile array.

16. Auvray, Hanneton, Lenay, & O'Regan, 2005. Other work using a device similar to the "The Vibe" has been done as a doctoral thesis by Barthélémy Durette with Jeanny Hérault at the INPG Gipsa-lab in Grenoble.

17. Charles Lenay has contributed highly interesting work on sensory substitution, in particular his "minimalist" system (Lenay, Canu, & Villon, 1997). Similar work has been done by Froese and Spiers (2007) and Siegle and Warren (2010).

18. For an inventory of current electronic mobility aids, see Roentgen, Gelderblom, Soede, and de Witte (2008). For an older review, see, for example, Kay (1985).

19. Ziat et al., 2007.

20. This work is being done at the Ishikawa Komuro Laboratory at the University of Tokyo (Cassinelli, Reynolds, & Ishikawa, 2006). See http://www.k2.t.u-tokyo.ac.jp/index-e.html. Another recent head-mounted device provides information about color and direction of surfaces to vibrators on the fingers is Zelek, Bromley, Asmar, and Thompson (2003). There are more and more laboratories in the world begin-ning to work on devices making use of tactile stimulation in innovative applications.

21. For a review, see Arias (1996).
22. A Web site devoted to Ben Underwood's memory (he died of cancer in 2009 at age 17) includes videos of his impressive skills: http://www.benunderwood.com/
23. See http://www.worldaccessfortheblind.org
24. For instance, consider the following quote cited by William James from the blind author of a treatise on blindness at the turn of the 20th century: "Whether within a house or in the open air, whether walking or standing still, I can tell, although quite blind, when I am opposite an object, and can perceive whether it be tall or short, slender or bulky. I can also detect whether it be a solitary object or a continuous fence; whether it be a close fence or composed of open rails, and often whether it be a wooden fence, a brick or stone wall, or a quick-set hedge . . . . The currents of air can have nothing to do with this power, as the state of the wind does not directly affect it; the sense of hearing has nothing to do with it, as when snow lies thickly on the ground objects are more distinct, although the footfall cannot be heard. I seem to perceive objects through the skin of my face, and to have the impressions immediately transmitted to the brain" (James, 1890, p. 204, Vol. 2). See also Kohler (1967). Since Diderot's "Letter on the blind," facial vision had often been considered to truly be a kind of tactile, or even possibly an extrasensory, form of perception. Echolation expert Daniel Kish gives an extensive discussion of facial vision in his master's thesis of which an update is provided by Kish (2003).
25. For a historical review, see Arias (1996).
26. These devices are briefly described, along with other prosthetic devices using tactile stimulation, in Jones and Sarter (2008). See also the interesting review by Gallace, Tan, and Spence (2007).
27. Lane & Bahan, 1998; Tucker, 1998.
28. The cochlear nerve only sends about 30,000 fibres to the brain, compared to the optic nerve, which sends about a million. This might suggest that an auditory substitution system has about 30 times less to process than a visual substitution system, although differences in type of processing in the two channels might very well invalidate this argument.
29. Priplata, Niemi, Harry, Lipsitz, & Collins, 2003; Tyler & Danilov, 2003; Wall III & Weinberg, 2003.
30. Bach-y-Rita, Tyler, & Kaczmarek, 2003; Lundborg, Rosén, & Lindberg, 1999.
31. Buck & Axel, 1991.
32. Nagel, Carl, Kringe, Martin, & König, 2005.
33. This view has been suggested by Lenay, Gapenne, Hanneton, Marque, and Genouëlle (2003) and by Auvray and Myin (2009). For a more cognitive rather than sensory context, and for applications of this view in society in general, see Clark (2003) and Menary (2007).
34. For a review of work on cortical plasticity, including the work on blind persons, see Pascual-Leone, Amedi, Fregni, and Merabet (2005). See also Amir Amedi's work at the Hebrew University (http://brain.huji.ac.il/press.asp).
35. Merabet et al., 2009. See also Pat Fletcher with Alvaro Pascual-Leone, a neuroscientist from Harvard Medical School and a specialist in transcranial magnetic stimulation, at http://www.seeingwithsound.com/cbc2008.html.
36. For an excellent discussion of the alternative ways in which the brain might underlie the sensory quality of a sensory modality, see Hurley and Noë (2003).
37. Sharma, Angelucci, & Sur, 2000; von Melchner, Pallas, & Sur, 2000. For further references, see also the commentary by Merzenich (2000).

38. For example, see Frost, Boire, Gingras, and Ptito (2000) and Slotnick, Cockerham, and Pickett (2004).
39. The most publicity was given to the cortical implant that was developed by Dobelle (2000), which provided sufficient acuity for a blind person to distinguish very large letters.
40. Hossain, Seetho, Browning, & Amoaku, 2005; Schiller & Tehovnik, 2008; Weiland & Humayun, 2008; Zrenner, 2002.

Chapter 13

The Localization of Touch

What seems like a very stupid question can sometimes be very profound. I once asked my 16-year-old daughter why, when I touched her arm, she felt the sensation on her *arm*. After all, touch sensation is caused by nerve receptors that send information up to the *brain*. So why didn't my daughter feel the touch in her *brain* instead of on her arm?

My daughter suggested that perhaps once information got up to the brain, the brain sent a message back down to the arm telling it that it was being touched. She agreed there was something circular about her answer: How would the arm then "know" that it was being touched? After all, the arm itself is not conscious. Would it have to send yet another message up to the brain?

Penfield's Somatosensory Homunculus

Neuroscientists have the following answer to the question. Their story is based on the concept of the "somatosensory map" or "somatosensory homunculus" discovered by Wilder Penfield—the same Canadian neurosurgeon who elicited memories in epileptic patients by directly stimulating neurons in their brains. Penfield's somatosensory map is an area along the central sulcus in parietal cortex (see Fig. 13.1), which seems to "represent" the different parts of the body in a map-like fashion: Parts of the body that are near each other are also near each other on the map. When a particular body part is touched, the neurons in the map become active. Conversely, when a surgeon electrically stimulates these neurons, people feel they are being touched on that body part.

Since Penfield's discovery, many such maps have been found and much research has been done on the way they work.[1] Several facts confirm that the particular map discovered by Penfield in parietal cortex is related to how we localize touch on the body.

A fundamental fact concerns the relation between touch sensitivity and the size of the areas devoted to different body parts on the map. We all know that the fingers have good touch sensitivity; we can accurately localize touch on the fingers and make fine discriminations with them. On the other hand, have you ever tried asking a friend to touch one of your toes while you close your eyes? You may be surprised to find that you may not be able to tell which toe was touched. On your back you may not be able to tell whether you are being touched with one or several fingers simultaneously.

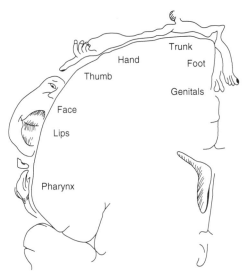

Figure 13.1 Penfield-type sensory homunculus. A vertical section of the left hemisphere showing the parietal cortex near the central sulcus, and the areas that are activated when different body regions are touched. Note the different relative sizes of the different areas, with lips, tongue, pharynx, and hands occupying large areas. Note also that the hand region is bordered by the face region and by the trunk and shoulder region. People whose hands have been amputated sometimes feel sensation in the area of their missing hands when stimulated in these regions of the map. Notice also that the genital region is near the feet. (From Ramachandran and Hirstein, 1998, adapted with permission of Macmillan press).

These differences in touch sensitivity correlate with the size of the corresponding areas of the somatosensory map. The fingers, the face, and the tongue and pharynx occupy large regions of the map. The parts of the map that represent areas like the feet or back occupy smaller areas. When you draw out the whole map, you get a distorted little man or "homunculus," with large lips and enormous hands.[2] These discoveries are a first line of evidence showing the importance of the somatosensory map in explaining touch sensation.

Adaptation of the Map

Another line of research consolidates this idea, namely research showing that the map is highly adaptable and can change rapidly depending on how the body part is used.[3] For example, research on monkeys shows that when two fingers are strapped together for several weeks, the part of the map that corresponds to the hand restructures itself to resemble a map for a single finger, with a corresponding loss in ability to distinguish stimulations on the two fingers. When a finger is amputated, the neural territory previously occupied by the representation of that finger is quickly invaded by neurons from the two nearby fingers. The same is true for other body parts.

Despite these changes, the sensation of the missing body part sometimes does not completely disappear. Immediately after amputation of a limb, people often have the impression that their limb is still present, sometimes in a painful posture. The feeling usually subsides, but when it doesn't, people can, even years later, still have the illusion that they can move and grab things with this "phantom limb." They will even move the rest of their body to avoid bumping into objects with their phantom limb. This suggests that the somatosensory map corresponding to the amputated limb is still partly present and functioning.[4]

In addition, if you gently touch the face of a person who has a phantom hand, the person will sometimes feel the stimulation *on that missing hand*. Figure 13.2 shows that with care, you can map out the different parts of the phantom hand on the face. An explanation may lie in the way the human somatosensory map is arranged: The area for the face in the map is close to the area for the hand. Presumably when the hand is amputated, the hand area is gradually invaded by neurons from the face area.

Part of the reason for the proximity of hand and face areas in the cortical map might be that in the womb, the fetus spends a lot of time with its hands near its face. During maturation of the fetus's brain, simultaneous excitation of face and hand neurons might bring these areas together in the cortical map. A related argument has been made about why foot massages might be erotic. In the womb, the fetus is curled up with its feet near its genitals, bringing the foot area on the somatosensory map close to the area for the genitals.[5] This and other results showing rapid adaptability of the somatosensory map, even to include tools that one holds,[6] concur to show the importance of such maps in explaining touch sensation.

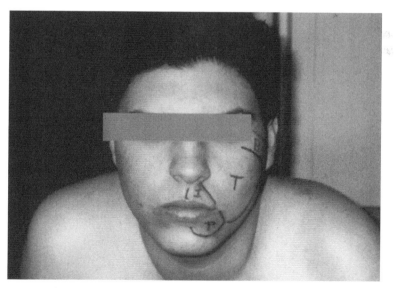

Figure 13.2 After amputation of his hand, when this person was touched lightly on his face at positions I, P, T, and B, he felt sensation on his phantom index finger, pinkie, thumb, and ball of thumb, respectively. (From Ramachandran and Hirstein, 1998, with permission of Oxford University Press.)

Multisensory Maps

A recent discovery about somatosensory maps concerns their *multisensory nature*.[7] This is the fact that the somatosensory map receives input not only from the touch receptors over the body but also from other senses, in particular from vision and from the proprioceptive system in the brain that keeps track of body posture.

Evidence for an influence of *vision* comes from experiments showing how visual distortions affect the organization of the maps. For example, experiments show that if you spend time looking through special video apparatus that makes your hand look larger than it is, a corresponding modification occurs in the size of the area that represents the hand in the somatosensory map. This kind of effect is familiar to people who play video games. After playing a game where you incarnate a giant lobster with enormous claws, for a while you will have the feeling that you move your arms and legs in an awkward, claw-like way.[8] It may be that a similar phenomenon occurs with prisoners. After spending months in a prison, they develop a feeling that the walls are part of their body, and when liberated they will unconsciously tend to hug walls when they walk along the street.[9]

Evidence for the effect of *posture* and proprioception on the somatosensory map comes from a wealth of experiments that show how one's ability to make tactile judgments is modified when one adjusts body positions. For example, the time it takes you to sense that someone has tapped you on your hand is longer if you put it in an abnormal pose, such as when you cross your arms. This kind of effect may partly explain the phenomenon of "Japanese hands." In this arrangement, you stretch your arms out in front of you and cross them. Then, keeping them crossed, twist your hands so your palms come together, and intertwine your fingers. Then bend your arms back toward yourself, so that you end up looking at your fingers in a completely unusual posture. If someone now touches one of your fingers, you will have a hard time knowing which hand it is on, and if someone points to a particular finger without touching it, you will have a hard time knowing how to move that finger rather than one on the other hand.

The Mystery Remains

We have seen that neurophysiological evidence converges on the idea that our sensations of bodily location are determined by the structure of a somatosensory map that represents the body anatomy. The distorted structure of the map, its adaptability, the influence of vision and proprioception, all concur to suggest that the reason we feel things where we do on the body is related to the existence of this cortical map.

But the question I discussed with my daughter still remains. Why should activation of neurons in a map in the *brain* somehow induce sensations in some *body* location? For example, why do the neurons in the arm area of the map create sensation on the arm rather than on the face, the foot, or anywhere else for that matter? Something is missing, and my daughter captured it conceptually by suggesting that the neurons in the map would have to send their information back down to the body part to tell it that it was being touched.

To add to the mystery, compare the case of touch with the case of seeing. It is known that there is a cortical map in area V1 of the occipital cortex at the back of the brain that represents the visual field. When neurons are active in this visual map, we have sensations that are referred outside to *the world*. Compare this to the Penfield map whose activation provides sensation *on the body*.

What accounts for this difference? And why do neurons in the Penfield map give rise to *tactile* sensations, whereas the neurons in visual areas give rise to *visual* sensations?

The Sensorimotor Approach: What Is the Feel of Touch?

One could say that having something touching a location of our body is a physical state of affairs that can be described by a particular set of sensorimotor dependencies. Like the law of gravity that describes how objects fall, these laws describe how changes made by our body provoke changes in the information coming into our sensors. They link different kinds of movements we might make to different kinds of sensory inputs that might be affected. The sensors involved are mainly tactile sensors, but visual, vestibular (measuring body motion), proprioceptive (measuring limb positions), and to a smaller extent, auditory sensors are also involved. Here is a partial list of the kinds of laws that apply when something is touching you at a particular body location:

- *Active motion by the body part:* If you actively move the part of the body being touched, the incoming sensory stimulation will change. Moving other parts of the body will not change the incoming sensory stimulation. For example, if your arm is being touched and you move it under the touch, the incoming stimulation from the touch will change. But if you move your foot, the incoming information from your arm will generally not change.
- *Active motion by a different body part:* Nevertheless, there are very specific movements of other body parts that *do* change stimulation at the touched location, namely movements to that location. For example, when something tickles you on your arm, you can move your *other* hand and scratch the tickled location.[10]
- *Passive motion:* The incoming stimulation changes if the body part is caused to move by some external agency (someone else moves your arm, for example, or it gets bumped away from what is touching it).
- *Vision:* If you look at the part of the body being touched, there are changes that occur in your visual field that are temporally correlated with the tactile changes (i.e., if the touch is a tapping kind of touch, the visual stimulation changes at the same rate as the tapping). Looking elsewhere will not provide such temporally correlated visual changes.
- *Audition:* When you feel something on some part of the body, you may be able to hear temporally correlated scratching or other auditory stimulation coming from the general direction of that body part.

When we feel something at a given body location, all these lawful relations between things we can do and resulting sensory changes are concurrently applicable (even if none of them are actually currently being exercised).

And now the idea of the sensorimotor theory is this: Instead of emphasizing the fact—and it is certainly a fact—that when we are touched, there is activation of neurons in a cortical map, the sensorimotor approach notes that what *constitutes* the fact of having a feel is that changes like those I have just listed will occur when we do certain things. I am not just saying what is obvious, namely that a certain state of affairs applies when one feels touch. What I'm saying is that this state of affairs *constitutes* the feel. What is *meant* by feeling touch is that these laws currently apply. There is nothing more to feeling a touch than the fact that the brain has registered that the laws currently apply.

And why do we feel the touch on our arm rather than in the brain? Because what we mean by feeling something in a particular place in our bodies is precisely that certain sensorimotor laws apply. The felt location is determined by which laws apply.

At first the idea seems strange. It doesn't seem right to claim that *nothing need be going on at all* in the brain at any given moment in order for the feel to be occurring, and that all that is necessary is that the brain should have registered that certain things might happen if the body moved or if there was a change in the environment. The idea seems strange because when we feel something touching us, we have the impression that, while it lasts, the feeling is *continuous*. One expects that this would require something likewise *going on* in the brain.

But remember what the philosophers call the "content-vehicle confusion" mentioned in Chapter 5. It is the philosophical error of thinking that for us to see redness, say, there must be something red being somehow activated or liberated in the brain. In the same way, it is a mistake to think that for us to see something as ongoing and continuous, there must also be something ongoing and continuous happening in the brain.

This still may be difficult to swallow. We are so used to reasoning in terms of machines buzzing and whirring and this giving rise to effects, that we are prisoners of this same analogy when it comes to thinking about the brain. Nevertheless, we have seen, with regard to vision in the first part of the book, how it is possible to have the feel of continually seeing, despite nothing "going on" in the brain. The reason we see things in a continuous fashion is because if at any moment we want to know whether there is something out there in the world, we can obtain information about it by moving our attention and our eyes to it. That is what we *mean* by continually seeing.

Of course, although nothing is "going on" (in that machine-like, humming and whirring fashion), the brain is nevertheless serving some purpose. It is in a certain state, which is different from the state it is in when we are feeling something else. The particular state has the property that it corresponds to the fact that certain seeing-type sensorimotor dependencies currently apply.

Another analogy is the feeling at home analogy also mentioned in Chapter 5. I have the *continuous* feel of being at home because I'm in a state of knowing that potentially there are things that I can do which confirm that I'm at home (like go into the kitchen). The reason I have the impression that this feel is "going on" is that if I should wonder whether I'm at home, I would immediately confirm that I have these potentialities.

And so, more explicitly, how do we answer my daughter's question?

If you were to touch me on my arm, the information would indeed be sent up to the somatosensory map in my parietal cortex, and it would activate the area devoted to the arm. But the reason I feel the touch on my arm is not because of that activation itself. The reason I feel it on my arm is that the brain has previously registered the fact that when such activation occurs, certain laws apply:

- *Active motion of the body part:* If I were to actively move my arm (but not my foot) under the touch, that same group of neurons will also be activated.
- *Active motion to the body part:* If I moved my other hand, say, to that location on my arm that was touched, I would also get the same kind of incoming changes that would occur.
- *Passive motion of the body part (proprioception):* If someone pushed my arm away, the sensation would cease.
- *Vision:* If I looked at my arm, I would see something touching it, and changes in the visual stimulation would temporally correlate with the tactile sensation.
- *Audition:* There are changes in auditory input coming from the direction of my arm, which are temporally correlated with the tactile changes.

So, suppose an activation occurs in the somatosensory map. Because such activation has previously been associated with all of these kinds of dependencies (even though at this moment none of them may actually apply), a person will know implicitly that he or she is in a situation where these particular laws apply. If the person then attends to that fact, he or she will be having the feel of touch. Furthermore, the felt location of the touch will be determined by which particular laws apply.

Multisensory Nature of Somatosensory Maps and Their Adaptability

For the brain to have coded the dependencies concerning touch on the arm, connections must previously have been established between the arm-representing neurons in the somatosensory map and those brain areas that are concerned with each of the dependencies I have just listed. This provides an explanation for why recent work shows that the somatosensory map is multisensory: It gets input from sense modalities other than touch, in particular from vision and proprioception, because such input is actually necessary for the feel of touch to occur.

How are the connections built up? Though there may be some connections that are present at birth, most will have been created by accumulating experiences over time. Because the connections are determined by the innumerable laws that determine, at any given body location, how incoming sensory changes may be influenced by one's own actions on the one hand, and by environmental changes on the other, learning more details of possible laws is an ongoing process. For this process to be possible, the somatosensory map has to be adaptable. It has to be able to respond to modifications in the different ways a body part is used, and in the ways our sensory organs change throughout life and over different environmental conditions.

Neurophysiology confirms that the system is continually recalibrating itself, with adaptation occurring very quickly, within a matter of hours. Such continual recalibration may represent an important evolutionary advantage, given that humans grow and that their body shape changes quite dramatically over time. Injury can also modify the shape of a limb or the way it can be used, and it makes sense that the localization of sensation should rapidly adapt to such changes.

I mentioned in the previous chapter that adaptability of the sensed location of touch can actually go as far as encompassing a tool like a pen or a whole vehicle like an automobile. From a simplistic neurophysiological point of view, it is surprising that one should ever be able to sense something at the tip of the pen or below the wheels of the car where there are in fact no sensors at all. The effect is even more surprising given the way the pen touches different parts of different fingers or the palm. The pressure changes on these different surface areas are very complex and depend on how one holds the pen, but somehow the brain is able to "project" them out to a single point at the tip of the pen. Of course, this "projection" requires familiarization with holding a pen in one's hand. If you try to write with a pen in your mouth, having had little practice with this way of writing, you feel the vibrations on your tongue, rather than at the tip of the pen. But with time you come again to feel the touch at the tip of the pen. The sensorimotor approach makes this phenomenon of appropriation of a tool or of extension or expansion of the body boundaries easy to understand. From the sensorimotor point of view such phenomena *are precisely the same* as the phenomena that allow us to feel our bodies the way we do.

The reason is that the very notion of "feeling something somewhere" is only indirectly determined by the location of the sensors themselves. After all, visual and auditory sensors are located in the body (in the retina, in the ear), but we see and hear things outside of the body. Similarly I feel something on my fingertip, not because the sensors happen to be at the fingertips, but because certain laws are obeyed, namely the sensorimotor dependencies that together describe what is actually meant by having a feel of touch on the fingertip: physical facts like the fact that if you move your fingertip, the input changes, but if you move your toe, nothing happens to that input. Or the fact that if your eyes are directed toward your fingertip there will be changes in (visual) input which are temporally correlated with the tactile input.[11]

Using one's hands and whole body, and all of one's sensory organs, including hearing and vestibular system, to register the laws that govern the position of my car wheels near the curb, is no different from using these same action systems and sensory systems to register the laws that govern the position of touch on my body.

The Rubber Hand Illusion and Out-of-Body Experiences

Confirmation of this approach to understanding touch localization comes from a very active recent literature on what is called the rubber hand illusion. The idea of this illusion harks back at least to experiments by French psychologist J. Tastevin,[12] who in the 1930s described how one could get the curious sensation that outside objects might actually be part of one's own body. He gave an example where an individual might be wearing a long raincoat that drapes down to his feet. He looks down and sees his two shoes sticking out from underneath. Gradually he moves his feet apart. He takes off one shoe and moves it further and further from the other. He can do this in such a way that he continues to really feel his foot in the shoe, and finally he has the peculiar feeling that his legs are spread abnormally across the room.

Today a whole literature has sprung up developing the idea that it is possible to transfer one's feeling of owning a body part to an outside object, with the paradigmatic phenomenon being Botvinick and Cohen's brilliant "rubber hand illusion."[13] The principle is as follows: A replica of a human hand and lower arm (the "rubber arm") is set on a table in front of an observer, whose own hand is hidden from view (see Fig. 13.3).

The observer looks at the rubber hand while the experimenter strokes it, usually with a paintbrush. At the same time, and in synchronous fashion, the experimenter also strokes the observer's real hand. After as little as one minute of stroking, the observer begins to have the curious impression that the rubber hand is her own hand. If the apparatus is covered and the observer is asked to say where under the cover she feels her own hand to be, she makes a systematic error in the direction of the rubber hand.

Multiple variations of the experiments have now been done in order to determine the conditions that are necessary for the illusion of transfer of ownership

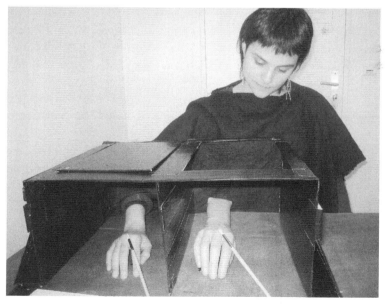

Figure 13.3 Rubber hand experiment. Camila Valenzuela-Moguillansky looking at the rubber hand. Her real hand (on the left) is hidden from her view. The paintbrushes are used to stroke her hand and the rubber hand synchronously so as to create the illusion that the rubber hand is her own.

to occur. The posture of the rubber hand has to correspond to a realistic posture of the observer's body, since if the hand is placed perpendicular to the body in a nonanatomically realistic position, the induction of the sensation of ownership fails. The hand must also not look like a hairy green, alien hand, although it can be of slightly different color and build than the observer's. When the observer does induce ownership into a hand that has different characteristics than his own, this can affect how he subsequently perceives his hand. For example, in experiments in my laboratory I've induced ownership of a larger or smaller rubber hand and shown that this affects the visually perceived size of the observer's own hand, as well as the size of the observer's grasp when he or she picks up an object.[14]

We have also shown something similar with feet. We had people wear little chest "bibs" with sand-filled babies' socks attached to them. They lie down with their back somewhat arched so that they can only see the babies' socks and not their own feet, and the experimenter simultaneously strokes the socks and their real feet. We find that people rapidly get the impression that the babies' feet are their own. Furthermore, when asked to estimate where their own feet are, they make systematic errors toward their own chest, so that essentially they perceive themselves to be shorter than they really are.

Other literature in this field concerns what are called "out-of-body" or autoscopic experiences. Such experiences are not so rare; in a group of 50 people, several may have experienced one. They sometimes happen after near-death situations, after neurological damage, and in situations of drug taking or severe stress. The different ways in which they can manifest themselves have been classified by neurologist Olaf Blanke at the Ecole Polytechnique Fédérale de Lausanne (see Fig. 13.4).[15] Blanke has shown that very circumscribed brain areas are involved in the phenomenon.

What is interesting for the sensorimotor approach is the fact that the phenomenon can be induced artificially by a method similar to the rubber hand illusion, but using techniques from virtual reality. People are, for example, fitted with head-mounted virtual reality spectacles in which they see a video image of themselves taken by a camera mounted behind them. As the experimenter strokes the participants on the back, they see an image of themselves from behind, being stroked at the same time as they feel the stroking on their back. People experience a curious

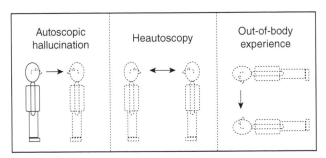

Figure 13.4 Three types of autoscopic phenomenon as illustrated by Blanke and Mohr (2005). The black lines represent the physical body and the dotted lines the experienced position of the disembodied body. The arrow indicates the position in space from which the patient has the impression to see.

out-of-body feeling in this situation, and furthermore, when asked to estimate where they themselves are located in the room, they make a systematic error forward, toward their virtual selves. In other experiments it is possible to transfer body ownership to a plastic mannequin or to another person, even of a different sex.[16]

The phenomena associated with the rubber hand illusion and the related phenomena of felt location of the body or its parts confirm that the localization of touch and the sensation of body ownership are built up by the brain from correlations between different sensory channels. But such multisensory correlations are not the only important factor; also very important should be the correlation with *voluntary action*. I would suggest that, instead of passive stroking, active sensorimotor interactions should be even more effective in transferring ownership. Unfortunately, however, current work has not thoroughly investigated to what extent action is important.[17] Another prediction that I might make would be that all aspects of sensed body awareness should be constituted in a similar way from sensorimotor correlations. For example, the approach predicts that, in addition to size, perceived smoothness, softness, elasticity, or weight of one's body parts should be adaptable and depend on such correlations. These predictions need to be tested in future work.

A promising line of research that we are starting in my laboratory concerns pain. The idea is that if the sensed location of a stimulation can be transferred outside the body, then perhaps this transfer could be done with pain. We have found that by using the rubber arm illusion to transfer ownership of an observer's arm to a rubber arm, painful thermal stimulation on the real arm is also transferred to the rubber arm. If this scientific form of voodoo can be generalized and developed, it might have useful applications in the clinical treatment of pain.

Notes

1. For an easy-to-read overview, see Blakeslee and Blakeslee (2007).
2. In addition to Penfield's homunculus in parietal cortex, other areas in the brain exist that also represent the body, but generally not in such a detailed way (e.g., Longo, Azañón, & Haggard, 2010).
3. For reviews of this work see, Kaas, Merzenich, and Killackey (1983); Merzenich and Jenkins (1993); and Wall, Xu, and Wang (2002).
4. An amusing book that summarizes this work is by Ramachandran and Blakeslee (1998).
5. Farah (1998) makes this proposal, but see a recent convincing critique by Parpia (in press).
6. See the review by Maravita and Iriki (2004).
7. For a review of multisensory interactions in the brain, see Bavelier and Neville (2002) and Pascual-Leone and Hamilton (2001).
8. This experience is described by Jaron Lanier, the coiner of the term "virtual reality" (Blakeslee & Blakeslee, 2007).
9. This was pointed out to me by developmental psychologist André Bullinger.
10. From the brain's point of view, this is quite an impressive feat. Imagine the complexity involved when I absent-mindedly swat a mosquito that lands on my arm.

The brain is able to direct my other arm accurately to that location. This is something that newborns are not able to do (they just agitate their whole bodies when they are stimulated locally). It takes about eight months before a baby is able to react in a way that shows that its brain knows how to attain particular body parts with another body part.

11. Note that here I did not say: You will see something changing that is temporally correlated with the *sensation coming from the fingertip*. The reason is that the brain cannot predispose the issue. It cannot take for granted that the incoming sensation is coming from the fingertip, since that is precisely what it has to establish.

12. Tastevin, 1937.

13. Botvinick & Cohen, 1998. You can see an excellent video demonstration given by Olaf Blanke of the rubber hand illusion on youtube (http://www.youtube.com/watch?v=TCQbygjG0RU). For a review, see Makin, Holmes, and Ehrsson (2008). For similar phenomena using virtual reality, see the review by Slater, Perez-Marcos, Ehrsson, and Sanchez-Vives (2009).

14. These experiments were done by my ex-student Ed Cooke, and they are currently being replicated with Thérèse Collins in my lab and in collaboration with Tobias Heed at the University of Hamburg. Related to these experiments, Lackner (1988) and Ramachandran and Hirstein (1997) mention an amusing "Pinocchio" phenomenon, in which, with a stroking technique similar to that used in the rubber hand illusion, one can get the impression of having a longer nose.

15. Blanke & Mohr, 2005. Philosopher Thomas Metzinger discusses these types of experiences in detail in order to bolster his theory that our selves are self-consistent cognitive illusions (Metzinger, 2004). The point of view I have taken with regard to the self in this book is fairly consistent with Metzinger's ideas, at least as far as I, a nonphilosopher, can understand them (Metzinger, 2004, 2009). What my sensorimotor approach adds is a way of explaining the characteristic presence or "what it's like" of sensory experiences.

16. Ehrsson, 2007; Lenggenhager, Tadi, Metzinger, & Blanke, 2007; Slater et al. 2009, 2010. See the Associated Press and New Scientist videos on youtube: http://www.youtube.com/watch?v=rawY2VzN4-c&feature=fvw; http://www.youtube.com/watch?v=mHP2liY0oDE&feature=related

17. Tsakiris, Prabhu, and Haggard (2006) suggest that depending on the kind of action (fingers, whole hand), the effect generalizes in different ways across fingers. The effect of action on the rubber hand illusion has been considered also by Sanchez-Vives et al. cited in Slater et al. (2009). See also Dummer, Picot-Annand, Neal, and Moore (2009).

Chapter 14

The Phenomenality Plot

I have described how the sensorimotor approach to raw feel explains four mysteries: why there's something it's like to have a raw sensory feel (presence); why different raw feels feel different; why there is structure in the differences; and why raw feel is ineffable. Of these four mysteries, the one philosophers consider to be the most mysterious is the first one, namely the question of why there's "something it's like" to have an experience. I would like to devote more space to this here.

First, recall the reason why the new approach has helped with this mystery. It has helped because it uses a definition of raw feel that essentially already contains the solution. If we take experiencing a raw feel to be an activity of interacting with the world, then by this very definition, there must be something it's like for this interaction to be happening: Interactions always have some quality or other.

But philosophers are saying more than simply that experience has a quality. They are saying that there is something very special about the quality, namely, in the case of sensory experiences, that the quality imposes itself on us in a very special way— the "something it's like" to have the experience involves what is sometimes called "phenomenality" or *presence*. I suggested that four aspects of sensory interactions could explain this presence of raw feel: richness, bodiliness, insubordinateness, and grabbiness. Sensory experiences possess these properties strongly, whereas thoughts and autonomic neural functions do not.

Now if richness, bodiliness, insubordinateness, and grabbiness are the basis for the "what it's like" of sensory feels, then we can naturally ask whether these concepts can do more work for us. In particular we would like them to explain, in the case of other, nonsensory types of experiences, the extent to which people will claim these have a "something it's like." In the following I shall be showing how proprioception and the vestibular sense, despite being real sensory systems, possess little if any sensory presence. I shall consider also the cases of emotions, hunger and thirst, and pain. We shall see that the low or intermediate values of richness, bodiliness, insubordinateness, and grabbiness possessed by such experiences explain why people will tend to say that these experiences only have intermediate values of sensory presence.

I shall be concentrating mostly on bodiliness and grabbiness, which we shall see tend to be the critical factors. I shall be plotting them on what I call a "phenomenality plot" (see Fig. 14.1). This graph indicates on the x axis the amount of bodiliness a given type of mental or neural activity has, and on the y axis the amount of grabbiness that activity has. I have chosen a scale of 0 to 10, with 0 meaning no bodiliness or grabbiness, and 10 meaning maximum bodiliness or grabbiness. For the moment the values I shall be plotting are very crude estimates that are open to debate. Further work would require defining a precise way of quantifying these notions—they are, I should emphasize, not psychological constructs but objectively quantifiable by physical and physiological measurements.

If the theory is right, we would expect that the more bodiliness and grabbiness a mental or neural activity has, that is, the more the activity is to be found up in the top right-hand portion of the graph, the more "what it's likeness" or "presence" or "phenomenality" the activity should be perceived as having. For example, I've already previously discussed the five basic senses as having high bodiliness and grabbiness, and so here I have plotted them with values in the range of 8–10, high up on the diagonal corresponding to high phenomenality (note that they have less bodiliness than proprioception—see later). By contrast, memory, thought, and autonomic functions, which have low phenomenality, are both plotted near the lower left-hand corner.

Before discussing other cases, I should make a note about one of the basic senses, namely smell. Smells possess strong grabbiness, since our attention and cognitive processing can be incontrovertibly diverted by nasty smells. But there is an issue about bodiliness: Body motions probably influence the incoming signal of smell much less than they do in other sense modalities. There is some degree of sniffing in smell, and it has been shown that humans use the speed of sniffing, and the differences in such speeds between the nostrils, to help optimize sensitivity to different smells and to determine their direction.[1] But I think globally the degree of change produced by body and head movements is somewhat less than in the other sense modalities. I have for that reason plotted smell with a bodiliness of about 6.

And this, I suggest, is why smelling is an experience that is perceived as not being strongly localized. Of course, by approaching an object and sniffing it, one can determine that the smell comes from a particular location, but more often the impression one has with smell is unlocalized. It is an impression of just being there accompanying us. Other sense impressions have a more definite spatial localization, either in the outside world, or, in the case of touch or taste, on the body.

Also, I should add a note about driving. Even though I used Porsche driving as an analogy in order to make the new approach more plausible, the feel of driving is not at all as perceptually "present" as seeing red or hearing a bell. Its level of grabbiness and bodiliness is low compared to those sensory experiences. You might think that grabbiness of driving is high, because when there is a sudden bump in the road or an obstacle, you react immediately. But such events do not correspond to the grabbiness of driving itself. The feel of driving a Porsche, say, resides in the particular quality of interaction you have with the car as you drive. If someone were suddenly, by mechanical wizardry, to replace the Porsche with a Volkswagen as you drive, nothing would grab your attention to tell you that this switch had happened until you tried to actually press on the accelerator and found that now nothing much happened, or until you tried to turn the wheel and experienced a much more sluggish response than with the Porsche. Thus, driving has relatively low grabbiness because what happens when there is a change in the driving experience is quite different from what happens when there is a change in sensory modalities like vision, hearing, and touching, where any sudden change will incontrovertibly grab your attention.

Bodiliness of driving is also relatively low, because although moving the wheel and the accelerator has an immediate effect, the majority of your body motions while driving have no effect. So long as you keep your hands and feet in the same place, you can move your head, eyes, and body without this changing the driving experience.

Now consider some other types of experience and test whether the notions of richness, bodiliness, insubordinateness, and grabbiness really are diagnostic of the degree of sensory presence that these different experiences possess.

Proprioception and the vestibular sense

Every time we move, proprioceptive information from muscles and joints signals to the brain whether the movements are correctly executed so that slight errors in muscle commands can be taken into account, as might be caused when we carry weights or encounter resistance to a limb. Yet we are completely unaware of the existence of this complex signaling that accompanies every single one of our motions.

The vestibular sense provides us with information about head and body acceleration, and it is essential to ensure balance and posture. Yet here again we are completely unconscious of this important sense modality.

Why do we not "feel" these two important sense modalities with the same sensory presence as our other senses? It's no use replying that the sensors involved are somehow not connected to the special brain circuitry that provides conscious sensations. If that were somehow true, then we would have to explain what it was about that special brain circuitry that made it "conscious." Saying that it was, perhaps, richly connected to other brain areas might explain why it is "access conscious" in the sense discussed in Chapter 6, but the phenomenal aspect or the lack of "raw feel" involved cannot be explained this way.

Thus, it will be a good test of the sensorimotor approach to see whether we have something more useful to say about proprioception and the vestibular sense by plotting their bodiliness and grabbiness on the phenomenality plot. Do they have bodiliness? Clearly proprioception does, because by its very nature, it is exquisitely sensitive to body motions. I have plotted it at a value of 10, the maximum of bodiliness scale. The vestibular sense perhaps has less bodiliness because only whole-body and head accelerations affect it. I have given it a value of 6.

Does proprioception have grabbiness? To my knowledge this is not something that has been explicitly measured. One would have to cause a sudden change in proprioceptive input without other (tactile, vestibular) changes occurring. Certainly it seems that passive motion of a limb is something that we are not very sensitive to. For example, if you are totally relaxed, and someone moves your arm, while taking care not to modify tactile pressure at the same time, I think there is nothing that grabs your attention or incontrovertibly occupies your thoughts. To test for grabbiness, such an experiment would have to be performed by making very sudden motions. As a guess, I would suggest that proprioception has little grabbiness. I have given it a value of 2 on the phenomenality plot.

Does the vestibular sense have grabbiness? Not very much, I think. Certainly if your airplane suddenly hits an air pocket, you feel a sinking feeling. But you are feeling the tactile feeling caused by the change in pressure your body exerts on the seat, or by the fact that the acceleration causes your stomach to shift inside your body, not by the vestibular sense itself. Closer to the actual feel of the vestibular sense is what happens when the airplane banks and goes into a curve: You feel the cabin as rotating, even though in fact your actual position with respect to it remains identical. But this feeling is not grabby; it doesn't cause any kind of orienting response in the same way as a loud noise or a bright light would. A way really to get an idea of the grabbiness of the vestibular sense is to induce dizziness by twirling around several times and then stopping. The resulting feeling of the world turning about is certainly perturbing, but I would suggest that it doesn't have the same grabbiness as a loud noise or a bright light, which cause you incontrovertibly to orient your attention. For these reasons, though I admit the issue can be debated, I have plotted the vestibular sense with a value of 3 on the grabbiness scale.

So we see that proprioception and the vestibular sense are not up in the top right-hand area of the phenomenality plot. We therefore expect these experiences not to have the same kind of sensory presence as the five basic sense modalities. And indeed it is true that we only really feel these senses in exceptional circumstances, if at all. Even though proprioception tells us where our limbs are in space, this feeling is more a kind of implicit knowledge than a real feeling, and certainly it does not have the same sensory presence as seeing a light or hearing a bell. The vestibular sense contributes to dizziness and the sense of orientation of our bodies, and it may have a little bit of grabbiness. But with only moderate bodiliness, the experience we have of it is not localized anywhere in space or the body.

In conclusion, plotting proprioception and the vestibular sense on the phenomenality plot helps explain why they have the particular feels that they do, and why we don't count them as having the same kind of sensory presence as the basic five senses. We don't need to appeal to differences in hypothetical consciousness properties of different brain areas. Of course, it's true that the differences are due to brain properties, but they are not due to these brain properties differing in their degrees of "consciousness." They are due to differences in the way proprioception and the vestibular sense are wired up to impact on our attentional and cognitive processes. Unlike the basic sense modalities, which are wired to be able to incontrovertibly interfere with our attention and thoughts, proprioception and the vestibular sense do not have this capacity.[2]

Emotions

I would like to devote some space to how emotions fit into the sensorimotor framework. Emotions are a very active and complex topic in the cognitive sciences, with numerous points of view and debates. Important current studies are probing the neurobiological and neurochemical basis of emotions and seeking their cognitive, social, and evolutionary role as well as the possibility of building emotions into robots.[3]

Compared to simple sensations like the red of a tomato, the sound of a bell, or the smell of lemon, emotional experiences have an intrinsic bodily component: Emotions involve changes in perceived body state. They also have a motivational component, often involving a propensity to initiate certain actions. Indeed, one of the historical debates about emotions is precisely the question of whether there is anything more to emotions than these bodily states and potential actions. William James famously claimed that fear, for example, was nothing more than the sum total of the bodily states and actions that are characteristic of fear: It's not that you run away when you're afraid, it's that you're afraid when you run away.[4]

There has been much debate around James's claim, and his view has been considered rather extreme. Nevertheless, today's neuroscientists confirm the importance of basic bodily states and actions that underlie emotions. Tremendous progress has been made in mapping out the brain structures that participate in these states. In particular, there is much talk of the important role of the amygdalae, the two small, almond-shaped neural structures tucked under the brain's temporal lobes that are phylogenetically old in mammals with equivalents in reptiles and birds. Information from the outside world related to danger, food, and sex, for example, seems to be immediately recognized by this structure and used to automatically trigger the appropriate behavioral, endocrine, and autonomic bodily reactions, such as fleeing or freezing, and changes in facial expressions as well as in the workings of the body's internal organs and glands, hormonal functions, sweating, blood pressure, and heartbeat.

The way the amygdalae are involved in the bodily manifestations associated with fear has been extensively studied by Joseph Ledoux in rats. Ledoux's idea is that one should distinguish between the emotion of fear itself, which is simply a *response* triggered by the amygdalae, and the *feeling* of fear.[5] He says that the feeling of fear comes about when higher mental processes involved with attention and short-term memory of the present moment, probably situated in prefrontal brain areas, get access to the signals from the body and viscera (internal organs and glands), and interpret these as corresponding to the fear response. In other words, Ledoux essentially complements William James's idea by saying that the feeling of fear comes from one's realizing that one's body is reacting with a fear response. Other scientists today agree that the automatic bodily responses are one thing, but that what we call the *feeling* of an emotion involves cognitively monitoring of the associated bodily reactions.[6]

The sensorimotor view agrees that cognitively monitoring an experience is what allows one to become conscious of the experience. But whereas Ledoux and others with related approaches cannot explain why cognitively monitoring something suddenly gives it a feel and makes it "something it's like" to experience, the sensorimotor approach can explain the phenomenon by saying that what is being monitored is not a brain state, but an ongoing interaction with the environment whose qualities constitute the experienced feel.

But in the case of emotions, is this experienced quality really the same kind of quality as the feel of red or of the sound of a bell? I suggest that whereas people do say that they feel emotions, in fact on closer analysis, the feel involved does not have the same kind of sensory presence as the feels possessed by the basic senses.

To see this, consider their bodiliness and grabbiness. Certainly emotions have grabbiness. Fear, if it is the prototypical emotion, may completely grab your attentional and cognitive resources and prevent you from functioning normally. The grabbiness is perhaps slightly different from the grabbiness of a sensory feel, because the grabbiness of fear requires a cognitive and probably a social interpretation.[7] You are only afraid when you have recognized and interpreted a situation, and realized that it is of a nature to be dangerous to you. This may happen very quickly, and the process, which may be accomplished in part by the amygdalae, may have been automatized by previous experience with dangerous stimulations. On the other hand, a loud noise or a bright flash attracts your attention in a totally automatic fashion and does not require any cognitive or social interpretation. I would suggest that in these cases the neurophysiology might be much more genetically hard-wired than in the case of emotions where previous experience is involved. For this reason I have plotted the grabbiness of fear at a value around 5, being significantly lower than that of basic sensations.

As concerns bodiliness, it is clear that emotions possess very little. Moving your body in no way immediately changes your fear or anger. The only role of motion would be if you move your body out of the dangerous or irritating situation (perhaps easier to do with fear than with anger). As we have seen before, the lack of bodiliness of an experience correlates with the fact that it is not perceived as being localized anywhere in particular. Though we clearly need a more precise way of measuring bodiliness, and a better definition than what I have been using here, this approach is a first approximation to explaining why emotions, having low bodiliness, are somewhat like smell and (we shall see, hunger and thirst); they are less spatially localized than the sensory experiences of seeing, hearing, touching, and tasting.

In conclusion, emotions like fear and anger do not fall high up on the diagonal representing high degree of sensory presence. They are, of course, very real, but my suggestion, in agreement with Ledoux and Damasio, and ultimately with William James, is that their feel can be accounted for essentially as the sum total of the feels of the bodily states that correspond to them. Being *conscious* of having an emotion then additionally requires one to become cognitively aware of the fact that one is in the associated mental state. But, because of its low amount of bodiliness and more cognitively linked type of grabbiness, the feel of an emotion is different from the feel of the basic sensory experiences: The feel is not phenomenally present in the same way, and it is not precisely localized anywhere. Perhaps this is why, at least in English, we tend to say: "I am afraid" rather than "I feel afraid." In Romance languages people say the equivalent of: "I have fear." We say, "I'm angry" rather than "I feel angry." Language here captures a subtle difference that corresponds to the position of fear and anger on the phenomenality plot.

Hunger and Thirst (and Other Cravings)

Are hunger and thirst emotions? Or are they just bodily states? Hunger and thirst are perhaps different from emotions like fear and anger in the sense that they are less cognitively complex, less determined by social situations, and more directly triggered by basic physiological mechanisms. Nevertheless, like emotions, hunger and thirst possess a motivational and an evaluative component. The motivational component consists in the fact that being hungry or thirsty presses us to engage in specific activities (eating, drinking) to relieve our hunger or thirst. The evaluative component is constituted by our cognitive and perhaps social evaluation of the state we are in: In the case of hunger and thirst, we cognitively consider that these are states which ultimately should be relieved.

But what of the sensory component: Do we really "feel" hunger and thirst? Do they have sensory presence in the same way as seeing red or hearing a bell? Under the approach I am taking, having a sensory experience is an activity of interacting with the world, and the degree to which this activity can be said to have a real sensory presence will be determined by the amount of richness, insubordinateness, bodiliness, and grabbiness that the activity possesses.

Again, focusing just on the latter two aspects, I suggest hunger and thirst have very little bodiliness. Moving parts of your body does not change the signals of hunger or thirst. It's true that by eating or drinking you can modify the signals. But the modification is not immediate in the way it is in the case of the classic senses. For this reason, the experience (if we can call it that) of feeling one's hunger or thirst does not involve the same kind of bodily engagement with the environment as the experience of seeing, hearing, touching, and tasting.

A point related to bodiliness concerns the localization of hunger and thirst. Certainly thirst has no specific localization. This is understandable, because what I mean by a feeling having a localization[8] is that we should be able to change that feeling by doing something with respect to its location: for example moving my hand to it, looking at it, or moving the location with respect to an outside object. In the case of thirst, there is no body motion that can modify the thirst signal: I have given thirst a low bodiliness rating of 1. In the case of hunger, there is perhaps a little bit of bodiliness owing to the fact that you can press on your stomach and somewhat alleviate the hunger signal: I have given hunger a value of 2.

Do hunger and thirst have grabbiness? Yes, they do: Strong hunger and thirst can prevent you from attending to other things and they can seriously interfere with your thought. But compared to the five classic senses, the effect is more phasic, or "dull," compared to the extreme attention-grabbing capacity that sudden sensory changes possess.

In sum, then, hunger and thirst are off the main diagonal of the phenomenality plot because of their relative lack of bodiliness and somewhat lower grabbiness. We can understand that they don't present themselves to us with the same presence as sensations from the basic sense modalities.[9] Though hunger and thirst can very strongly affect us, the effect is similar to that of emotions like fear and anger, say, which also have little bodiliness. More than really "feeling" our hunger and thirst, we "know" of them, and this state motivates us to alleviate the feelings by searching for food and drink.

This analysis of hunger and thirst can probably also be extended to other bodily desires, like craving for alcohol or nicotine when one is addicted. Like hunger and thirst such cravings are very real, but they present themselves with a rather different kind of sensory presence than the red of red or the sound of a bell.

Pain, Itches, and Tickles

Pain represents an enormous field of research with medical, neurophysiological, cognitive, social, and philosophical facets, to which I cannot do justice here. Like emotions, pains possess a motivational and evaluative component: They motivate us to stop the pain, and they are cognitively evaluated as bad. There may be a strong social contribution in this evaluation as well. But the sensory component of pain is clearly much more acute and present than the sensory components of emotions like fear and anger, and the sensory components of bodily states like hunger and thirst. The fact is that pain hurts. How can we account for this?

As for all sensations, it makes no sense to search for brain structures that might generate the qualitative "hurt" associated with pain. It's no use saying that the "hurt" is generated by special nociceptive pathways or pain circuits. To hope to find an explanation for "hurt" in these pathways and circuits themselves would lead us into an infinite regress of questions, as I have already emphasized at many places in this book when discussing what might generate raw feel. Moreover, the argument some make that our species has survived because the hurt of pain has prevented us from continually damaging ourselves also fails to answer the question of what the hurting feels like and why. Such an argument only tells us what the hurting causes us to do.

The idea is to examine what the hurt of pain really consists of. As illustrated in the phenomenality plot, pain has only a moderate amount of bodiliness. Moving one's body can somewhat modify the pain (one can remove one's finger from the fire, rub the aching limb, and change the incoming sensations), but many pains change only moderately (one cannot remove them completely) when one moves the body part itself or when one touches the affected body part. I suggest that this reduced ability to modulate the sensory stimulation of pain by body motions, that is, its reduced bodiliness, explains the sometimes unlocalized quality of the hurt of pain, contrary to the clearly localized quality of touch, vision, hearing, and taste.

If pains have only moderate bodiliness, then why are they still experienced as having a *sensory* quality? Why are they not more like thoughts, which have very little bodiliness and so are not perceived as spatially localized? Because unlike thoughts, pains have the other characteristics of sensory experiences: They have richness and partial insubordinateness,[10] and, most important, they have grabbiness to an extraordinary degree. I have given pain a value of 10 on the grabbiness scale. It is virtually impossible to prevent oneself from attending to a noxious stimulation. One's cognitive processing is interrupted and one cannot function properly as long as there is a pain.[11]

So we see that pain is somewhat different from the basic senses, in having a little less bodiliness, but much more grabbiness. Is this really sufficient to account for the very strong specificity of pain: for the fact that pain *hurts*? Intuitively, extreme grabbiness does not seem sufficient. Hurting is more than just having one's attention very strongly grabbed by a sensory stimulation whose localization may not be strongly defined. As evidence, consider, for example, an extremely piercing sound, like a burglar-alert siren. Such a sound does not hurt; it merely is extremely grabby. Or consider the sound of chalk or fingernails scraping on a blackboard. This is a stimulation that is extraordinarily grabby for some reason and makes many people cringe, though it is clearly not painful. We need a better characterization than just extreme grabbiness to account for the "hurt" of pain.

A possibility is an additional component that I call *automaticity*. The strong motivational component of pain, like that of emotions, causes us to change our course of action, but with pain, this component does so in a way that is much more automatic and hard-wired. For example, there are automatic reactions that cause our finger to jerk out of the fire, or that cause our twisted ankle to resist applied pressure. Painful stimuli cause us to incontrovertibly and automatically modify the way we use our bodies. We limp, we hold our breath, we adopt a different posture. These modifications in our body dynamics, and even perhaps in our vocalizations like screaming, are not cognitively determined (they occur even in simple animals). They seem to be genetically determined; they are automatic.

Could we say, then, that what we mean by "hurt" is a mode of interaction with the environment which has the characteristics of normal sensations (albeit with a little less bodiliness), has extreme grabbiness, but in addition has automaticity? Unfortunately this assertion is not sufficient to account for the hurt of pain either. Consider itches and tickles. Everything I have said about pain also applies to them. They can be just as grabby as pains, and they too provoke automatic reactions of the body. Why then do these experiences not *hurt*?[12]

I cannot think of any other objective aspect of the interaction we have with the environment when we suffer pain that could constitute the hurt of pain. If we add richness and insubordinateness to bodiliness, grabbiness, and automaticity, I think I have characterized the what it's likeness of pain as much as possible along the spectrum of possible *sensory* aspects to pain. And yet a full account of the experience still seems lacking.

I therefore make the following suggestion, which is very much in line with what several physiologists and certain philosophers have recently proposed[13]: In fact, the *sensory* component of pain does not hurt! It does all the same things that extremely grabby sensory stimulations do, like itches and tickles, the chalk on the blackboard, or extremely piercing sounds. But I suggest that what makes pain hurt is simply its additional evaluative, cognitive, and possibly its social components.

This is a rather shocking assertion, since it suggests that anything that has enough grabbiness should also be liable to hurt if it is cognitively evaluated as "bad." For example, one could imagine a culture that considers that itches and tickles are somehow damaging to the soul, and that they should be avoided as much as physical injury to the body. People would then feel that itches and tickles hurt in the same way as a real physical injury. I don't know whether such cultures exist. The suggestion also puts forth the counterintuitive idea that the actual "hurt" of pain should correspond to something mental, determined by cognitive evaluation and therefore in some sense unreal and potentially modifiable and modulable. It's difficult to accept that something purely mental could cause a feeling that is so acutely "real."

However, in defense of the idea that a strong negative mental evaluation might really be at the basis of "hurt," consider phobias. My aversion to having thin needles stuck into my body is so strong that just thinking about them makes me physically cringe. People can suffer considerable anguish from ideas that do not correspond to any physical stimulation. Imagine children's very real fear of the dark, or the irrational

fears of spiders or of flying. These are really "felt," are they not? If we imagine com-
bining such anguish with the grabbiness and automaticity that characterize a physical injury, and also with the bodiliness, insubordinateness, and richness that
characterize sensory presence, we can conceive that we might well have sufficient
ingredients to constitute the hurt of pain.

Morphine provides more evidence in favor of the idea that the "hurt" of pain is
largely due to a cognitive-evaluative component. People who take morphine will
generally have normal automatic avoidance reactions to sudden noxious stimuli.
Measurements of their thresholds for pain will be normal. They will say that they
can feel the pain, but, curiously, they will say that it does not bother them. This is
precisely what one would expect if pain is a particular kind of sensory stimulation
(namely one having a very high degree of grabbiness, and also having "automaticity,"
in the sense of provoking automatic hard-wired avoidance reactions), coupled with
a cognitive evaluative component. It would seem that under morphine use, the
sensory component is fully present, but the cognitive-evaluative component loses
its negative evaluation. Other conditions where this may happen are under
hypnosis,[14] and following lobotomy and cingulectomy.

Two other clinical conditions are also of interest because they present the opposite situation; that is, the deficit is in the *sensory* component. In congenital insensitivity to pain and in pain asymbolia, it would seem that the "automaticity" of the
sensory component does not function normally. Even though patients suffering
from these conditions show appropriate autonomic reactions—tachycardia, hyper-
tension, sweating, and mydriasis—and even though they can recognize the pain,
and their thresholds for detection of pain are the same as for normal people, the
patients will manifest none of the automatic avoidance reactions that are normally
present in response to a sudden noxious stimulation.[15]

Other, anecdotal evidence in favor of the view that the hurt of pain resides in
the cognitive-evaluative component is probably familiar to everyone. For instance,
consider the experience one can sometimes have of sustaining a bad injury but of
being so mentally involved in something else as not to notice the wound; only upon
seeing it later does one suddenly feel its pain. Soldiers at the front apparently sometimes report this experience. The converse is also well known: A child's pain will
often miraculously disappear when he or she is distracted.

Conclusion

The discussion in this chapter has shown that by looking at the bodiliness and grabbiness
of various mental or neural processes, we can gain insight into what they feel like. If
what we mean by having a real sensory feel is to have a high degree of bodiliness and
grabbiness (coupled with richness and partial insubordinateness), then we can see on
the "phenomenality plot" that really only the five basic senses of seeing, hearing, touching, tasting, and smelling possess these qualities to a significant extent. Only they will
have the sensory "presence" that we associate with prototypical sensations.

But plotting other mental states on the phenomenality plot can shed light on what
they feel like as well. In the very interesting case of pain, the phenomenal quality

would seem to be well described by its very high grabbiness, plus the additional component of automaticity, plus, finally, a very important cognitive-evaluative component that, I suggest, provides the real *hurt* and is what differentiates pains from itches and tickles.

Emotions like fear and anger, and bodily states like hunger and thirst, also have a what-it's-like quality that is well captured by considering their bodiliness and grabbiness. Owing to their comparatively low amount of bodiliness, they have less sensory presence. They have a quality of not being so precisely localized as compared to the five basic senses.

Appealing to bodiliness and grabbiness to explain the degree of sensory presence of a mental or neural process also provides an explanation of why proprioception and the vestibular sense are not perceived in the same way as the basic sensory modalities. This difference with the basic sensory modalities is surprising: after all, proprioceptive and vestibular signals originate from sensors in the muscles and joints or in the inner ear which are quite comparable to the sensors involved in touch and in hearing. The explanation resides in the fact that these signals do not have the grabbiness that is required for a neural signal to appear to us as being of a sensory nature.

Speculatively I suggest that the phenomenality plot also can track phenomena whose sensory nature is not so clear, for example, embarrassment, happiness, loneliness, love, and feeling rich, to name but a few. I have tentatively included these experiences in Figure 14.1. Consider feeling rich, for example. People do say that they "feel rich"—or slangily, they may say they "feel flush" or "feel in the money"—and intuitively it does make sense to use such expressions. If we examine the bodiliness and grabbiness involved, it would seem that feeling rich involves a small amount

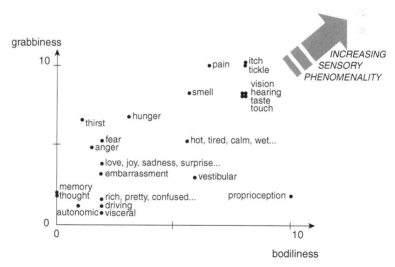

Figure 14.1 The phenomenality plot. Mental states that are located high up on the main diagonal, that is, states that objectively possess high bodiliness and high grabbiness, are precisely those that people will tend to say have a real sensory feel, that is, they have high "phenomenality," or "something it's like."

of bodiliness. There are things one can do when one is rich, such as buy an expensive car or a second home. Of course, such actions have nothing like the immediate and intimate link that action has on sensory input from vision, for example. Nor is there very much grabbiness in feeling rich, because no warning signal occurs when there are sudden fluctuations in one's bank account; we have to actively take out our bank statement and look at it. As a consequence, feeling rich only has a very limited amount of sensory presence, and it is more like purely mental processes. Perhaps greater sensory presence to feeling rich occurs when one is more engaged in actually doing the various things that are possible when one is rich.

I suggest that there are a variety of other mental conditions—such as feeling pretty, handsome, well-dressed, uncertain, confident, determined, relieved, confused, preoccupied, concerned, worried, busy, poor, abandoned, sociable—where one could apply the same kind of analysis, and in each case find that the degree of sensory presence would also be fairly low, as predicted from the phenomenality plot. Perhaps there is a class of mental states where the degree of sensory presence is somewhat greater: for example, feeling hot, cold, tired, sleepy, drowsy, nervous, restless, calm, wet, dry, comfortable, energetic or invigorated. Why do we say that we *feel* such states with more sensory presence than when we say we feel rich or abandoned? An obvious aspect of these states is that, like emotions, they involve bodily manifestations that one can to a certain degree modify by one's own bodily actions. I would like to claim that this greater degree of bodiliness may explain part of the reason for their greater sensory "presence." Perhaps love, joy, sadness, and surprise have somewhat more grabbiness, in that they can interfere significantly in our thoughts.

I have been tentatively sketching an approach here in which I try to use a small number of objective criteria—principally bodiliness and grabbiness—that characterize an interaction with the world in order to try to explain what it's like to have the associated experience. We have seen that bodiliness and grabbiness are essential features in determining what one intuitively would conceive of as the degree of sensory presence, or phenomenality. Bodiliness also determines the degree to which an experience is perceived as being localized at a precise location and being either on our bodies or exterior to ourselves, rather than being sensed as "interior" feelings that somehow simply accompany us without having a precise localization. Here the approach has been very tentative and approximate, for lack of an objective definition and measure of bodiliness and grabbiness. Perhaps with further work we would be able to make a finer link between such objective aspects of sensorimotor interactions and the subtle differences in how a mental state feels. Certainly it is the contention of the sensorimotor approach that potentially everything people will tend to say about the feel of mental states should be accounted for by such objective qualities of the activity that constitute them.

Note that I say that the qualities are objective. They are objective because they are qualities of the interaction a person has with the environment that can conceivably be objectively measured, for example, by a physicist. They are not psychological constructs or properties. What gives the sensorimotor approach its advantage over an approach based on neural correlates of consciousness is precisely the fact that objective physical characteristics of a sensorimotor interaction, describable in everyday language, can be linked to the kinds of things people will tend to say about their feels.

Notes

1. Porter et al., 2007; Schneider & Schmidt, 1967; Sobel et al., 1998.

2. Further analysis would be necessary to understand the experienced status of proprioception and the vestibular sense. Consider, for example, whether proprioception has insubordinateness. What would this mean? It would mean that influx from proprioceptive sensors would not always be correlated with your voluntary body motions. This is true during passive body motion, that is, when someone else moves one of your body parts. Does the vestibular sense have insubordinateness? Yes, since there are cases when vestibular input occurs independently of when you yourself move, namely when you are, for example, in a vehicle being accelerated, as in a boat. Perhaps the feeling of dizziness or of swaying corresponds to feeling your vestibular sense. On the other hand, it could be that one component of the feels of dizziness and swaying results from your vision being perturbed by the compensating eye movements that vestibular changes produce. Further thought is necessary on these issues, but overall, the sensorimotor approach aims to account for why proprioception and vestibular sense have much less perceptual presence, if any, than the other senses. For this account, the sensorimotor approach would draw only on objectively measurable aspects of the agent's sensorimotor interaction with the environment, like richness, bodiliness, partial insubordinateness, and grabbiness.

3. See, for example, the review by Scherer (2000). Some currently often cited books are by LeDoux (1996), Damasio (1994), Prinz (2004), Panksepp (2004), Lazarus (1991), Plutchik (1991), Rolls (2005), and Lane and Nadel (2002). Arbib and Fellous (2004) and Fellous and Arbib (2005) overview the functional, neuroanatomical, and neuromodulatory characteristics of emotions that could be built into a robot architecture.

4. Here is a quote from his essay "What is an emotion?" (James, 1884): "What kind of an emotion of fear would be left, if the feelings neither of quickened heart-beats nor of shallow breathing, neither of trembling lips nor of weakened limbs, neither of goose-flesh nor of visceral stirrings, were present, it is quite impossible to think. Can one fancy the state of rage and picture no ebullition of it in the chest, no flushing of the face, no dilatation of the nostrils, no clenching of the teeth, no impulse to vigorous action, but in their stead limp muscles, calm breathing, and a placid face? The present writer, for one, certainly cannot. The rage is as completely evaporated as the sensation of its so-called manifestations, and the only thing that can possibly be supposed to take its place is some cold-blooded and dispassionate judicial sentence, confined entirely to the intellectual realm, to the effect that a certain person or persons merit chastisement for their sins." (p. 193).

5. Joseph Ledoux's excellent Web site contains a song called "All in a nut" expounding the importance of the amygdala. See http://www.cns.nyu.edu/home/ledoux/Ledouxlab.html

6. Proponents of this view include Ledoux, Damasio, and Rolls. For example, Damasio says: *"That process of continuous monitoring, that experience of what your body is doing while thoughts about specific contents roll by, is the essence of what I call a feeling"* (Damasio, 1994, p. 145). Those against this view include Arbib and Fellous (2004) and Fellous and Arbib (2005). An excellent review of the relation of emotions and feelings is by Sizer (2006).

7. An interesting suggestion concerning the basic mechanism whereby an emotion can be socially constructed has been put forward, in the context of minimalist approaches

to sensory supplementation, by Charles Lenay and his collaborators (Auvray, Lenay, & Stewart, 2009; Lenay et al., 2007).

8. A related argument has been made by Pacherie and Wolff (2001).

9. Are hunger and thirst insubordinate? Yes, they are, since they are clearly not under our immediate direct control. Do hunger and thirst have richness? I think it's true that the body adjusts its food and liquid intake in different ways to adapt to its needs. So there must be, as a matter of objective fact, a degree of richness in the sensory signals that correspond to these differences. On the other hand, I think most people will agree that the subjective feelings we have are not highly differentiated. We do differentiate, for example, hunger from thirst, but certainly we don't feel very much richness in our hunger and thirst sensations. You are either hungry or not hungry. When you're hungry, you're not hungry in any *particular* way. It's true that you can have a craving for meat and not for strawberries, say, but the actual hunger feeling, I suggest, is not *itself* different. The idea you want meat rather than strawberries, I would submit, is more of a cognitive addition to the basic hunger feeling. The same is true for thirst, or for people who crave for a cigarette or for an alcoholic drink. Their actions will be to try to obtain whatever they are craving for, but the feeling will be more of a blunt craving-feeling, rather than a specific feeling for different subspecies of what they are craving for.

10. Pains have richness because like any other sensation coming from the outside world, our minds cannot imagine all their details. Pains have partial insubordinateness because, being caused by something outside our own minds, they have a life of their own and partially escape our mental control.

11. Obsessive thoughts are also grabby, but they are perceived as thoughts, and not as having sensory presence. Why is this? Because bodiliness, richness, and partial insubordinateness are also necessary in order for such thoughts to be perceived as having sensory presence. Clearly obsessive thoughts, as obsessive as they are, still are perceived as under our control.

12. I have heard that there are forms of torture that could fit the description I'm suggesting, namely the mythical Chinese "water torture" and "tickle torture." Both of these are presumably extremely attention grabbing but not physically noxious. Do they *hurt*? Chinese water torture was confirmed to be effective by the Discovery Channel program "Mythbusters" (see http://en.wikipedia.org/wiki/Chinese_water_torture).

13. For an excellent review of the arguments dissociating the sensory from the evaluative components of pain, see Aydede (2010). See also Dennett (1978); Grahek (2007); Hardcastle (1999); and Auvray, Myin, and Spence (2010).

14. Hardcastle (1999) authoritatively devotes a chapter to expounding the extraordinary effectiveness of hypnosis, which, she says, surpasses all other methods of pain control.

15. The difference between congenital insensitivity and pain asymbolia seems to be that though people with these conditions do not have the normal withdrawal reactions, those with pain asymbolia claim that in some sense they can feel it, whereas this is not so among patients with congenital insensitivity. For a detailed description that, unfortunately, still leaves this distinction unclear, see Grahek (2001, 2007).

Chapter 15

Consciousness

The topic of consciousness has generated a massive amount of attention, with numerous conferences all over the world that draw large numbers of people with a wide range of interests, including philosophy, neuroscience, psychology, psychiatry, physics, hypnosis, meditation, telepathy, levitation, religion, lucid dreaming, altered states, panpsychism, parapsychology, hallucinations, and auras. In addition to articles in the many specialized journals, discussions on various aspects of consciousness appear regularly in the mass media. Films like *AI* by Steven Spielberg, and books like *Thinks* by David Lodge, have generated considerable debate. Most surprising of all, philosophically quite technical books such as Daniel Dennett's *Consciousness Explained* have become bestsellers. Consciousness clearly captures the interest of a wide range of people.

Despite all this interest, no clear understanding of consciousness has emerged. Neuroscientists believe they are making advances in charting the brain regions involved in consciousness, but no single brain area nor any conceivable brain mechanism has been suggested that might fit the bill for producing consciousness.

Why are we making so little progress? The problem is that consciousness has until recently been the domain of philosophers, not scientists. When defining a concept, philosophers look at all the possible definitions irrespective of their potential for empirical verifiability. A plethora of concepts has thus emerged, upon which no one can agree.[1] Scientists, however, need a few clear concepts that can be investigated scientifically and applied to precise situations that allow empirical progress to be made.

Confusion surrounding definitions is not restricted to the concept of consciousness. For example, during the middle of the 19th century, the term *force* was used in different ways, sometimes meaning energy, sometimes power, sometimes force in the sense that physicists use it today. In fact, in German, the word *Kraft* retains these different meanings. It was through restricting the technical use of the word to the Newtonian concept of something that accelerates mass, and distinguishing it from energy and power, that physicists began to make progress. After these distinctions were made, it became possible for Hermann von Helmholtz to advance the law of Conservation of Energy, which is probably the cornerstone of contemporary science. It is amazing to realize that one of the most important discoveries in physics was made by restricting the definition of a word.[2]

Of course, there is more to understanding consciousness than choosing and precisely defining useful words and concepts to work on. A scientific theory is only successful if these words and concepts can be related to how we use them every day. To create a scientific theory of consciousness, we must find a way of defining terms that is both reasonably related to everyday use, yet simple and precise enough to be investigated empirically and to generate interesting further scientific work. This is what I have tried to do in the second half of this book.

I needed to dissect the different concepts underlying the notion of consciousness to see which could be accounted for by current scientific methods and which required something extra. To do this, I imagined trying to build a robot that was conscious. Investigating what would be involved in this task, I determined that thought, perception, language, and the self, though complicated and difficult, seemed amenable to the scientific method. It does seem possible in the foreseeable future to build devices that have these capacities; indeed, at least in a rudimentary way, some current devices already have these capacities. The same can be said of what is called access consciousness—the knowledge that an agent (an animal, robot, or human) has of the fact that it can make decisions, have goals, make plans, and communicate this knowledge to other agents. As progressively we become able to provide robots with these capacities, we will be advancing along the path to what is commonly understood as consciousness.

However, something essential is still missing, namely what I have called "feel." I tried to determine what aspects of feel are amenable to scientific explanation. I considered the mental associations that feel creates, the decisions made on account of it, the knowledge gained from it, and the things said as a result. I also considered the actions taken on account of feel, as well as the physical tendencies and the physiological states that are associated with feel. All of these things, though certainly very complex, are potentially understandable within a view of brains as information-processing, symbol-manipulating devices, acting in a real physical and social environment.

But in pushing these ideas further, it became clear that there remained one problem that seemed inaccessible to scientific explanation, namely what I called "raw feel." Raw feel seems to be what is left after we have peeled away the parts of feel that we can explain scientifically. It is probably very close to what philosophers call "phenomenal consciousness," or "qualia." This, they agree, constitutes the "hard" problem of consciousness, the problem of understanding the perceived quality of sensory experience.

Exactly what is so difficult for science to explain about raw feel? There are four properties of raw feel that I call the four mysteries:

1. Raw feels feel like something rather than feeling like nothing.
2. Raw feels have different qualities.
3. There is structure in the differences between the qualities of raw feels.
4. Raw feels are ineffable.

These four mysteries pose a problem for science because it seems difficult to imagine a physical mechanism in the brain that could give rise to raw feels with these properties.

Even worse, if we did ever manage to find a mechanism in the brain that we thought could give rise to raw feels with these properties, we would have no way of testing it. For example, if I found a mechanism that I thought generated the feel of red, how would I explain why it generated the red feel rather than, say, the green feel? It is difficult to understand how any explanation could go further than saying why the brain generated different actions, action tendencies, physical or physiological states, and mental states or tendencies. The underlying raw feel itself would not be explained.

The difficulty comes from the very definition of raw feel as whatever is left after science has done all it can. This is a basic logical difficulty, not just a matter of current ignorance about neurophysiology.

Some philosophers, most famously Daniel Dennett, argue that the way out of this situation is to claim that raw feel doesn't actually exist at all, or more accurately, that the notion itself makes no sense. Thus, when we have peeled away everything that can be scientifically said about feel, there is nothing left to explain. But many people consider this argument to be unsatisfactory because we all have the impression that there is actually something it is like to experience red or to have a pain. Many are thus not satisfied with Dennett behavioristically explaining away this impression of what it is like as nothing more than what one can potentially either do or say when experiencing red or having a pain.

It is for this reason that I suggest thinking of feel in a new way. The new way was inspired by the way of thinking about seeing that I developed in the first part of the book. My idea is that we should not think of feel as something that happens to us, but rather as a thing that we do. This means that the quality of a sensory feel, the impression we have, is the quality of our way of interacting with the environment. As a quality, it is something abstract and therefore not something that can be generated in any way, let alone by the brain.

Understanding sensory feel as a quality of something that we do allows us to understand why feels possess the four apparently mysterious properties that posed a problem for science. As we saw in detail in Chapter 9:

1. Feels feel like something rather than feeling like nothing because the modes of interaction we have with the environment when we are experiencing sensory feels always involve our body interacting with the environment. These interactions have the special properties of richness, bodiliness, insubordinateness, and grabbiness. These qualities are objective properties of our interactions with the environment and our sensory apparatus. They account for the particular felt "presence" of sensory experience—the fact that there is "something it's like" to have an experience. If you think about what you really mean by this "presence" or "something it's like," it turns out that it corresponds precisely with these qualities of richness, bodiliness, insubordinateness, and grabbiness.

The other mysteries are also solved with this way of thinking:

2. and 3. Feels have different qualities, and the qualities have particular structures because the associated interactions with the environment are of different natures and have different structures.

4. Raw feels are ineffable because interactions our bodies have with the environment are complex: We do not have cognitive access to every single detail of the interactions.

When is a feel conscious? A feel is conscious when we, as agents with selves, know that we are able to make use—in our judgments, reasoning, planning, and communication—of the fact that the feel is occurring. Having such knowledge requires nothing magical, and is, moreover, on the way to being realized in today's robots.

If some kind of magic was needed to explain consciousness, it was needed in understanding the "raw feel," since under the traditional view this was something that seemed impossible to generate in any biological or physical system. But I hope to have shown in this book how the sensorimotor approach, by taking feel as an abstract quality of our interaction with the environment, provides a way out of this difficulty. Furthermore, I showed how, far from being simply a philosophical stance, the sensorimotor approach makes empirically verifiable predictions and opens new research programs in topics such as visual attention, sensory substitution, color, tactile perception, and robotics.

Notes

1. This has been eloquently pointed out by Sloman (2010).
2. This point is made in the excellent biography of Helmholtz by Koenigsberger (1902).

REFERENCES

Arbib, M., & Fellous, J. (2004). Emotions: From brain to robot. *Trends in Cognitive Sciences, 8*(12), 554–561. doi:10.1016/j.tics.2004.10.004.

Arias, C. (1996). L'écholocation humaine chez les handicapés visuels [Human echolocation in cases of visual handicap]. *L'année psychologique, 96*(4), 703–721. doi:10.3406/psy.1996.28926.

Armstrong, D. M. (1968). *A materialist theory of mind* (Rev. ed.). London, England: Routledge.

Armstrong, D. M., & Malcolm, N. (1984). *Consciousness and causality: A debate on the nature of mind.* Oxford, England: Blackwell.

Auvray, M., Hanneton, S., Lenay, C., & O'Regan, K. (2005). There is something out there: Distal attribution in sensory substitution, twenty years later. *Journal of Integrative Neuroscience, 4*(4), 505–521.

Auvray, M., Hanneton, S., & O'Regan, J. K. (2007). Learning to perceive with a visuo-auditory substitution system: Localisation and object recognition with "The vOICe." *Perception, 36*(3), 416.

Auvray, M., Lenay, C., & Stewart, J. (2009). Perceptual interactions in a minimalist virtual environment. *New Ideas in Psychology, 27*(1), 32–47.

Auvray, M., & Myin, E. (2009). Perception with compensatory devices: From sensory substitution to sensorimotor extension. *Cognitive Science, 33*(6), 1036–1058. doi:10.1111/j.1551-6709.2009.01040.x.

Auvray, M., Myin, E., & Spence, C. (2010). The sensory-discriminative and affective-motivational aspects of pain. *Neuroscience and Biobehavioral Reviews* [Special issue], *34*(2), 214–223.

Auvray, M., & O'Regan, J. (2003) L'influence des facteurs sémantiques sur la cécité aux changements progressifs dans les scènes visuelles [The influence of semantic factors on blindness to progressive changes in visual scenes]. *L'Année Psychologique, 103*(1), 9–32.

Aydede, M. (2010). Pain. In E. N. Zalta (Ed.), Stanford encyclopedia of philosophy. Retrieved from http://plato.stanford.edu/archives/spr2010/entries/pain/

Baars, B. J. (1988). *A cognitive theory of consciousness.* Cambridge, England: Cambridge University Press.

Baars, B. J. (1997). *In the theater of consciousness.* New York, NY: Oxford University Press.

Baars, B. J. (2002). The conscious access hypothesis: Origins and recent evidence. *Trends in Cognitive Sciences, 6*(1), 47–52.

Bach-y-Rita, P. (1972). *Brain mechanisms in sensory substitution.* New York, NY: Academic Press.

Bach-y-Rita, P. (1997). Substitution sensorielle, qualia. In J. Proust (Ed.), *Perception et intermodalité. Approches actuelles de la question de Molyneux* (pp. 81–100). Paris, France: Presses Universitaires de France.

Bach-y-Rita, P. (2002). Sensory substitution and qualia. In A. Noë & E. Thompson (Eds.), *Vision and mind* (pp. 497–514). Cambridge, MA: MIT Press.

Bach-y-Rita, P., Danilov, Y., Tyler, M. E., & Grimm, R. J. (2005). Late human brain plasticity: Vestibular substitution with a tongue BrainPort human-machine interface. *Intellectica, 40,* 115–122.

Bach-y-Rita, P., Tyler, M. E., & Kaczmarek, K. A. (2003). Seeing with the brain. *International Journal of Human-Computer Interaction, 15*(2), 285–295.

Bach-y-Rita, P., & W. Kercel, S. (2003). Sensory substitution and the human-machine interface. *Trends in Cognitive Sciences, 7*(12), 541–546. doi:10.1016/j.tics.2003.10.013.

Barabasz, A. F., & Barabasz, M. (2008). Hypnosis and the brain. In M. R. Nash & A. J. Barnier (Eds.), *The Oxford handbook of hypnosis: Theory, research and practice* New York, NY: Oxford University Press. (pp. 337–364).

Bargh, J. A., & Chartrand, T. L. (1999). The unbearable automaticity of being. *American Psychologist, 54*(7), 462–479. doi:10.1037/0003-066X.54.7.462.

Barlow, H. (1990). A theory about the functional role and synaptic mechanism of visual after-effects. In C. Blakemore (Ed.), *Vision: Coding and efficiency.* Cambridge. England: Cambridge University Press.

Baron-Cohen, S. (1997). *Mindblindness.* Cambridge. MA: MIT Press.

Bauby, J. (1998). *The diving bell and the butterfly.* New York, NY: Vintage Books.

Bavelier, D., & Neville, H. J. (2002). Cross-modal plasticity: Where and how? *Nature Reviews Neuroscience, 3*(6), 443–452.

Becklen, R., & Cervone, D. (1983). Selective looking and the noticing of unexpected events. *Memory and Cognition, 11*(6), 601–608.

Bekoff, M., & Sherman, P. W. (2004). Reflections on animal selves. *Trends in Ecology and Evolution, 19*(4), 176–180.

Benham, G., & Younger, J. (2008). Hypnosis and mind–body interactions. In M. R. Nash & A. J. Barnier (Eds.), *The Oxford handbook of hypnosis: Theory, research and practice* (pp. 393–435). Oxford, England: Oxford University Press.

Berkeley, E. C. (1949). *Giant brains; or, Machines that think.* New York, NY: Wiley.

Berlin, B., & Kay, P. (1991). *Basic color terms.* Berkeley, CA: University of California Press.

Bischof, N., & Kramer, E. (1968). Untersuchungen und Überlegungen zur Richtungswahrnehmung bei willkürlichen sakkadischen Augenbewegungen [Investigations and considerations on visual direction during voluntary eye saccades]. *Psychological Research, 32*(3), 185–218.

Blackmore, S. J., Brelstaff, G., Nelson, K., & Troscianko, T. (1995). Is the richness of our visual world an illusion? Transsaccadic memory for complex scenes. *Perception, 24*(9), 1075–1081.

Blackmore, S. J. (2000). *The meme machine.* Oxford, England: Oxford University Press.

Blakeslee, S., & Blakeslee, M. (2007). *The body has a mind of its own.* New York, NY: Random House.

Blanke, O., & Mohr, C. (2005). Out-of-body experience, heautoscopy, and autoscopic hallucination of neurological origin. Implications for neurocognitive mechanisms of corporeal awareness and self-consciousness. *Brain Research Reviews, 50*(1), 184–199.

Block, N. (1996). On a confusion about a function of consciousness. *Behavioral and Brain Sciences, 18*(02), 227–247.

Block, N. (2001). Paradox and cross purposes in recent work on consciousness. *Cognition, 79*(1–2), 197–219.

Block, N. (2007). Consciousness, accessibility, and the mesh between psychology and neuroscience. *Behavioral and Brain Sciences, 30*(5-6), 481–499.

Bompas, A., & O'Regan, J. (2006a). Evidence for a role of action in color perception. *Perception, 35*(65–78).

Bompas, A., & O'Regan, J. K. (2006b). More evidence for sensorimotor adaptation in color perception. *Journal of Vision, 6*(2), 5.

Botvinick, M., & Cohen, J. (1998). Rubber hands "feel" touch that eyes see. *Nature, 391*(6669), 756. doi:10.1038/35784.

Brandt, S. A., & Stark, L. W. (1997). Spontaneous eye movements during visual imagery reflect the content of the visual scene. *Journal of Cognitive Neuroscience, 9*(1), 27–38. doi:10.1162/jocn.1997.9.1.27.

Breazeal, C., & Scassellati, B. (2002). Robots that imitate humans. *Trends in Cognitive Sciences, 6*(11), 481–487.

Bridgeman, B., Van der Heijden, A. H. C., & Velichkovsky, B. M. (1994). A theory of visual stability across saccadic eye movements. *Behavioral and Brain Sciences, 17*(02), 247–258.

Broackes, J. (1992). The autonomy of colour. In K. Lennon & D. Charles (Eds.), *Reduction, explanation, and realism* (pp. 421–465). Oxford, England: Oxford University Press.

Buck, L., & Axel, R. (1991). A novel multigene family may encode odorant receptors: A molecular basis for odor recognition. *Cell, 65*(1), 175–187.

Cairney, P. T. (2003). *Prospects for improving the conspicuity of trains at passive railway crossings* (Australian Transport Safety Bureau, Road Safety Research Report No. CR 217).

Cairney, P., & Catchpole, J. (1996). Patterns of perceptual failures at arterial roads and local streets. *Vision in Vehicles, 5*, 87–94.

Carr, J. E. (1978). Ethno-behaviorism and the culture-bound syndromes: The case of amok. *Culture, Medicine and Psychiatry, 2*(3), 269–293.

Carruthers, P. (2000a). *Phenomenal consciousness: A naturalistic theory*. Cambridge, England: Cambridge University Press.

Carruthers, P. (2000b). Replies to critics: Explaining subjectivity. Psyche, *6*(3). Retrieved from http://www.theassc.org/files/assc/2463.pdf

Carruthers, P. (2008). Meta-cognition in animals: A skeptical look. *Mind and Language, 23*(1), 58.

Carruthers, P. (2009). Higher-order theories of consciousness. In E. N. Zalta (Ed.), The Stanford encyclopedia of philosophy. Retrieved from http://plato.stanford.edu/archives/spr2009/entries/consciousness-higher/

Cassinelli, A., Reynolds, C., & Ishikawa, M. (2006). Augmenting spatial awareness with haptic radar. *10th IEEE International Symposium on Wearable Computers* (pp. 61–64). Montreux, Switzerland. doi:10.1109/ISWC.2006.286344.

Castet, E. (2009). Perception of intra-saccadic motion. In U.J. Llg and G.S. Masson (Eds.), *Dynamics of visual motion processing: Neuronal, behavioral, and computational approaches* (pp. 213–238). New York, NY: Springer Science+Business Media.

Cavanagh, P., Hunt, A. R., Afraz, A., & Rolfs, M. (2010). Visual stability based on remapping of attention pointers. *Trends in Cognitive Sciences, 14*(4), 147–153. doi:10.1016/j.tics.2010.01.007

Chabris, C. F., & Simons, D. J. (2010). *The invisible gorilla: and other ways our intuitions deceive us.* New York, NY: Crown Publishers.

Chalmers, D. J. (1996). *The conscious mind*. Oxford, England: Oxford Univ. Press.

Chalmers, D. J. (1997). *The conscious mind: In search of a fundamental theory*. New York, NY: Oxford University Press.

Clark, A. (1993). *Sensory qualities*. New York, NY: Oxford University Press.

Clark, A. (2003). *Natural-born cyborgs*. New York, NY: Oxford University Press.

Cooke, E., & Myin, E. (in press). Is trilled smell possible? A defense of embodied odour. *Journal of Consciousness Studies.*

Crick, F., & Koch, C. (1995). Why neuroscience may be able to explain consciousness. *Scientific American, 273*, 84–85.

Crick, F., & Koch, C. (2003). A framework for consciousness. *Nature Neuroscience, 6*(2), 119–126. doi:10.1038/nn0203-119.

Damasio, A. R. (1994). *Descartes' error: Emotion, reason, and the human brain*. New York, NY: Putnam Adult.

Dawkins, R. (1976). *The selfish gene*. Oxford, England: Oxford University Press.

Dehaene, S., Changeux, J. P., Naccache, L., Sackur, J., & Sergent, C. (2006). Conscious, preconscious, and subliminal processing: a testable taxonomy. *Trends in Cognitive Sciences, 10*(5), 204–211.

Dennett, D. C. (1978). Why you can't make a computer that feels pain. *Synthese, 38*(3), 415–456.

Dennett, D. C. (1989). The origins of selves. *Cogito, 3*, 163–173.

Dennett, D. C. (1991). *Consciousness explained*. Boston, MA: Little, Brown & Co.

Dennett, D. C. (1992). The self as a center of narrative gravity. In F. Kessel, P. Cole, & Johnson (Eds.), *Self and consciousness: Multiple perspectives* (pp. 103–115). Hillsdale, NJ: Erlbaum.

Derbyshire, S. W., & Furedi, A. (1996). Do fetuses feel pain? "Fetal pain" is a misnomer. *BMJ, 313*(7060), 795.

Derbyshire, S. W. G. (2008). Fetal pain: Do we know enough to do the right thing? *Reproductive Health Matters, 16*(31), 117–126.

Descartes, R. (1637/1965). Discourse on method, optics, geometry and meteorology (P. J. Olscamp, Trans.). Indianapolis, IN: Bobbs-Merrill Co. Inc.

Dobelle, W. H. (2000). Artificial vision for the blind by connecting a television camera to the visual cortex. *ASAIO Journal, 46*(1), 3–9.

Dolezal, H. (1982). *Living in a world transformed: Perceptual and performatory adaptation to visual distortion*. New York, NY: Academic Press.

Dreyfus, H. L. (1972). *What computers can't do*. New York, NY: Harper & Row.

Dreyfus, H. L. (1992). *What computers still can't do*. Cambridge, MA: MIT Press.

Dummer, T., Picot-Annand, A., Neal, T., & Moore, C. (2009). Movement and the rubber hand illusion. *Perception, 38*(2), 271.

Durgin, F., Tripathy, S. P., & Levi, D. M. (1995). On the filling in of the visual blind spot: Some rules of thumb. *Perception, 24*, 827–840.

Eastwood, B. (1986). Al Hazen, Leonardo, and late-medieval speculation on the inversion of images in the eye. *Annals of Science, 43*(5), 413. doi:10.1080/00033798600200311.

Edsinger, A., & Kemp, C. (2006). *What can I control? A framework for robot self-discovery*. Paper presented at the 6th International Conference on Epigenetic Robotics, Paris, France.

Ehrsson, H. H. (2007). The experimental induction of out-of-body experiences. *Science, 317*(5841), 1048.

Etnier, J. L., & Hardy, C. J. (1997). The effects of environmental color. *Journal of Sport Behavior, 20*(3). 299–312.

Farah, M. J. (1998). Why does the somatosensory homunculus have hands next to face and feet next to genitals? A hypothesis. *Neural computation, 10*(8), 1983–1985.

Faymonville, M. E., Fissette, J., Mambourg, P. H., Roediger, L., Joris, J., & Lamy, M. (1995). Hypnosis as adjunct therapy in conscious sedation for plastic surgery. *Regional Anesthesia and Pain Medicine, 20*(2), 145.

Feigl, H. (1967). *The mental and the physical: The essay and a postscript*. Minneapolis, MN: University of Minnesota Press.

Fellous, J. M., & Arbib, M. A. (2005). *Who needs emotions? The brain meets the robot*. New York, NY: Oxford University Press.

Fernandez-Duque, D., & Thornton, I. M. (2003). Explicit mechanisms do not account for implicit localization and identification of change: An empirical reply to Mitroff et al. (2002). *Journal of Experimental Psychology-Human Perception and Performance, 29*(5), 846–857.

Fitzpatrick, P., & Metta, G. (2003). Grounding vision through experimental manipulation. *Philosophical Transactions of the Royal Society London A: Mathematical, Physical and Engineering Sciences,* (361), 2165–2185.

Fletcher, P. (2002). Seeing with sound: A journey into sight. Invited presentation at *Toward a Science of Consciousness 2002 "Tucson V"*. April 8–12, Tucson, Arizona, USA.

Froese, T., & Spiers, A. (2007). *Toward a phenomenological pragmatics of enactive perception*. Paper presented at the 4th International Conference on Enactive Interfaces, Grenoble, France.

Frost, D. O., Boire, D., Gingras, G., & Ptito, M. (2000). Surgically created neural pathways mediate visual pattern discrimination. *Proceedings of the National Academy of Sciences USA, 97*(20), 11068–11073. doi:VL – 97.

Gallace, A., Tan, H. Z., & Spence, C. (2007). The body surface as a communication system: The state of the art after 50 years. *Presence: Teleoperators and Virtual Environments, 16*(6), 655–676. doi:10.1162/pres.16.6.655.

Gallagher, S. (2000). Philosophical conceptions of the self: Implications for cognitive science. *Trends in Cognitive Sciences, 4*(1), 14–21.

Gallagher, S., & Shear, J. (1999). *Models of the self*. Exeter, England: Imprint Academic.

Gegenfurtner, K. R., & Kiper, D. C. (2003). Color vision. *Annual Review of Neuroscience, 26*(1), 181–206.

Gennaro, R. J. (2004). *Higher-order theories of consciousness*. Philadelphia, PA: John Benjamins.

Grahek, N. (2007). *Feeling pain and being in pain*. Cambridge, MA: MIT Press.

Greene, J., & Cohen, J. (2004). For the law, neuroscience changes nothing and everything. *Philosophical Transactions of the Royal Society B: Biological Sciences, 359*(1451), 1775–1785.

Grimes, J. (1996). On the failure to detect changes in scenes across saccades. In K. Akins (Ed.), *Vancouver studies in cognitive science, Vol. 5. Perception* (pp. 89–110). New York, NY: Oxford University Press.

Grossberg, S., Hwang, S., & Mingolla, E. (2002). Thalamocortical dynamics of the McCollough effect: Boundary-surface alignment through perceptual learning. *Vision Research, 42*(10), 1259–1286.

Grüsser, O. J. (1987). Afterimage movement during saccades in the dark. *Vision Research, 27*(2), 215–226.

Guarniero, G. (1974). Experience of tactile vision. *Perception, 3*(1), 101–104.

Guarniero, G. (1977). Tactile vision: A personal view. *Visual Impairment and Blindness, 71*(3), 125–130.

Hacking, I. (1986). Making up people. In T. Heller, M. Sosna, & D. Wellbery (Eds.), *Reconstructing individualism* (pp. 222–236). Stanford, CA: Stanford University Press.

Haines, R. (1991). A breakdown in simultaneous information processing. In G. Obrecht & L. W. Stark (Eds.), *Presbyopia research. From molecular biology to visual adaptation* (pp. 171–175). New York, NY: Plenum Press.

Hamid, P. N., & Newport, A. G. (1989). Effects of colour on physical strength and mood in children. *Perceptual and Motor Skills, 69*, 179–185.

Hansen, T., Pracejus, L., & Gegenfurtner, K. R. (2009). Color perception in the intermediate periphery of the visual field. *Journal of Vision, 9*(4), 26.

Hardcastle, V. (1999). *The myth of pain*. Cambridge, MA: MIT Press.

Hardin, C. L. (1988). *Color for philosophers: Unweaving the rainbow*. Indianapolis, IN: Hackett Publishing Company.

Hartocollis, L. (1998). The making of multiple personality disorder: A social constructionist view. *Clinical Social Work Journal, 26*(2), 159–176. doi:10.1023/A:1022819001682

Hatta, T., Yoshida, H., Kawakami, A., & Okamoto, M. (2002). Color of computer display frame in work performance, mood, and physiological response. *Perceptual and Motor Skills, 94*(1), 39–46.

Hawkins, P. J., Liossi, C., Ewart, B. W., Hatira, P., & Kosmidis, V. H. (2006). Hypnosis in the alleviation of procedure related pain and distress in paediatric oncology patients. *Contemporary Hypnosis, 15*(4), 199–207.

Hayek, F. A. (1999). *The sensory order*. Chicago, IL: University of Chicago Press.

Held, R. (1980). The rediscovery of adaptability in the visual system: Effects of extrinsic and intrinsic chromatic dispersion. In C. Harris (Ed.), *Visual coding and adaptability*. Hillsdale, NJ: Lawrence Erlbaum Associates.

Helmholtz, H. (1867/1962). *Treatise on physiological optics* (Vol. 3). Mineola, NY: Dover.

Herslund, M. B., & Jørgensen, N. O. (2003). Looked-but-failed-to-see-errors in traffic. *Accident Analysis and Prevention, 35*(6), 885–891.

Heyes, C. M. (1998). Theory of mind in nonhuman primates. *Behavioral and Brain Sciences, 21*(01), 101–114.

Hofer, H., & Williams, D. (2002). The eye's mechanisms for autocalibration. *Optics and Photonics News, Jan*, 34–39.

Hossain, P., Seetho, I. W., Browning, A. C., & Amoaku, W. M. (2005). Artificial means for restoring vision. *BMJ, 330*(7481), 30–33. doi:10.1136/bmj.330.7481.30

Hume, D. (1793/2003). *A treatise of human nature*. Mineola, NY: Dover Publications.

Humphrey, N. (1992). *A history of the mind*. New York, NY: Simon & Schuster.

Humphrey, N. (2000). How to solve the mind—body problem. *Journal of consciousness Studies, 7*(4), 5–5.

Humphrey, N. (2005). Sensation seeking. *New Scientist*. Issue 2486, February 12.

Humphrey, N. (2006a). *Seeing red: A study in consciousness*. Belknap Press.

Humphrey, N. (2006b). Seeing red, a postscript. Retrieved from http://www.humphrey.org.uk/papers_available_online.htm

Humphrey, N. (2008, January 28). Questioning consciousness. SEED Magazine. Retrieved from http://seedmagazine.com/content/article/questioning_consciousness/

Hurley, S., & Noë, A. (2003). Neural plasticity and consciousness. *Biology and Philosophy, 18*(1), 131–168.

Husserl, E. (1989). *Ideas pertaining to a pure phenomenology and to a phenomenological philosophy* (R. Rojcewizc & A. Schuwer, Trans.) Dordrecht, Netherlands: Kluwer.

Hutchins, J. (2003). Has machine translation improved? Some historical comparisons. In MT Summit IX: Proceedings of the Ninth Machine Translation Summit, New Orleans, USA, September 23–27 (pp. 181–188). AMTA: East Stroudsburg, PA.

Ibbotson, M. R., & Cloherty, S. L. (2009). Visual perception: Saccadic omission—suppression or temporal masking? *Current Biology, 19*(12), R493–R496.

IJsselsteijn, W. A. (2002). Elements of a multi-level theory of presence: Phenomenology, mental processing and neural correlates. In F. Gouveia & F. Biocca (Eds.) *Presence 2000 Proceedings*. (pp. 245–259). University of Fernando Pessoa Press: Porto, Portugal.

Irwin, D. E. (1991). Information integration across saccadic eye movements. *Cognitive Psychology, 23*(3), 420–456.

James, W. (1884). What is an emotion? *Mind, 9*(34), 188–205.

James, W. (1890). *The principles of psychology*. Mineola, NY: Dover Publications.

Jameson, K., D'Andrade, R. G., Hardin, C. L., & Maffi, L. (1997). It's not really red, green, yellow, blue: An inquiry into perceptual color space. In C. L. Hardin & L. Maffi (Eds.) *Color categories in thought and language* (pp. 295–319). Cambridge, England: Cambridge University Press.

Järvilehto, T. (1998a). The theory of the organism-environment system: II. Significance of nervous activity in the organism-environment system. *Integrative Psychological and Behavioral Science, 33*(4), 335–342.

Järvilehto, T. (1998b). The theory of the organism-environment system: I. Description of the theory. *Integrative Psychological and Behavioral Science, 33*(4), 321–334.

Järvilehto, T. (2009). The theory of the organism-environment system as a basis of experimental work in psychology. *Ecological Psychology, 21*(2), 112. doi:10.1080/10407410902877066

Jones, L. A., & Sarter, N. B. (2008). Tactile displays: Guidance for their design and application. *Human Factors: The Journal of the Human Factors and Ergonomics Society, 50*(1), 90–111. doi:10.1518/001872008X250638.

Kaas, J. H., Merzenich, M. M., & Killackey, H. P. (1983). The reorganization of somatosensory cortex following peripheral nerve damage in adult and developing mammals. *Annual Review of Neuroscience, 6*, 325–356.

Kassan, P. (2006). AI gone awry: The futile quest for artificial intelligence. *Skeptic, 12*(2), 30–39.

Kay, L. (1985). Sensory aids to spatial perception for blind persons: Their design and evaluation. In D. Warren & E. Strelow (Eds.), *Electronic spatial sensing for the blind* (pp. 125–139). Dordrecht, Netherlands: Martinus Nijhoff.

Kenny, M. G. (1983). Paradox lost: The latah problem revisited. *The Journal of Nervous and Mental Disease, 171*(3), 159.

Kepler, J. (1604/1980). *Paralipomena ad Vitellionem (Les fondements de l'optique moderne: Paralipomènes à Vitellion)* (C. Chevalley, Trans.). L'Histoire des Sciences, Textes et Etudes. Paris, France: J. Vrin.

Kish, D. (2003). Sonic echolocation: A modern review and synthesis of the literature. Update of unpublished Master's thesis, University of Southern California. Retrieved from http://www.worldaccessfortheblind.org/sites/default/files/echolocationreview.htm

Kitagawa, N., Igarashi, Y., & Kashino, M. (2009). The tactile continuity illusion. *Journal of Experimental Psychology: Human Perception and Performance, 35*(6), 7.

Knoblauch, K., Sirovich, L., & Wooten, B. R. (1985). Linearity of hue cancellation in sex-linked dichromacy. *Journal of the Optical Society of America A, 2*(2), 136–146.

Koch, C. (2004). *The quest for consciousness.* Greenwood Village, CO: Roberts and Company Publishers.

Koenderink, J. J. (1984). The concept of local sign. In A. van Doorn, W. van de Grind, & J. Koenderink (Eds.), *Limits in perception* (pp. 495–547). Zeist, Netherlands: VNU Science Press.

Koenderink, J. J. (1990). The brain a geometry engine. *Psychological Research, 52*(2), 122–127.

Koenigsberger, L. (1902). *Hermann von Helmholtz.* (Vols. 1-3). Braunschweig, Germany: F. Vieweg & Sohn.

Koestler, A. (1968). *The sleepwalkers: A history of man's changing vision of the universe.* London, England: Penguin.

Kohler, I. (1962). Experiments with goggles. *Scientific American, 206*(5), 62–72.

Kohler, I. (1967). Facial vision rehabilitated. In R. Busnel (Ed.), *Les systèmes sonars animaux* (pp. 187–196). Jouy-en-Josas, France: Laboratoire de Physiologie Acoustique.

Kohler, I. (1974). Past, present, and future of the recombination procedure. *Perception, 3*(4), 515–524. doi:10.1068/p030515.

Kohut, H. (2009). *The analysis of the self.* Chicago, IL: University of Chicago Press.

Komatsu, H. (2006). The neural mechanisms of perceptual filling-in. *Nature reviews neuroscience, 7*(3), 220–231.

Kosslyn, S. M., Thompson, W. L., & Ganis, G. (2006). *The case for mental imagery.* New York, NY: Oxford University Press.

Kottenhoff, H. (1961). *Was ist richtiges Sehen mit Umkehrbrillen und in welchem Sinne stellt sich das Sehen um?* (Vol. 5). Meisenheim am Glan, Germany: Anton Hain.

Kuehni, R. G. (2004). Variability in unique hue selection: A surprising phenomenon. *Color Research and Application, 29*(2), 158–162.

Lackner, J. R. (1988). Some proprioceptive influences on the perceptual representation of body shape. *Brain*, *111*(2), 281–297. doi:10.1093/brain/111.2.281.

Lamme, V. A. F. (2006). Towards a true neural stance on consciousness. *Trends in Cognitive Sciences*, *10*(11), 494–501.

Lane, H., & Bahan, B. (1998). Ethics of cochlear implantation in young children: A review and reply from a deaf-world perspective. *Otolaryngology-Head and Neck Surgery*, *119*(4), 297–313.

Lane, R. D., & Nadel, L. (2002). *Cognitive neuroscience of emotion*. New York, NY: Oxford University Press.

Lazarus, R. S. (1991). *Emotion and adaptation*. New York, NY: Oxford University Press.

LeDoux, J. (1996). *The emotional brain*. New York, NY: Simon and Schuster.

Lee, S. J., Ralston, H. J. P., Drey, E. A., Partridge, J. C., & Rosen, M. A. (2005). Fetal pain: A systematic multidisciplinary review of the evidence. *Journal of the American Medial Association*, *294*(8), 947.

Legrand, Y. (1956). *Optique physiologique*. Paris, France: Editions de la Revue d'Optique.

Lenay, C., Canu, S., & Villon, P. (1997). Technology and perception: The contribution of sensory substitution systems. In Second International Conference on Cognitive Technology (pp. 44–53). Los Alamitos, CA: IEEE. Retrieved from http://www.computer.org/portal/web/csdl/doi/10.1109/CT.1997.617681

Lenay, C., Gapenne, O., Hanneton, S., Marque, C., & Genouëlle, C. (2003). Sensory substitution: Limits and perspectives. In Y. Hatwell, A. Streri, & E. Gentaz (Eds.), *Touching for knowing: Cognitive psychology of haptic manual perception* (pp. 275–292). Philadelphia, PA: John Benjamins Publishing Company.

Lenay, C., Thouvenin, I., Guénand, A., Gapenne, O., Stewart, J., & Maillet, B. (2007). Designing the ground for pleasurable experience. In I. Koskinen & T. Keinonen (Eds.) Proceedings of the 2007 Conference on Designing Pleasurable Products and Interfaces (pp. 35–58). New York, NY: ACM. Retrieved from http://doi.acm.org/10.1145/1314161.1314165

Lenggenhager, B., Tadi, T., Metzinger, T., & Blanke, O. (2007). Video ergo sum: Manipulating bodily self-consciousness. *Science*, *317*(5841), 1096.

Leslie, A. M. (1994). ToMM, ToBy, and agency: Core architecture and domain specificity. In L. Hirschfeld & S. Gelman (Eds.), *Mapping the mind: Domain specificity in cognition and culture* (pp. 119–148). Cambridge, England: Cambridge University Press.

Levin, D. T., Momen, N., Drivdahl, S. B., & Simons, D. J. (2000). Change blindness blindness: The metacognitive error of overestimating change-detection ability. *Visual Cognition*, *7*(1), 397–412.

Levin, D. T., & Simons, D. J. (1997). BRIEF REPORTS Failure to detect changes to attended objects in motion pictures. *Psychonomic Bulletin and Review*, *4*(4), 501–506.

Levine, J. (1983). Materialism and qualia: The explanatory gap. *Pacific Philosophical Quarterly*, *64*, 354–361.

Lifton, R. J. (1986). *The Nazi doctors: Medical killing and the psychology of genocide*. New York, NY: Basic Books.

Lifton, R. J. (1989). *Thought reform and the psychology of totalism: A study of "brainwashing" in China*. Chapel Hill, NC: University of North Carolina Press.

Lifton, R. J. (1991). *Death in life: Survivors of Hiroshima*. Chapel Hill, NC: University of North Carolina Press.

Lindberg, D. C. (1981). *Theories of vision from al-Kindi to Kepler*. Chicago, IL: University of Chicago Press.

Linden, D. E. J., Kallenbach, U., Heinecke, A., Singer, W., & Goebel, R. (1999). The myth of upright vision. A psychophysical and functional imaging study of adaptation to inverting spectacles. *Perception*, *28*(4), 469–481.

Liossi, C., Santarcangelo, E. L., & Jensen, M. P. (2009). Bursting the hypnotic bubble: Does hyp-notic analgesia work and if yes how? *Contemporary Hypnosis, 26*(1), 1–3. doi:10.1002/ch.376.

Longo, M. R., Azañón, E., & Haggard, P. (2010). More than skin deep: Body representation beyond primary somatosensory cortex. *Neuropsychologia, 48*(3), 655–668. doi:10.1016/j.neuropsychologia.2009.08.022.

Luck, S. J., & Vogel, E. K. (1997). The capacity of visual working memory for features and conjunc-tions. *Nature, 390*(6657), 279–281.

Lundborg, G., Rosén, B., & Lindberg, S. (1999). Hearing as substitution for sensation: A new prin-ciple for artificial sensibility. *Journal of Hand Surgery, 24*(2), 219–224.

Lungarella, M., Metta, G., Pfeifer, R., & Sandini, G. (2003). Developmental robotics: A survey. *Connection Science, 15*(4), 151–190. doi:10.1080/09540090310001655110

Lycan, W. G. (1987). *Consciousness.* Cambridge, MA: MIT Press.

Lycan, W. G. (1996). *Consciousness and experience.* Cambridge, MA: MIT Press.

Lynn, S. J., Rhue, J. W., & Weekes, J. R. (1990). Hypnotic involuntariness: A social cognitive analy-sis. *Psychological Review, 97*(2), 169–184.

Mack, A., & Rock, I. (1998). *Inattentional blindness.* MIT Press/Bradford Books series in cognitive psychology. Cambridge, MA: The Mit Press.

MacKay, D. M. (1967). Ways of looking at perception. In W. Wathen-Dunn (Ed.), *Models for the perception of speech and visual form* (pp. 25–43). Cambridge, MA: The MIT Press.

MacKay, D. M. (1972). Visual stability and voluntary eye movements. In R. Jung (Ed.), *Handbook of sensory physiology* (Vol. 3, pp. 307–331). New York, NY: Springer.

Makin, T. R., Holmes, N. P., & Ehrsson, H. H. (2008). On the other hand: Dummy hands and peripersonal space. *Behavioural Brain Research, 191*(1), 1–10.

Maloney, L. T., & Ahumada, A. J. (1989). Learning by assertion: Two methods for calibrating a linear visual system. *Neural Computation, 1*(3), 392–401.

Mamlouk, M. (2004). On the dimensions of the olfactory perception space. *Neurocomputing, 58,* 1019–1025.

Maravita, A., & Iriki, A. (2004). Tools for the body (schema). *Trends in Cognitive Sciences, 8*(2), 79–86. doi:10.1016/j.tics.2003.12.008.

Markman, A. B., & Dietrich, E. (2000). Extending the classical view of representation. *Trends in Cognitive Sciences, 4*(12), 470–475.

Matin, L. (1986). Visual localization and eye movements. *Handbook of perception and human perfor-mance., 1,* 20–21.

McConkie, G. W., & Currie, C. B. (1996). Visual stability across saccades while viewing complex pictures. *Journal of Experimental Psychology: Human Perception and Performance, 22*(3), 563–581.

von Melchner, L., Pallas, S. L., & Sur, M. (2000). Visual behaviour mediated by retinal projections directed to the auditory pathway. *Nature, 404*(6780), 871–876. doi:10.1038/35009102.

Menary, R. (2007). *Cognitive integration: Mind and cognition unbounded.* Basingstoke, England: Palgrave Macmillan.

Merabet, L. B., Battelli, L., Obretenova, S., Maguire, S., Meijer, P., & Pascual-Leone, A. (2009). Functional recruitment of visual cortex for sound encoded object identification in the blind. *NeuroReport, 20*(2), 132–138. doi:10.1097/WNR.0b013e32832104dc.

Merleau-Ponty, M. (1962). *The phenomenology of perception* (Colin Smith, Trans.) London, England: Routledge.

Merzenich, M. (2000). Cognitive neuroscience: Seeing in the sound zone. *Nature, 404*(6780), 820–821. doi:10.1038/35009174.

Merzenich, M. M., & Jenkins, W. M. (1993). Reorganization of cortical representations of the hand following alterations of skin inputs induced by nerve injury, skin island transfers, and experience. *Journal of Hand Therapy: Official Journal of the American Society of Hand Therapists*, 6(2), 89–104.

Metzinger, T. (2004). *Being no one: The self-model theory of subjectivity*. Cambridge, MA: MIT Press.

Metzinger, T. (2005). Précis: Being no one. Psyche, 11(5). Retrieved from: http://www.theassc. org/files/assc/2608.pdf.

Metzinger, T. (2009). *The ego tunnel*. New York, NY: Basic Books.

Minsky, M. (1988). *The society of mind*. New York, NY: Simon and Schuster.

Mollon, J. (2006). Monge: The Verriest lecture, Lyon, July 2005. *Visual neuroscience*, 23(3-4), 297–309.

Montgomery, G. H., Bovbjerg, D. H., Schnur, J. B., David, D., Goldfarb, A., Weltz, C. R., Schechter, C., ... Silverstein, J. H. (2007). A randomized clinical trial of a brief hypnosis intervention to control side effects in breast surgery patients. *JNCI Journal of the National Cancer Institute*, 99(17), 1304.

Morgan, M. (1977). *Molyneux's question. Vision, touch and the philosophy of perception*. Cambridge, England: Cambridge University Press.

Morin, A. (2006). Levels of consciousness and self-awareness: A comparison and integration of various neurocognitive views. *Consciousness and Cognition*, 15(2), 358–371.

Murray, M. M., Wylie, G. R., Higgins, B. A., Javitt, D. C., Schroeder, C. E., & Foxe, J. J. (2002). The spatiotemporal dynamics of illusory contour processing: combined high-density electrical mapping, source analysis, and functional magnetic resonance imaging. *Journal of Neuroscience*, 22(12), 5055–5073.

Nagel, S. K., Carl, C., Kringe, T., Martin, R., & König, P. (2005). Beyond sensory substitution— learning the sixth sense. *Journal of Neural Engineering*, 2(4), R13–R26.

Nagel, T. (1974). What is it like to be a bat? *Philosophical Review*, 83, 435–456.

Nakshian, J. S. (1964). The effects of red and green surroundings on behavior. *The Journal of general psychology*, 70, 143–161.

Nash, M. R., & Barnier, A. J. (2008). *The Oxford handbook of hypnosis: Theory, research and practice*. Oxford, England: Oxford University Press.

Natsoulas, T. (1997). The presence of environmental objects to perceptual consciousness: A difference it makes for psychological functioning. *The American Journal of Psychology*, 110(4), 507–526.

Neisser, U. (1988). Five kinds of self-knowledge. *Philosophical Psychology*, 1(1), 35–59.

Neisser, U., & Becklen, R. (1975). Selective looking: Attending to visually-specified events. *Cognitive Psychology*, 7, 480–494.

Noë, A. (2004). *Action in perception*. Cambridge, MA: MIT Press.

Noë, A. (2009). *Out of our heads*. Hill and Wang: New York, NY.

Noë, A., & O'Regan, J. (2000). Perception, attention, and the grand illusion. Psyche, 6(15) Retrieved from: http://www.theassc.org/files/assc/2472.pdf.

Noton, D., & Stark, L. (1971). Scanpaths in saccadic eye movements while viewing and recognizing patterns. *Vision Research*, 11(9), 929–942.

Oakley, D. A. (2008). Hypnosis, trance and suggestion: Evidence from neuroimaging. In M. R. Nash & A. J. Barnier (Eds.), *The Oxford handbook of hypnosis: Theory, research and practice* (pp. 365–392). Oxford, England: Oxford University Press.

O'Regan, J., Rensink, R., & Clark, J. (1999). Change-blindness as a result of "mudsplashes." *Nature*, 398, 34.

O'Regan, J. K. (1990). Eye movements and reading. In E. Kowler (Ed.), *Eye movements and their role in visual and cognitive processes* (pp. 395–453). New York, NY: Elsevier Science Publishers BV.

O'Regan, J. K. (1992). Solving the "real" mysteries of visual perception: The world as an outside memory. *Canadian Journal of Psychology*, 46(3), 461–488.

O'Regan, J. K., Deubel, H., Clark, J. J., & Rensink, R. A. (2000). Picture changes during blinks: Looking without seeing and seeing without looking. *Visual Cognition*, 7(1–3), 191–211.

O'Regan, J. K., & Noë, A. (2001). A sensorimotor account of vision and visual consciousness. *Behavioral and Brain Sciences*, 24(5), 883–917.

Pacherie, E., & Wolff, F. (2001). Peut-on penser l'objectivité sans l'espace? [Can we conceive of objectivity without space?]. In F. Wolff (Ed.) *Philosophes en liberté - Positions et arguments 1* (pp. 46–66). Paris, France: Ellipses.

Palmer, S. E. (1999). Color, consciousness, and the isomorphism constraint. *Behavioral and Brain Sciences*, 22(06), 923–943.

Panksepp, J. (2004). *Affective neuroscience: The foundations of human and animal emotions.* New York, NY: Oxford University Press.

Parfit, D. (1986). *Reasons and persons.* New York, NY: Oxford University Press.

Parpia, P. (in press). Reappraisal of the somatosensory homunculus and its discontinuities. *Neural Computation*.

Pascual-Leone, A., & Hamilton, R. (2001). The metamodal organization of the brain. *Progress in Brain Research*, 134, 427–445.

Pascual-Leone, A., Amedi, A., Fregni, F., & Merabet, L. B. (2005). The plastic human brain cortex. *Annual Review of Neuroscience*, 28, 377–401.

Patterson, D. R., & Jensen, M. P. (2003). Hypnosis and clinical pain. *Psychological Bulletin*, 129(4), 495–521.

Paul, G. L. (1963). The production of blisters by hypnotic suggestion: Another look. *Psychosomatic Medicine*, 25(3), 233–244.

Pellegrini, R. J., Schauss, A. G., & Miller, M. E. (1981). Room color and aggression in a criminal detention holding cell: A test of the "tranquilizing pink" hypothesis. *Journal of Orthomolecular Psychiatry*, 10(3), 8.

Penfield, W. (1958). Some mechanisms of consciousness discovered during electrical stimulation of the brain. *Proceedings of the National Academy of Sciences USA*, 44(2), 51–66.

Pessoa, L., Thompson, E., & Noë, A. (1998). Finding out about filling-in: A guide to perceptual completion for visual science and the philosophy of perception. *Behavioral and Brain Sciences*, 21(06), 723–748.

Petkov, C. I., O'Connor, K. N., & Sutter, M. L. (2007). Encoding of illusory continuity in primary auditory cortex. *Neuron*, 54(1), 153–165.

Petrovic, P., & Ingvar, M. (2002). Imaging cognitive modulation of pain processing. *Pain*, 95(1–2), 1–5.

Philipona, D., O'Regan, J. K., & Nadal, J. P. (2003). Is there something out there? Inferring space from sensorimotor dependencies. *Neural Computation*, 15(9), 2029–2049.

Philipona, D., O'Regan, J. K., Nadal, J. P., & Coenen, O. (2004). Perception of the structure of the physical world using unknown multimodal sensors and effectors. *Advances in Neural Information Processing Systems*, 16, 945–952.

Philipona, D. L., & O'Regan, J. (2006). Color naming, unique hues, and hue cancellation predicted from singularities in reflection properties. *Visual Neuroscience*, 23(3-4), 331–339.

Pierce, D., & Kuipers, B. J. (1997). Map learning with uninterpreted sensors and effectors. *Artificial Intelligence*, 92(1–2), 169–227.

Platt, J. R. (1960). How we see straight lines. *Scientific American*, 202(6), 121–129.

Plutchik, R. (1991). *The emotions.* Lanham, MD: University Press of America.

Pola, J. (2007). A model of the mechanism for the perceived location of a single flash and two successive flashes presented around the time of a saccade. *Vision Research*, 47(21), 2798–2813. doi:10.1016/j.visres.2007.07.005.

Porter, J., Craven, B., Khan, R. M., Chang, S., Kang, I., Judkewitz, B., Volpe, J., Settles, G., Sobel, N. (2007). Mechanisms of scent-tracking in humans. *Nature Neuroscience, 10*(1), 27–29. doi:10.1038/nn1819.

Press, J. K. (2008). The scientific use of "representation"and "function": Avoiding explanatory vacuity. *Synthese, 161*(1), 119–139.

Prinz, J. J. (2004). *Gut reactions: A perceptual theory of emotion.* New York, NY: Oxford University Press.

Priplata, A. A., Niemi, J. B., Harry, J. D., Lipsitz, L. A., & Collins, J. J. (2003). Vibrating insoles and balance control in elderly people. *The Lancet, 362*(9390), 1123–1124.

Proulx, M. J., Stoerig, P., Ludowig, E., & Knoll, I. (2008). Seeing "where" through the ears: Effects of learning-by-doing and long-term sensory deprivation on localization based on image-to-sound substitution. *PLoS ONE, 3*(3), e1840. doi:10.1371/journal.pone.0001840.

Ramachandran, V. S., & Hirstein, W. (1997). Three laws of qualia: What neurology tells us about the biological functions of consciousness. *Journal of Consciousness Studies, 4*(5-6), 429–457.

Ramachandran, V., & Blakeslee, S. (1998). *Phantoms in the brain.* New York, NY: William Morrow & Co.

Ramachandran, V., & Hirstein, W. (1998). The perception of phantom limbs. The D. O. Hebb lecture. *Brain, 121*(9), 1603–1630. doi:10.1093/brain/121.9.1603.

Ratner, C. (1989). A sociohistorical critique of naturalistic theories of color perception. *Journal of Mind and Behavior, 10*(4), 361–372.

Regier, T., Kay, P., & Cook, R. S. (2005). Focal colors are universal after all. *Proceedings of the National Academy of Sciences USA, 102*(23), 8386.

Regier, T., Kay, P., & Khetarpal, N. (2007). Color naming reflects optimal partitions of color space. *Proceedings of the National Academy of Sciences USA, 104*(4), 1436–1441.

Rensink, R. (2000). The dynamic representation of scenes. *Visual Cognition, 7*, 17–42.

Rensink, R. A. (2002). Change detection. *Annual Review of Psychology, 53*(1), 245–277.

Rensink, R. (2005). Change blindness. In *McGraw Hill yearbook of science and technology* (pp. 44–46). New York, NY: McGraw Hill.

Rensink, R. A., O'Regan, J. K., & Clark, J. (1997). To see or not to see: The need for attention to perceive changes in scenes. *Psychological Science, 8*(5), 368–373.

Rensink, R. A., O'Regan, J. K., & Clark, J. J. (2000). On the failure to detect changes in scenes across brief interruptions. *Visual Cognition, 7*(1-3), 127–145.

Richters, D. P., & Eskew, R. T. (2009). Quantifying the effect of natural and arbitrary sensorimotor contingencies on chromatic judgments. *Journal of Vision, 9*(4), 1–11. doi:10.1167/9.4.27.

Roentgen, U. R., Gelderblom, G. J., Soede, M., & de Witte, L. P. (2008). Inventory of electronic mobility aids for persons with visual impairments: A literature review. *Journal of Visual Impairment and Blindness, 102*(11), 23.

Rollman, G. B. (1998). Culture and pain. In S. Kazarian & D. Evans (Eds.), *Cultural clinical psychology: Theory, research, and practice* (pp. 267–286). Oxford, England: Oxford University Press.

Rolls, E. T. (2005). *Emotion explained.* Oxford, England: Oxford University Press.

Ronchi, V. (1991). *Optics, the science of vision* (E. Rosen, Trans.). Mineola, NY: Dover Publications.

Rosenthal, D. (1997). A theory of consciousness. In N. Block, O. Flanagan, & G. Güzeldere (Eds.), *The nature of consciousness: Philosophical debates* (pp. 729–753). Cambridge, MA: MIT Press.

Rosenthal, D. M. (2002). How many kinds of consciousness? *Consciousness and Cognition, 11*(4), 653–665.

Rosenthal, D. M. (2005). *Consciousness and mind.* Oxford, England: Oxford University Press.

Sabey, B. E., & Staughton, G. C. (1975). *Interacting roles of road environment, vehicle and road user in accidents*. Paper presented at the 5th International Conference of International Association for Accident and Traffic Medicine, London, England.

Sampaio, E., & Dufier, J. L. (1988). Suppléance sensorielle électronique pour les jeunes enfants aveugles. [An electronic sensory substitute for young blind children]. *Journal Français D'ophtalmologie, 11*(2), 161–167.

Sampaio, E., Maris, S., & Bach-y-Rita, P. (2001). Brain plasticity: "Visual" acuity of blind persons via the tongue. *Brain Research, 908*(2), 204–207.

Sanchez-Vives, M. V., & Slater, M. (2005). From presence to consciousness through virtual reality. *Nature Reviews Neuroscience, 6*(4), 332–339.

Scassellati, B. (2003). Investigating models of social development using a humanoid robot. Paper presented at the 2003 International Joint Conference on Neural Networks (IJCNN), Portland, OR. Retrieved from http://cs-www.cs.yale.edu/homes/scaz/papers/Scassellati-IJCNN-03.pdf

Schall, J. D. (2004). On building a bridge between brain and behavior. *Annual Review of Psychology, 55*(1), 23–50. doi:10.1146/annurev.psych.55.090902.141907.

Scherer, K. R. (2000). Psychological models of emotion. In J. Borod (Ed.) *The neuropsychology of emotion* (pp. 137–162). New York, NY: Oxford University Press.

Schiller, P. H., & Tehovnik, E. J. (2008). Visual prosthesis. *Perception, 37*(10), 1529.

Schneider, R. A., & Schmidt, C. E. (1967). Dependency of olfactory localization on non-olfactory cues. *Physiology and Behavior, 2*(3), 305–309. doi:10.1016/0031-9384(67)90084-4.

Segond, H., Weiss, D., & Sampaio, E. (2007). A proposed tactile vision-substitution system for infants who are blind tested on sighted infants. *Journal of Visual Impairment and Blindness, 101*(1), 32.

Sharma, J., Angelucci, A., & Sur, M. (2000). Induction of visual orientation modules in auditory cortex. *Nature, 404*(6780), 841–847.

Siegle, J. H., & Warren, W. H. (2010). Distal attribution and distance perception in sensory substitution. *Perception, 39*(2), 208–223. doi:10.1068/p6366.

Simons, D. J., & Ambinder, M. S. (2005). Change blindness. *Current directions in psychological science, 14*(1), 44.

Simons, D. J., & Chabris, C. F. (1999). Gorillas in our midst: Sustained inattentional blindness for dynamic events. *Perception, 28*(9), 1059–1074.

Simons, D. J., Franconeri, S. L., & Reimer, R. L. (2000). Change blindness in the absence of a visual disruption. *Perception, 29*(10), 1143–1154.

Simons, D. J., & Levin, D. T. (1998). Failure to detect changes to people during a real-world interaction. *Psychonomic Bulletin and Review, 5*, 644–649.

Simons, D. J., & Rensink, R. A. (2005). Change blindness: Past, present, and future. *Trends in Cognitive Sciences, 9*(1), 16–20.

Simons, R. C. (1980). The resolution of the latah paradox. *The Journal of Nervous and Mental Disease, 168*(4), 195.

Simons, R. C., & Hughes, C. C. (1985). *The culture-bound syndromes: Folk illnesses of psychiatric and anthropological interest*. New York, NY: Springer.

Sizer, L. (2006). What feelings can't do. *Mind and Language, 21*(1), 108–135.

Slater, M., Perez-Marcos, D., Ehrsson, H. H., & Sanchez-Vives, M. V. (2009). Inducing illusory ownership of a virtual body. *Frontiers in Neuroscience, 3*(2), 214–220. doi:10.3389/neuro.01.029.2009.

Slater, M., Spanlang, B., Sanchez-Vives, M. V., & Blanke, O. (2010). First person experience of body transfer in virtual reality. *PLoS One, 5*(5), e10564.

Sloman, A. (2010). Phenomenal and access consciousness and the "hard" problem: A view from the designer stance. *International Journal of Machine Consciousness, 02*(01), 117. doi:10.1142/S1793843010000424.

Slotnick, B., Cockerham, R., & Pickett, E. (2004). Olfaction in olfactory bulbectomized rats. *Journal of Neuroscience, 24*(41), 9195.

Smith, E. (1998). Spectacle lenses and emmetropization: The role of optical defocus in regulating ocular development. *Optometry and Vision Science, 75*(6), 388–398.

Sobel, N., Prabhakaran, V., Desmond, J. E., Glover, G. H., Goode, R. L., Sullivan, E. V., & Gabrieli, J. D. E. (1998). Sniffing and smelling: Separate subsystems in the human olfactory cortex. *Nature, 392*(6673), 282–286. doi:10.1038/32654.

Somera, E. (2006). Culture-bound dissociation: A comparative analysis. *Psychiatric Clinics of North America, 29*(1), 213–226.

Stark, L., & Bridgeman, B. (1983). Role of corollary discharge in space constancy. *Perception and Psychophysics, 34*(4), 371–380.

Stokes, M., Thompson, R., Cusack, R., & Duncan, J. (2009). Top-down activation of shape-specific population codes in visual cortex during mental imagery. *Journal of Neuroscience, 29*(5), 1565.

Stratton, G. M. (1896). Some preliminary experiments on vision without inversion of the retinal image. *Psychological Review, 3*(6), 611–617.

Stratton, G. M. (1897). Vision without inversion of the retinal image. *Psychological Review, 4*(4), 341–360.

Strawson, G. (1999). The self and the SESMET. *Journal of Consciousness Studies, 6*, 99–135.

Tastevin, J. (1937). En partant de l'expérience d'Aristote les déplacements artificiels des parties du corps ne sont pas suivis par le sentiment de ces parties ni par les sensations qu'on peut y produire. [Starting from Aristotle's observations, artificial displacements of parts of the body are not followed by sensations on those body parts nor by sensations that can be produced there]. *L'Encéphale, 32*(2), 57–84; 140–158.

Taylor, J. (1962). *The behavioral basis of perception.* New Haven, CT: Yale University Press.

Teller, D. Y. (1984). Linking propositions. *Vision Research, 24*(10), 1233–1246.

Thomas, N. J. T. (1999). Are theories of imagery theories of imagination? An active perception approach to conscious mental content. *Cognitive Science: A Multidisciplinary Journal, 23*(2), 207–245.

Thomas, N. (2010). Mental imagery. In E. N. Zalta (Ed.), The Stanford encyclopedia of philosohy. Retrieved from http://plato.stanford.edu/archives/spr2010/entries/mental-imagery/

Thompson, P. (1980). Margaret Thatcher: A new illusion. *Perception, 9*(4), 483–484.

Todorovic, D. (1987). The Craik-O'Brien-Cornsweet effect: New varieties and their theoretical implications. *Attention, Perception, and Psychophysics, 42*(6), 545–560.

Tononi, G., & Koch, C. (2008). The neural correlates of consciousness-an update. *Annals of the New York Academy of Sciences, 1124*, 239–261.

Tootell, R. B., Silverman, M. S., Switkes, E., & De Valois, R. L. (1982). Deoxyglucose analysis of retinotopic organization in primate striate cortex. *Science, 218* (4575), 902–904.

Torrance, S. (2005). In search of the enactive: Introduction to special issue on enactive experience. *Phenomenology and the Cognitive Sciences, 4*(4), 357–368.

Triesch, J., Teuscher, C., Deak, G. O., & Carlson, E. (2006). Gaze following: Why (not) learn it? *Developmental Science, 9*(2), 125.

Tsakiris, M., Prabhu, G., & Haggard, P. (2006). Having a body versus moving your body: How agency structures body-ownership. *Consciousness and Cognition, 15*(2), 423–432.

Tucker, B. P. (1998). Deaf culture, cochlear implants, and elective disability. *The Hastings Center Report, 28*(4), 6–14.

Tye, M. (2009). Qualia. In E. N. Zalta (Ed.), *The Stanford encyclopedia of philosophy.* Retrieved from http://plato.stanford.edu/archives/sum2009/entries/qualia/

Tyler, M., & Danilov, Y. (2003). Closing an open-loop control system: Vestibular substitution through the tongue. *Journal of integrative neuroscience, 2*(2), 159.

Valberg, A. (2001). Unique hues: An old problem for a new generation. *Vision Research, 41*(13), 1645–1657.

Varela, F. J., Thompson, E., & Rosch, E. (1992). *The embodied mind: Cognitive science and human experience.* Cambridge, MA: MIT Press.

Vierkant, T. (2003). *Is the self real? An investigation into the philosophical concept of "self."* Münster, Germany: LIT Verlag.

Villemure, C., & Bushnell, M. C. (2002). Cognitive modulation of pain: How do attention and emotion influence pain processing? *Pain, 95*(3), 195–199.

Vladusich, T., & Broerse, J. (2002). Color constancy and the functional significance of McCollough effects. *Neural Networks, 15*(7), 775–809.

Volkmann, F. C. (1986). Human visual suppression. *Vision Research, 26*(9), 1401–1416.

Wall C., III, & Weinberg, M. S. (2003). Balance prostheses for postural control. *IEEE Engineering in Medicine and Biology Magazine, 22*(2), 84–90.

Wall, J. T., Xu, J., & Wang, X. (2002). Human brain plasticity: An emerging view of the multiple substrates and mechanisms that cause cortical changes and related sensory dysfunctions after injuries of sensory inputs from the body. *Brain Research Reviews, 39*(2-3), 181–215. doi:10.1016/S0165-0173(02)00192-3.

Wallman, J., Gottlieb, M. D., Rajaram, V., & Fugate Wentzek, L. A. (1987). Local retinal regions control local eye growth and myopia. *Science, 237*(4810), 73–77.

Warren, R. M., Wrightson, J. M., & Puretz, J. (1988). Illusory continuity of tonal and infratonal periodic sounds. *The Journal of the Acoustical Society of America, 84*, 1338.

Webster, M. A., Miyahara, E., Malkoc, G., & Raker, V. E. (2000). Variations in normal color vision. I. Cone-opponent axes. *Journal of the Optical Society of America A, 17*(9), 1535–1544.

Wegner, D. M. (2003a). The mind's best trick: How we experience conscious will. *Trends in Cognitive Sciences, 7*(2), 65–69.

Wegner, D. M. (2003b). *The illusion of conscious will.* Cambridge, MA: MIT Press.

Weiland, J., & Humayun, M. (2008). Visual prosthesis. *Proceedings of the IEEE, 96*(7), 1076–1084. doi:10.1109/JPROC.2008.922589.

Wierzbicka, A. (1996). *Semantics: Primes and universals.* New York, NY: Oxford University Press.

Wildsoet, C. F., & Schmid, K. L. (2001). Emmetropization in chicks uses optical vergence and relative distance cues to decode defocus. *Vision Research, 41*(24), 3197–3204.

Wuerger, S. M., Atkinson, P., & Cropper, S. (2005). The cone inputs to the unique-hue mechanisms. *Vision Research, 45*(25-26), 3210–3223.

Wurtz, R. H. (2008). Neuronal mechanisms of visual stability. *Vision Research, 48*(20), 2070–2089.

Zelek, J. S., Bromley, S., Asmar, D., & Thompson, D. (2003). A haptic glove as a tactile-vision sensory substitution for wayfinding. *Journal of Visual Impairment and Blindness, 97*(10), 1–24.

Zeman, A. (2004). *Consciousness: A user's guide.* New Haven, CT: Yale University Press.

Ziat, M., Lenay, C., Gapenne, O., Stewart, J., Ammar, A., & Aubert, D. (2007). Perceptive supplementation for an access to graphical interfaces. In C. Stephanidis (Ed.), *UAHCI'07 Proceedings of the 4th international conference on Universal access in human computer interaction: Coping with diversity* (pp. 841–850). Berlin, Germany: Springer Verlag.

Zrenner, E. (2002). Will retinal implants restore vision? *Science, 295*(5557), 1022–1025. doi:10.1126/science.1067996.

SUBJECT INDEX